No Longer Business as Usual

Fighting Bribery and Corruption

OECD

ORGANISATION FOR ECONOMIC CO-OPERATION AND DEVELOPMENT

ORGANISATION FOR ECONOMIC CO-OPERATION AND DEVELOPMENT

Pursuant to Article 1 of the Convention signed in Paris on 14th December 1960, and which came into force on 30th September 1961, the Organisation for Economic Co-operation and Development (OECD) shall promote policies designed:

- to achieve the highest sustainable economic growth and employment and a rising standard of living in Member countries, while maintaining financial stability, and thus to contribute to the development of the world economy;
- to contribute to sound economic expansion in Member as well as non-member countries in the process of economic development; and
- to contribute to the expansion of world trade on a multilateral, non-discriminatory basis in accordance with international obligations.

The original Member countries of the OECD are Austria, Belgium, Canada, Denmark, France, Germany, Greece, Iceland, Ireland, Italy, Luxembourg, the Netherlands, Norway, Portugal, Spain, Sweden, Switzerland, Turkey, the United Kingdom and the United States. The following countries became Members subsequently through accession at the dates indicated hereafter: Japan (28th April 1964), Finland (28th January 1969), Australia (7th June 1971), New Zealand (29th May 1973), Mexico (18th May 1994), the Czech Republic (21st December 1995), Hungary (7th May 1996), Poland (22nd November 1996) and Korea (12th December 1996). The Commission of the European Communities takes part in the work of the OECD (Article 13 of the OECD Convention).

Publié en français sous le titre :
AFFAIRISME : LA FIN DU SYSTÈME
Comment combattre la corruption

Foreword

The OECD first put international corruption on its agenda in 1989 and later evolved two basic objectives for its work: to fight corruption in international business and to help level the competitive playing field for all companies. After several years spent analysing the nature of corruption in international business and studying the measures that countries might take to combat it, OECD countries agreed in 1994 on an initial *Recommendation on Bribery in International Business Transactions*. Subsequently, in May 1996, they adopted a *Recommendation on the Tax Deductibility of Bribes to Foreign Public Officials*. In May, 1997, a revised *Recommendation on Combating Bribery in International Business Transactions* was adopted.

The *1997 Convention on Combating Bribery of Foreign Public Officials in International Business Transactions* was born out of the conviction that bribery of foreign public officials in international business transactions is a serious threat to the development and preservation of democratic institutions. Not only does it undermine economic development but it also distorts international competition by seriously misdirecting resources. The Convention was signed by all 29 OECD countries and five non-member countries and came into force on 15 February 1999.

The OECD takes a multidisciplinary approach to fighting corruption, addressing both the supply and the demand side of bribery. Corruption thrives where public institutions are weak or wherever poor governance is prevalent. The OECD helps countries to improve their systems of governance and public sector management. Ensuring the transparency of public procurement systems is another essential element in the fight against corruption as is the effective enforcement of money laundering legislation.

Preventing corruption and enforcing laws to punish it require concerted actions by government, international organisations, business and labour, and civil society. The OECD acknowledges the important initiatives launched by these various actors and this book is, in large measure, a tribute to them as well. Above all, sustained, high-level political will is needed to ensure that anti-corruption strategies can deliver on their promises.

This publication is the result of the collaborative efforts of many individuals. The project was managed by Enery Quinones, Head of the OECD Anti-Corruption Unit (ACU) in the Directorate for Financial, Fiscal and Enterprise Affairs and co-ordinated by Nicola Ehlermann-Cache. Editing was carried out by Robert Cornell. The ACU wishes to express its gratitude to the Centre for Co-operation with Non-Members for its collaboration and for the support of the Public Affairs and Communications Directorate which has made this publication possible.

The ACU is particularly grateful to the contributing authors. The views expressed are those of the authors and do not necessarily reflect those of governments of the OECD and associated Member countries. This book is published on the responsibility of the Secretary-General of the OECD.

Preface

Donald Johnston

In 1997 the OECD Members joined by five other countries negotiated and signed the *Convention on Combating Bribery of Foreign Public Officials in International Business Transactions*. These 34 countries sent a message to the world that the way international business was conducted would never be the same.

The Convention, which entered into force in February 1999, requires the parties to make bribery of foreign public officials a crime, levy significant penalties on those who bribe, and tighten up accounting procedures to make it harder to hide illegal payments. The OECD is actively monitoring the effective compliance with the Convention, first the conformity of national implementing legislation with the requirements of the Convention, and in a second phase the application of laws in practice. I believe the 1997 Bribery Convention is making an essential contribution to the broader effort undertaken by OECD Members and partner countries to build a more honest and fair global market place and achieve greater prosperity.

The OECD is playing a leading role in the fight against corruption. Not only has the Organisation addressed the supply of bribes with the Convention and its 1996 recommendation against the tax deductibility of bribes, it has also taken steps to address the demand side of the problem. It has adopted *Principles for Ethical Conduct in the Public Service,* and its SIGMA Program (Support for Improvement in Governance and Management) is helping the countries of Central and Eastern Europe strengthen public procurement systems, establish effective financial controls, and reform civil service laws.

The OECD's initiative has galvanised anti-corruption action in other international organisations, such as the Council of Europe, the Organisation of American States, the European Union, the United Nations, and many others. Co-operation on a global scale is crucial and must involve all actors in the fight against corruption – national governments, business and labour, non-governmental organisations, and the public.

No Longer Business As Usual provides a unique overview of the broad range of legal and regulatory measures taken by governments to combat all forms of bribery and corruption. It also gives a comprehensive description of various initiatives by business and labour groups as well as civil society representatives in support of government anti-corruption efforts. I hope this publication will prove to be a valuable tool in the international fight against bribery and corruption.

Table of Contents

Part IV.
SOCIETY'S GADFLIES

© OECD 2000

I

CORRUPTION: A ZERO SUM GAME

No Longer Business as Usual has encouraging things to say about successful initiatives in the anti-corruption battle, in which the OECD plays a major role.

This first part starts with a detailed analysis of the causes and consequences of corruption. The following chapters deal extensively with the 1997 *Convention on Combating Bribery of Foreign Public Officials in International Business Transactions,* which took the major step of making the bribery of foreign public officials a criminal act in all the signatory countries. Significant related areas such as tax deductibility and corruption in public procurement are also focused on.

Finally, the Organisation's strategy is examined as a dynamic component of the broadening international effort against corruption.

Chapter 1

The Causes and Consequences of Corruption: Economic Analyses and Lessons Learnt[1]

by

Jean Cartier-Bresson[*]

Introduction

Three events have become landmarks in recent anti-corruption history. In 1992, Italy's "Clean Hands" operation brought to light instances of illicit funding of political parties and abuse of office for private gain in the democracies. In 1996, Mr. Wolfensohn, President of the World Bank, committed the Bank to combat corruption, the "cancer" of developing countries, with measures ranging from public-sector reform to debt cancellation. In 1997, OECD Member countries and associated governments negotiated and signed *the Convention on Combating Bribery of Foreign Public Officials in International Business Transactions* [the 1997 Bribery Convention (Annex I)], a reminder that this international problem involves developing countries and multinational firms. These three events together reveal how the international community has begun to realise that corruption – until recently considered a painless, victimless problem – in fact exacts a very high price, which can differ radically from one country or sector to another.

While corruption in the developed countries arises mainly from flaws in the democratic system, it has more devastating and alarming consequences in developing countries. For example, it has an enormous impact on their sovereign functions, which is not the case in developed countries. Whatever their political regimes, developing countries show more vulnerability to corruption simply because they are more prone to government and market failures that create the conditions for sharp distortions.

---

[*] Jean Cartier-Bresson is Professor of Economics at the University of Reims, France.

Economists generally ask three questions in relation to corruption.[2] What economic conditions tend to lead to it? What are its economic consequences? How can we combat it? This chapter presents what they have learned about the first two of these questions; the rest of this book covers the third.

The Causes of Corruption

Interdependence in the economic and political spheres fosters incestuous relationships. A mixed economy, for instance, facilitates the exchange of both legal and illegal resources between them. Building on this, microeconomic research into the causes of corruption traditionally draws on the economics of information and agency models,[3] recently supplemented by empirical studies.[4]

Agency Models: An Overall Picture

For most economists, the root causes of corruption lie in the delegation of power. The possibility of corruption therefore arises from the diverging interests of agents and principals and because information asymmetry, to the advantage of the agents, gives them a great deal of discretionary power. Opportunities for corruption depend on the size of the rents in the control of public agents, the discretion they have in allocating them, and their lack of a sense of accountability to society (Klitgaard, 1988). Where social standards attach no stigma to corruption, agents will often have that lack. A market for corruption thus exists when people trade public goods illegally against payoffs, at the risk of having to pay a penalty. Unfortunately, the likelihood of penalties is slight, not only because information asymmetry protects corrupt agents and proof is scarce, but also, and chiefly, because it is difficult to mobilise large numbers of scattered victims against well-organised agents profiting from illegal gains. The passiveness of the victims is often a prime factor in encouraging corruption.

Rose-Ackerman (1978) explains how corruption spreads when the political, bureaucratic and economic markets come into contact. The Rose-Ackerman study develops a whole series of models, on legislative corruption – when politicians betray the electorate by selling to pressure groups their votes on regulatory or budget legislation – and administrative corruption – when public officials betray politicians by taking payoffs to allow someone to obtain a public service by jumping the queue, to secure a procurement contract or to gain immunity for tax dodging. Opportunities for corruption exist at every level of the hierarchy, from the highest public office to the lowest rung on the ladder. They give rise to both "grand" and "petty" corruption. International corruption has its source in international trade and investment.

In corrupt transactions, firms, pressure groups and citizens try to maximise their gains by paying bribes, while public officials try to maximise their illegal earnings and politicians their power (re-election or client bases) and wealth. In these cases (Rose-Ackerman, 1997) the motivations for paying bribes can be very different. Bribe payers may seek to avoid or reduce costs, through illegal reductions in taxes, lax enforcement of regulations, underestimated rent for public housing or the dropping of criminal charges. They may go after major contracts or overpayment for public procurement. They may try to equate supply and demand for scarce public goods, although this pushes costs up (*i.e.* import licences or subsidised loans). They may pay incentive bonuses for improving or speeding up administrative procedures; and they may be coerced to pay (extortion).

Analysts can classify countries according to whether payoffs are common (*i.e.* endemic or systemic) or non-existent. Incentive bonuses and extortion are rare in developed countries but frequent in developing ones, which have very different institutional environments and therefore incentives. Developed countries uphold human and property rights, and political parties have a long tradition of activism; there are no emerging markets; civil servants are well paid; the supply of goods and services, including public ones, is plentiful enough to avoid shortages; elections are democratic and the welfare state, even if affected by corruption, continues to manage the risks of total exclusion for vulnerable individuals. Corruption, when it occurs, exposes hitherto concealed flaws in the democratic system, rooted mainly in the illegal funding of political parties (see Cartier-Bresson, 1997*b*). Developing countries have more complex causes of corruption.

Weak Governance and Erosion of Property Rights

Three factors explain how bad governance acts as one of the root causes of the spread of corruption:

- *Weak checks and balances*. Property rights, at best just being established or at worst non-existent, often become sources of corruption. From a Weberian standpoint, political systems whose legitimacy derives from charisma and supposedly rational objectives are more permeable by corruption than those based on competence and performance. In many developing countries, the state's monopoly on enforcement is illegitimate because government uses it arbitrarily. Authoritarian regimes – with no tradition of the separation of powers, no culture of expertise and little or no freedom of the press or public participation and consultation – have precarious systems of checks and balances (World Bank 1997). The weakness of independent intermediaries and methods of representation gives more discretionary power to political middlemen, and the costs of denouncing them can be prohibitively high in terms of both time and money (Alam, 1995).

- *Departures from the Weberian model and difficulties in nation building.* Even when political regimes become more democratic they can remain rooted in clientism, patrimonialism or corporatism. Bribes collected to let major contracts both line the pockets of the elite and fund clientist redistribution networks which enable the political authorities to remain in power by buying political backing. These informal networks and the connections and alliances formed through them assume greater importance when major ethnic, religious or regional divisions persist. Administrations come under constant pressure from political, factional and family powers, which limits the application of the principles of meritocracy. Purchasing public office to have access to kickbacks becomes more widespread (Wade, 1982).

- *Inappropriate laws.* The rules by which a society operates must evolve constantly to keep pace with rapid changes. The more ambiguous, rigid or inappropriate they are, the more will informal arrangements dictate economic options and behaviour. Moreover, many formal rules are put in place precisely to facilitate predatory behaviour. They take the form of laborious procedures or regulations that the public sees as unjustified, while informal rules get formulated behind closed doors, with no procedures for monitoring their overall impact. Labour legislation too advanced for the current level of economic development, or too much fiscal pressure on new activities, fuels the informal sector and the corrupt arrangements necessary for it to operate.

Arbitrary behaviour and the precarious legitimacy of many states – which fail to protect rightful economic activity or provide organisational structures for negotiations – leave a gap that alternative protection or "self-help" systems will fill. Such systems have their roots in the micro-legitimation conferred by family, clan, ethnic or regional, criminal or guerrilla organisations. By their very nature, they exclude those who do not belong, either by choice (*i.e.* on principle) or because they fail to qualify with resources to offer. When people perceive private and public property rights as unfairly distributed to start with, that access to them is closed, increasing marginalisation, or that allocating new rights favours the emergence of an elite, the issue becomes one of standards of justice. If the lawful distribution of favours to certain elite factions does not indirectly benefit the population as a whole, through income-generating or redistribution mechanisms, then a real danger exists that people will owe no loyalty to the government's standards (Cartier-Bresson, 1997*a*).

Economic Lag, Scarcity of Public Goods and Poverty

The role assigned to the state for policies designed to make up the economic lag in developing countries, combined with the state's lack of resources, create an environment conducive to corruption. Five situations make corruption likely.

First, the exploitation of natural resources can become a source of rents when they are sold at prices substantially higher than cost. Bribes frequently accompany concession sales. Many observers think that this explains the rampant corruption that followed the discovery of oil in Mexico and Nigeria.

Second, low civil-service wages largely explain the spread of petty corruption (Klitgaard, 1989). The greater the difference between civil-service and private-sector pay, the greater the temptation to make it up illegally (in Gambia, private pay is three to six times public salaries), and opportunities for corruption become the primary motive for seeking civil-service employment. Faced with fiscal crisis and other adjustment measures, governments often prefer to let inflation erode their salaries rather than cut back on the number of civil servants. In Latin America, salaries in the public sector have fallen by 30% to 40% in real terms since the beginning of the 1980s, three times as much as in the private sector. In Africa, the salaries of top civil servants had fallen in real terms by 1983 to 5% of 1975 levels in Uganda, 11% in Ghana, 30% in Nigeria and 45% in Zambia.

Third, protectionist measures and industrial policies have provided incentives for the creation and corrupt purchase of rents (Krueger, 1974). When this happens, the weakness of the productive entrepreneurial class explains the relationship between the crude accumulation of capital, the allocation of public resources to that class and corruption (Khan, 1996). Major infrastructure projects have also given rise to international corruption (Transparency International Report).

Empirical studies confirm the importance of these factors. In a study of 52 countries Ades and Di Tella (1995) identified four variables that explain the origins of corruption: the likelihood of political sanctions and the levels of development, education and economic competition. They conclude that an increase in per capita income of US$4 400 would improve a country's ranking on the corruption index by two points (to 6/10, say, from 4/10, see footnote 4). An increase of one standard deviation in the competition to which a country's firms are exposed would improve its ranking by half a point (for example to 4.5/10 from 4/10). Given identical economic development and similar conditions of competition, corruption was greater in countries with markets dominated by a few firms or with domestic firms sheltered from foreign competition. Italy's lower exposure to such competition could account for a third of the difference in corruption between Italy and Austria. In a later study, Ades and Di Tella (1997) analysed the effects of active industrial policy on corruption along the same lines. The negative effects of corruption (lower investment, see Mauro, 1995) should be subtracted from the positive effects of active industrial policy. By including data on the preferential procurement policies that governments applied to "national champions", they found that an improvement of one standard deviation in a preferential-policy index would greatly reduce corruption. About half of the efforts of industrial policy and the number of people doing R&D are lost through corruption-induced distortions.

Fourth, the scarcity of public goods in less developed countries leads to long waiting lists. The longer the lists and the more essential the goods concerned (a house, a business telephone line, a hospital bed, a student grant, irrigation water), the more people stand ready to pay to jump the queue. Where there are both unregulated (official or parallel market) and regulated prices (interest rates, exchange rates, currency allocation, subsidised staple products, housing), few goods exchange at the regulated prices – lower than the free-market prices – and competition to procure them breeds corruption.

Fifth, reforms to streamline the public sector and regulatory policies should, in the long term, reduce the opportunities for corruption generated by centrally planned development, but the process of transition towards new standards will tend to give rise to new illicit arrangements. Privatisation and the licensing of banks, for example, have seen new forms of corruption. Where governance remains poor, the introduction of competition policy through regulatory agencies risks allowing the emergence of new forms of corruption on a wide scale.

The World Bank (1997) highlights four factors associated with low levels of corruption: the absence of distortions due to economic policy, a predictable judiciary, merit-based recruitment and little difference between public and private wages. Elliot (1997) tempers the critique of the state with evidence that, for 83 counties, low levels of corruption and central government spending are positively correlated. In the 16 most corrupt countries, central government spending averages 21% of GDP, less than the 32% average for the sample.

The Consequences of Corruption

Increasingly fewer commentators maintain that corruption has positive effects, and the costs that it generates are finally being recognised. Unfortunately, those costs are difficult to calculate, partly because corrupt transactions are secret but also because they cause both direct distortions through less competition and indirect ones through a general laxness, which increases non-accountability. Both causes affect the amounts that change hands. Recent economic studies generally conclude that the negative effects on the allocation and distribution of resources are as follows:

- The transaction costs of illegal exchanges are important for maintaining secrecy. Because corrupt contracts confer no property rights, the corrupt party may not provide the service, ask for more money or provide the service to a competitor. With no third party to which agents can appeal in the event of a dispute, such contracts are risky, especially if no further transactions are expected or very high amounts are involved. There are three ways to mitigate these risks. One can select agents by other than economic criteria, such as family, ethnic, religious or social connections. One can create social standards (honour amongst thieves), or pressures like the loss of reputation for agents who break faith, which carry the penalties of exclusion and loss of future income. Finally, one can delegate control and enforcement of contracts to a criminal organisation using threats or violence. These options make the market for corruption a very closed one.

- By increasing uncertainty and the costs of legal transactions, corruption reduces investment and therefore growth. Mauro (1995) shows a negative correlation between corruption and the rate of investment and between corruption and the growth rate in 67 countries in 1960-85. He finds that if a country like Egypt were to improve the efficiency of its administration and reduce corruption to the same level as in Argentina (*i.e.* an index rating of 6/10 rather than 4/10) the rate of investment would increase by 3% and the growth rate would increase by 0.5%. A paper by Wei (1997) studies the effects of both tax increases and the corruption level on investment in 45 host countries by multinational firms from fourteen source countries. It concludes that an increase in the corruption level from that of Singapore, which has a zero rating (10/10), to that of Mexico (3.25/10) would equate with raising the tax rate by 21 percentage points. That would sharply depress the flow of foreign direct investment, including flows to countries in Asia.

- Poor allocation of public resources results when governments award contracts to corrupt firms, which recover in the estimates they submit the costs of bribes they pay. When this occurs, political and economic collusion between public servants and archaic or rent-seeking cliques will hamper innovation.

- Corruption distorts the allocative role of government because it tilts the composition of public spending towards projects that make it easier to collect on bribes, at the expense of priority programmes. Interminable and inappropriate "white elephant" projects will proliferate. In major international transactions a preference arises for purchasing custom-built, high-tech equipment, because controls become difficult with no market prices against which to compare costs (Winston, 1979). Corruption also increases public deficits, as contracts are not let to the lowest bidders and the frequent insertion of additional clauses inflates the initial project costs. Mauro (1997) shows that corruption steers public expenditure towards areas that will facilitate corrupt transactions – typically, spending on defence rather than on education.

- Corruption distorts the redistributive role of the state, facilitates fraud and breeds tax evasion. Because it reduces government revenues, it places an increasingly heavier burden on a steadily decreasing number of taxpayers. This raises incentives to turn to the informal sector and starts a vicious circle. It also totally distorts programmes to combat poverty. It renders international aid much less effective by diverting growing amounts from their intended purposes, such as infrastructure, programmes to combat poverty or reconstruction from earthquakes and civil wars.

- Corruption lowers the quality of services provided and goods bought by administrations. Four hundred recent deaths when a building collapsed in Seoul have heightened awareness of corruption in Korea.

- In systems where rent seeking proves more lucrative than productive work, talent will be misallocated and the elite will turn to non-productive work, with adverse consequences for the social surplus and growth.

- Corruption of the enforcement apparatus (army, police and the courts) allows organised crime to extend its predatory activities of the private sector. It can even enable a symbiosis between organised crime and politicians that further encourages the abuse of power.

Complex socio-political consequences add to these economic costs: loss of legitimacy, instability or, conversely, closer co-operation between rival factions. Difficulty in gauging the costs of corruption arises because its political and economic consequences may differ greatly. Waterbury (1973) explained how the corruption that accompanied agrarian reform in Morocco contributed to political stability but not to economic growth. Nevertheless, political stability could well have boosted economic growth in the long term. It thus becomes important to differentiate between corrupt practices according to their political and economic effects, bearing in mind that the induced costs are by no means identical. This has prompted some economists to analyse the differential effects using the concept of market power.

Market Power and the Organisation of Corruption

Observers have found that given sets of identical circumstances (those described by the agency models above) will not produce the same levels of corruption. Moreover, corruption may be just as widespread in one place as another, but differ in strength; why does the percentage demanded in bribes rise from 10% to 20% in some countries or sectors but not in others? All of these differences can find explanation in the varied resources and/or capacity for action – market power – available to corrupt agents across sectors, countries or time.

Deliberate Corruption and Predatory Behaviour

Since Johnston (1986), economists have agreed that the consequences of corruption depend strongly on the characteristics of the transactions and the agents who conduct them. Exchanges can be highly organised, centralised among agents who abide by the established rules of the game, or relatively disorganised, decentralised or anarchic, involving constant bargaining over changeable amounts. The consequences of corruption depend on its predictability, the stability of the number of agents on both the supply and demand sides of the market, their social positions and the types of social relations that they maintain outside of corrupt transactions (*i.e.* impersonal or within the same social network). Factors such as whether transactions are regular or occasional and whether the market is inclusive (open to all) or exclusive (requiring some form of qualification) will also affect the consequences. Thus, the level of corruption depends not only on the potential for rents but also on 1) the political structures of the corruption market on the demand side, which sells favours and generates the demand for bribes, and 2) domestic and international market structures on the supply side, which demands favours and pays bribes.

Cartier-Bresson (1997) and Rose-Ackerman (1998) note four possible permutations of the relative market powers of the demand side (public officials) and the supply side (private agents):

- *Bilateral monopoly.* Both parties have identical market power and exchanges are mutually beneficial. Centralised transactions of this type occur most often when the political and economic elites are small and homogenous, with their legitimacy tied to performance, as in democracies. Here, the elites prohibit the petty corruption of bureaucrats.

- *Demand side stronger than supply side.* In kleptocratic systems, the recipients of bribes set the transaction prices, operating from a strong position of market power. This is extortion. It thrives on maintaining constant competition between rent seekers or on other methods, such as violence and intimidation. The prices and the numbers of corrupt transactions increase. This situation is frequent in either of two circumstances. First, civil society or the private sector may be weak, with under-developed human and property rights, or none at all. Second, political power may be highly fractionalised between regions, ethnic origins, parties or party factions, with all sides needing to extract the maximum resources in order to continue the struggle. This predatory situation leads to the most negative effects of all. Rents from raw materials or international aid dry up because they have either been over-exploited or exhausted. Tensions in their redistribution increase to breaking point, the social breakdown of the system begins and violence escalates, with civil war often the last stage. The tolerance of grand corrupters for petty corruption is part of the clientist domination strategy.

- *Supply side stronger than demand side.* Two cases may arise here. In the first, a position of social or economic power – a member of the elite versus a minor public official or a multinational firm versus the administration – allows the bribe payer to set the price. In the second, typically where the state is weak, corrupters, including organised criminals, gain their power using methods such as intimidation and violence. Because bribe payers dominate, levels of corruption and the prices are lower.

- *Supply and demand sides fragmented.* Here a fragmented government faces multiple bribe payers and the corruption market becomes highly competitive, generating a corruption spiral that results in a multitude of small bribes.

The relative strengths in those markets depend not just on the number of agents or their financial power but also on their political power, how efficiently they organise and whether they can align themselves with other pressure groups. The consequences of corrupt transactions depend on the political context in which the politically powerful and socio-economic groups compete, and on whether they can co-operate in a relatively stable and profitable way. When the objectives of those with political power are maximisation of personal gain or development, these become indivisible from the effects of corruption. This explains why corruption is particularly pernicious in developing countries, which seldom have bilateral monopolies, and why the most efficiently organised and controlled – and therefore less harmful – forms of corruption are found in the Western democracies.

The Corruption Trap in Developing Countries

Shleifer and Vishny (1993) and *Finance and Development* (1998) have demonstrated that the more disorganised the system of corruption, the higher its costs. Moreover, organised corruption through networks consisting of a mix of politicians and bureaucrats will have internal monitoring mechanisms able to detect and punish those who deviate from the norm of the aggregate bribe price, provided that the elites are small and the society is homogenous. According to these authors, the KGB controlled corruption in the former Soviet Union, while corruption in the transition period has been anarchic. Kaufmann (1997) and Kaufmann and Wei (1998) have shown that the more bribes firms pay, the more management time they have to spend negotiating with bureaucrats.

Based on cross-country data for 28 countries, Brunetti (1995) demonstrated that the uncertainty bred by regulatory instability, of which corruption is only one element, adversely affects investment more than does corruption itself. Thus, countries with endemic but predictable corruption, such as Thailand and Indonesia, have not seen a fall in investment or growth. The World Bank (1997) produced an index of the predictability of corruption for 69 countries, measuring the predictability of the extra amounts that one must pay and that of receiving the outcome one has paid for. For given levels of corruption, countries in which corruption is more predictable have higher investment rates. If the levels of corruption and its predictability are related with investment, a different investment rate emerges in each of four cases. High corruption and low predictability associate with an investment/GNP ratio of 12.3%. High corruption and high predictability yield a ratio of 19.5%, low corruption and low predictability one of 21.3%, and low corruption with high predictability one of 28.5%.

Corruption Networks and Price Restraints in Developed Countries

Developed countries have many social codes that act as restraints on competition in the corruption market, evidenced, for example, in low bribes compared with rents sold. The restriction of competition stems from both economic and social barriers to entry (Cartier-Bresson, 1997). All comers may not enter the race for rents, and social as well as technical (firm-specific) prerequisites operate; one must move in the right circles. Pre-selection guarantees transaction security and the reproduction of benefits within a small elite. Co-operation strategies between rent-seekers (cartels) restrict competition and outbidding. In social exchanges, the absence of maximising behaviour and the cultivation of adequately satisfactory routine relations (procedural rationality and mimesis) are frequent. The decision to cultivate privileged relationships over the long term curbs the opportunistic behaviour often characteristic of short-term relations.

Policy analyses that have looked at corruption in terms of social networks have been able to refine the concept of power as exercised on the corruption market and have particular pertinence for Western democracies. They see corruption as a socially reproduced mechanism that should be analysed in the context of each country's own construct of the state. The sheer diversity of the personal-relations networks that administer economic and political goods explains the varying patterns of corruption. To analyse the different types of market power operating on the supply and demand sides of the corruption market, one must study the structure and form of legal networks established by the intermediaries of public policy. These economic, social and political agents – who produce information both to inform and to assist decision-makers – exchange widely diverse goods under socially established codes. Their legal networks are the origin of the clandestine agreements that characterise corruption in the Western democracies.

In a corrupt bilateral monopoly, the tensions that arise from discrepancies between the symbolic order (*i.e.* "money has no place in politics") and the real-life practices of an elite foster the creation of illicit networks that take care of "arrangements". Bargaining gets avoided and contracts are honoured in obedience to social codes of good behaviour. Corruption becomes a social exchange, and the networks have the power to sanction agents who deviate from the contract price by exclusion from future transactions and loss of reputation. This often requires that business networks be inclusive and do not object to competition. Prices, normally stable, can rise as soon as firms start making higher bids and/or pressure comes from politicians or political parties. Situations in which private outsiders face politicians more interested in lining their pockets than in the prudent use of money will lead to a spiral of bribery.

In democratic countries, however, the economic exchange usually turns into a social one because the goal is as much to consolidate special relations as to make an immediate profit. The risks, the secrecy, the heterogeneity of the goods exchanged, which are not always commensurate (insider information as well as economic, political, social and symbolic resources) and the diversity of objectives make for a self-regulated, "customised market for arrangements". The existence of checks and balances, whether electoral, judicial, or ensured by the media, and the need to avoid dysfunctions or excessive surplus costs in administrations, restrict the bribery spiral in democracies.

Empirical Problems: The Use of Local Surveys

Securing Reliable Data

The effectiveness of an anticorruption agenda depends in part on accurate analysis of the causes and consequences of corruption in extremely varied political and economic contexts. Misperceptions of the underlying causes of corruption – industrial policy rather than a weak judiciary, for example – or incorrect appraisal of the most distortive effects (corruption of police or legislators) can mean that the entire anti-corruption agenda will simply be a string of abstract universal measures with no practical effect. Countermeasures must also guard against adverse collateral consequences. For example, one side-effect of the 1997 Bribery Convention (Annex I), in cutting the bribes paid by multinationals to political leaders in developing countries, could be the destruction of clientist redistribution channels which secure the allegiance of ethnic, regional or religious groupings in local populations. If turmoil and heightened insecurity were to ensue, that would reduce foreign direct investment, and the outcome would be the reverse of that sought.

The econometric analysis of the causes and consequences of corruption described in this chapter casts light on these questions, but does not identify the specific mechanisms of corruption or clarify their diverse configurations. It provides too general an overall picture of the problems to provide a basis for detailed remedies. A further weakness stems from the subjective and aggregated data used.[5] To overcome these problems, international agencies such as the World Bank, UNDP, USAID and Transparency International increasingly use diagnostic surveys of households, enterprise managers and public officials in developing countries. Such surveys increase practical knowledge of the causes and consequences of corruption, and can find use in discussion workshops to pave the way for reforms.

Country Surveys of Public Services

Efficient provision of public services entails appropriate administrative reforms. They require sharper evaluation of demand by local communities, diagnostic surveys of service quality, covering consumers and inspection units and evaluation of the effectiveness of reform. The surveys collect information, by sectors of administration, on the prevalence of bribery, the levels of officials involved, the amounts, the goods and services that bribery secures, trends and changes, the main victims, and so on. Repeat surveys are run 18 or 24 months after the launch of reforms, and then annually. Surveys of this kind have been conducted in 13 countries and provide both proofs of corruption's costs and information on perceptions about the sectors most affected, helping to set priorities for reforms.

The initial findings for Albania, Georgia and Latvia reveal that corruption takes many forms (World Bank, 1998). A weak judiciary is one of the main causes of corruption in Albania, but regulatory failures are more serious in Georgia and Latvia. In Georgia, for example, corruption is most prevalent in tax and financial inspectorates, customs, water and electricity services, fire and sanitary inspectorates, and the police. The survey, which covered between 350 and 450 enterprises, also showed that business would be willing to pay additional taxes if corruption were eliminated. Bribes take 7% of firms' revenue in Albania and Latvia and 15% in Georgia. Some 14% per cent of Georgian households admit to paying bribes and 11% in Latvia. Further information concerns the public offices (customs, tax inspectorates, etc.) that officials are keenest to obtain because of the opportunities for bribery; the more lucrative the position, the higher the price they will pay for it. Overall, the government sectors most affected are customs in Guinea Bissau, tax inspectorates in Latvia, the judiciary in Albania, Guatemala and Morocco, and procurement agencies in Benin, Georgia and Colombia. Along similar lines, Kaufmann (1997, 1999) presents considerable information on bribe taking in Ukraine.

In Uganda (World Bank, 1999) public spending on primary education trebled in 1991-93, but enrolment rates did not rise. A survey of 250 schools showed that over 70% of capital funding got misappropriated and that sinecures and clientist recruiting were widespread and damaging. Reforms relied on dismissals and regular radio announcements of the budgets allocated to each school. A survey of the health sector showed how staff diverted medicine and equipment to their own use (70% of medicines misappropriated). Last, VAT restitution to firms was deficient in 58% per cent of the cases (18% got none and 40% waited for many months).

Facts and Figures to Bolster Civil Society and Reformers

The World Bank posits that corruption can be brought under control only when citizens cease to tolerate it. That calls for dissemination of the information obtained from the diagnostic surveys and a stronger role for employers' groups, trade associations and NGOs. Under its mandate, and at the express request of governments, the Bank has organised integrity workshops through its Economic Development Institute (on national integrity systems, see Langseth *et al.*, 1997). These workshops bring together local NGOs and government representatives. They advocate the partnership approach as a means of exchanging previously confidential information, passing on data from the diagnostic surveys, presenting claims and resolving conflicts of interest. The Bank hopes that non-partisan anti-corruption coalitions will form, drawing on this range of facts and figures. In methodological terms, the proposed reforms are based on economic analysis of public management and a pro-democratic view of the creativeness and importance of mobilising civil society.

Conclusion

Economic analyses provide insight into the causes of corruption by examining the concepts of information asymmetry, discretionary power, monopolies and rent seeking. They highlight the roles of poverty, low civil-service pay and rent seeking. They catalogue the allocative and distributive ills caused by corruption, and suggest an approach to the study of the diverse consequences through classifying the various power structures that operate among the corrupters and the corrupted. As more empirical surveys appear over the next few years, a clearer picture of the overall costs of corruption should emerge, a measure that, unfortunately, remains one of the major unknowns.

Notes

1. This chapter owes much to discussions with Irène Hors (OECD Development Centre) that provided valuable input, but full responsibility for the views expressed in it remains, of course, the author's.

2. For a general introduction to economic analyses on corruption, see Cartier-Bresson, 1995; Bardham, 1997; and Goudies and Stasavage, 1997.

3. The economics of information and moral hazard studies work from two premises. First, not all agents have the same amount of information on their exchanges. Second, their actions and the effects are not easy to observe or quantify (for example achievement of an electoral programme or the costs of building an opera house). Under these assumptions, studies examine potential maverick behaviour in markets and in government, and then go on to analyse measures that could reduce such behaviour at the least possible cost.

4. Econometric research uses subjective data supplied by consultancies on investment and loan risks. It has ranked about 60 developed and developing countries on an index ranging from 0 (total corruption) to 10 (absolute integrity), based on evaluations by business executives.

5. The first problem in such analysis is the reliability of sources. Data on corruption are uncertain because transactions are, by definition, covert. Court proceedings cannot be taken as a basis, because legal definitions of corruption, and above all actual law enforcement, vary markedly from one country to another. A country that takes firm action against corruption, bringing numbers of court cases, would then be deemed more corrupt; a country with lax provisions on conflict of interest would be deemed honest. Similarly, using newspaper data would largely reflect public awareness of corruption, and press freedom. Econometric research has accordingly used indexes of perception of international corruption, as estimated by business. There are two types of bias here. First, countries with good economic performance and substantial corruption come out better than those with the same level of corruption but weaker performance, because lower growth heightens awareness and hence perceptions of corruption. Second, domestic corruption, impacting on citizens or local firms, gets disregarded.

Bibliography

ADES, A. and R. DI TELLA (1997),
   "National Champions and Corruption: Some Unpleasant Interventionist Arithmetic", *The Economic Journal*, July.

ADES, A. and R. DI TELLA (1995),
"Rent, Competition and Corruption", Oxford University, *mimeo.*

ALAM, M. S., (1995),
"A Theory of Limits on Corruption and Some Applications", *Kyklos*, No. 48, pp. 419-435.

BARDHAN, P. (1997),
"The Economics of Corruption in Less Developed Countries: A Review of the Issues", in *The Role of Governance in Economic Development*, OECD Development Centre Studies, Paris, OECD, pp. 15-44.

BRUNETTI, A. (1997),
Politics and Economic Growth, OECD Development Centre Studies, Paris, OECD.

CARTIER-BRESSON, J. (1995),
"The Economics of Corruption" in: D. DELLA PORTA and Y. MENY (eds.), *Democracy and Corruption in Europe, Pinter*, pp. 149-165.

CARTIER-BRESSON, J. (1997a),
"Corruption Networks, Transaction Security and Illegal Social Exchange", in *Political Studies*, v. 45, No. 3, pp. 463-476.

CARTIER-BRESSON, J. (1997b),
"A Few Suggestions for A Comparative Analysis of Corruption in Western Europe", *Revue Internationale de Politiques Comparées.*

ELLIOTT, K. (1997),
"Summary and Conclusion", in: ELLIOT, K. (ed.), *Corruption and the Global Economy.* Washington DC, Institute for International Economics, pp. 175-233.

FINANCE AND DEVELOPMENT,
March, 1998, 3-4.

GOUDIES, A., and D. STASAVAGE (1997),
Corruption, the Issues, OECD Development Centre Technical Papers, No. 122, Paris, OECD.

JOHNSTON, M. (1986),
"The Political Consequences of Corruption. A Reassessment", *Comparative Politics*, pp. 459-477.

KAUFMANN, D. (1997),
"Corruption: Some Myths and Facts", *Foreign Policy*, No. 107.

KAUFMANN, D. (1999),
"Anticorruption Strategies: Starting Afresh? Unconventional Lessons from Comparative Analysis", in STAPENHURST and KPUNDEH, *Curbing Corruption*, Washington, EDI, World Bank, pp. 35-49.

KAUFMANN, D. and WEI, S-J. (1999),
Does "Grease Money" Speed Up the Wheels of Commerce?, NBER Working Paper, No. 7093, April.

KHAN, M. (1996),
"A Typology of Corrupt Transactions in Developing Countries", *IDS Bulletin*, v. 27, pp. 12-21.

KLITGAARD, R. (1989),
"Incentive Myopia"*, World Development*, v. 17, No. 4, pp. 447-459.

KLITGAARD, R. (1988),
"Controlling Corruption", University of California Press.

KRUEGER, A. O. (1974),
"The political Economy of rent seeking society", *The American Economic Review*, 64, pp. 271-303.

LANGSETH, P. and R. STAPENHURST (1997),
National Integrity System Country Studies, Washington, EDI, World Bank.

LANGSETH, P., R. STAPENHURST and J. POPE (1997),
"The Role of A National Integrity System in Fighting Corruption", Washington, EDI, World Bank.

MAURO, P. (1997),
"The Effects of Corruption on Growth, Investment and Government Expenditure", in ELLIOT, *op. cit.*, pp. 83-108.

MAURO, P. (1995),
"Corruption and Growth", *Quarterly Journal of Economics*, v. 3, No. 442, pp. 681-712.

ROSE-ACKERMAN, S. (1978),
"Corruption: A Study in Political Economy", New York, Academic Press.

ROSE-ACKERMAN, S. (1997),
Corruption and Good Governance. UNDP.

ROSE-ACKERMAN, S. (1998),
"Corruption and Development", in PLESKOVIC, B. and STIGLITZ, J., *Annual World Bank Conference on Development Economics*, Washington, World Bank.

SHLEIFER A. and R. VISHNY (1993),
"Corruption", *Quarterly Journal of Economics*. August, pp. 599-617.

TANZI, V. (1995),
"Corruption, Governmental Activities and Markets", *Finance and Development*, December, pp. 24-26.

TRANSPARENCY INTERNATIONAL REPORT,
Berlin, Annual.

WADE R. (1982),
"The System of Administrative and Political Corruption: Canal Irrigation in South India", *The Journal of Development Studies*, v. 18, No. 3, pp.287-328.

WATERBURY J. (1973),
"Endemic and Planned Corruption in A Monarchical Regime", *World Politics*, pp. 534-555.

WEI S-J. (1997),
"How Taxing Is Corruption on International Investors?", *NBER Working Paper*, No. 6030.

WORLD BANK (1997),
World Bank Development Report, Washington, World Bank.

WORLD BANK (1998),
New Frontiers in Diagnosing and Combating Corruption. Premnotes No. 7, Washington.

WORLD BANK (1999),
Using Surveys for Public Sector Reform, Premnotes No. 23, Washington.

Chapter 2

To Bribe or not to Bribe?

by
Giorgio Sacerdoti[*]

The Role of the OECD in Anti-Corruption Work

Since 15 February 1999, the answer to the question "to bribe or not to bribe?" is "NO". That is the date on which the Convention on Combating Bribery of Foreign Public Officials in International Business Transactions (the 1997 Bribery Convention, see Annex I) entered into force, imposing criminal penalties on those who bribe foreign public officials in order to obtain business deals. This Convention, signed in Paris on 17 December 1997 under the auspices of the OECD, thus became the first tangible and most important global result of international initiatives that developed when, under pressure from global public opinion, a number of scandals and investigations revealed much about corruption in international affairs. Yet the OECD has not worked alone. The European Union (EU) approved a Convention on combating corruption on 26 May 1997 (ECOJ, 1997*a*), while the Council of Europe in Strasbourg laboured actively on a regional convention on corruption in general, which it later finalised on 5 November 1998. Although the 1997 Bribery Convention covers a narrower range of offences – for example, unlike the EU convention, it criminalises only active and not passive corruption – its signatories include 29 OECD Members plus five other countries,[1] it is open to accession by other states, and it covers corruption of public officials of any state, not just of the states that are parties on the basis of reciprocity as in the EU convention.

The OECD began this work in 1989 at the initiative of the United States, whose companies complained that only they, among firms based in the major

---

[*] Giorgio Sacerdoti is Professor of International Law at the Bocconi University, Milan, Italy and Vice-Chairman of the OECD Working Group on Bribery in International Business Transactions.

trading countries, faced criminal sanctions for bribes paid abroad, under the US Foreign Corrupt Practices Act of 1977 (FCPA). Almost all other countries aimed the offence of corruption only at safeguarding the integrity of their own public administrations. No specific rules criminalised the corruption of foreign officials, even where this behaviour involves countries other than that of the official, as occurs when a company obtains a market or a contract abroad at the expense of more deserving competitors in a third country. Moreover, the justifications for developing and expanding internationally the rules against corruption go beyond only commercial arguments. Other relevant factors include growing economic interdependence, the use of public funds for aid to developing countries and the emergence of common values of good government, transparency of public administration and democracy.

Against this background, the lack of interest displayed until recently by many of the largest countries, whose companies export and invest abroad, seems difficult to justify any longer. In the global economy, such benign neglect finds no justification in the two main contentions used to support it. One holds that states individually bear the principal responsibility to assure that their own houses are in order. The other asserts that practices and sensibilities are not the same everywhere – *i.e.* the meaning of "corruption" varies – and the corruption phenomenon links narrowly to the political and administrative organisation of each country.

On the contrary, international co-operation is necessary to cope effectively with corruption. Unilateral actions, which incriminate behaviour outside a country's territory (even if enforcement remains domestic) easily lay that country open to criticism of interference, the more so when they implicate high foreign political dignitaries. Unilateral action taken in isolation can also be ineffective in practice. The legal and factual limitations (on collecting evidence, for example) of even indirect extra-territorial exercise of national penal jurisdiction are well known, especially where the foreign authorities involved do not collaborate. Without international co-operation, business and investment freedom, the use of groups and companies with subsidiaries in off-shore centres, and recourse to obliging intermediaries permit companies to elude obligations enacted in their home countries. While unilateral measures may have succeeded in the United States, thanks to its economic and political power, this is not so for most other countries.

The general background to the OECD effort thus included not only the specific request of the United States for discussions, but also a recognised increase in corruption globally, heightened public awareness of it, the perceived weakening of the major arguments against taking anti-corruption action multilaterally and a growing sense that unilateral measures were inadequate. The effort had as its purpose to organise effective co-operation between the principal actors in the international economy. That co-operation, building a consensus based on shared objectives, would work to promulgate an effective legal instrument containing reciprocal and comparable legal commitments to combat transnational bribery (see Yannaca-Small, 1994).

From an *Ad Hoc* Working Group to the 1997 Ministerial Recommendation

The work began modestly but thoroughly. An *ad hoc* Working Group, established in 1989, started with a comparative review of Members' national legislation and of the concepts fundamental both to the offence of corruption and to the exercise of national jurisdiction over offences committed wholly or partially abroad. The examination covered participating countries' criminal, civil and commercial laws, administrative laws, accounting requirements, banking and financial provisions, and laws and regulations relating to public subsidies and contracts. It resulted in the most complete survey done to that date. It revealed more potential reach in law to the bribery of foreign public officials than was previously known. Existing laws, including criminal laws, would apply in a number of countries, even if they did not specifically address the bribery of foreign public officials. Effective action, however, required further, more specific efforts.

The OECD possesses only limited powers to pass decisions binding on its members, as they must be unanimous. Proceeding to such "consensus", in OECD parlance, presents a long and formidable negotiating task, however. Members therefore decided to seek as the first objective a "soft law" instrument, *i.e.* a recommendation inviting Member states to confront bribery with dissuasive actions outside of criminal law, to remove any provisions that might facilitate bribery. A point of contention arose over the tax deductibility of corrupt payments abroad, allowed by certain countries as inherent to procuring contracts. Although such deductibility has only arguable practical value, it seems contradictory to allow as legitimate expense payments which the business community and states consider unacceptable in terms of morality and the good conduct of business. This question encompasses the more general one of accounting practices and controls, given that these payments are normally hidden by accounting devices, the use of false invoices or non-transparent documents.

In 1994, the OECD Council adopted at ministerial level a first Recommendation, inviting Member states to adopt "effective measures to detect, prevent and combat bribery of foreign public officials in international business". Those measures were to apply both to national political institutions and legislation (criminal and commercial law, the tax system when it favoured corruption and the regulation of procurement contracts) and to the reinforcement of international co-operation. It represented a first important signal, completed by the renewal of the Working Group's mandate. Prof. Mark Pieth of Basel, who had guided its work efficiently from the start, continued as the Chairman, leading a group of knowledgeable Member delegates, most often experts in the field. The new mandate charged the Group with examining how Member countries intended to follow the recommendation, studying critical areas for feasible further initiatives and formulating co-ordinated criminal-law principles to combat corruption.

Questions remained about the best way to "criminalise the corruption of foreign public officials in an effective and co-ordinated manner", as had been decided. Should a classic international convention on criminal law be negotiated, or would a recommendation to Members suffice for them to adopt autonomous internal rules, based on a model prepared by the Group (the Working Group on Bribery in International Transactions is refered to by the author as the Group) to guarantee basic uniformity? Clearly, the different structures of the Member countries' criminal-law systems would render impossible any agreement on the inclusion of identical provisions, either in a treaty or in national legislation. To resolve this conundrum, the Group developed the concept of "functional equivalence". Differences would not matter and would be admitted, provided they led to equivalent results, namely effective prosecution and sanctions.

This concept allowed the Group to move ahead with original work to negotiate key elements of minimal uniformity (in regulation, for example), independently of whether the provisions would go into a convention or serve as a model for internal law. It entrusted this task to a sub-group of experts, chaired by this author, which completed its work over three sessions between the autumn of 1996 and the spring of 1997. The sub-group formulated eight "Agreed Common Elements of Criminal Law and Related Measures". The Group itself pushed work ahead on the non-deductibility of illicit payments (as agreed with the OECD Fiscal Affairs Committee), accounting and auditing practices, procurement contracts and civil remedies. The OECD Council at ministerial level approved all of the Group's proposals on 23 May 1997, in its "Revised Recommendation on Combating Bribery in International Business Transactions", to which the "Agreed Common Elements" are annexed (see Annex II).

A compromise resolved the choice between the convention and its alternative. The United States supported using the Recommendation. With a law (the FCPA) already in place, it urged the other Members to equip themselves as rapidly as possible with domestic criminal provisions inspired by the "Agreed Common Elements". It feared that resort to a convention might entail further delays, not only in lengthy negotiations but also in the time needed to ratify it for entry into force. Other countries, France and Germany in particular, insisted that only a convention could guarantee the binding character of precise and equivalent obligations by Member states. Still others, such as Italy, held an intermediate position. They recognised that adequate national arrangements could be adopted under the umbrella of the Recommendation, but they highlighted the greater efficiency of a convention, both in application and in showing a firm commitment against corruption to national parliaments and public opinion.

The compromise involved giving the Recommendation a dual effect: that Members, in any event, adopt national laws by the end of 1998; and that they open negotiations immediately to conclude a convention by the end of 1997 in order for it to enter into force by the end of 1998. Both initiatives would use the "Agreed Common Elements" as a basis, and, obviously, successful negotiation of the Convention would render autonomous national legislation superfluous, except as needed to conform to the Convention itself.

Negotiation and Signature of the 1997 Convention

On the basis of this political commitment by the Member states and the work already accomplished by the Group, progress came rapidly. The Group, transformed into a negotiating conference of both the Member countries and those non-members already participating in its work, concluded negotiations on the text of the Convention in November 1997, and it was officially signed on 17 December.[2]

Despite the "Agreed Common Elements", which determined the content of the Convention, the negotiation was tough. Certain important residual divergences persisted, as well as different approaches to several issues by various delegations in light of different national traditions – on jurisdiction and the criminal responsibility of legal persons, for example. The negotiators managed to resolve these difficulties by drafting explanatory notes, later transformed into "Commentaries" on the Convention and adopted by the negotiating conference at the same time as the text of the Convention. These Commentaries do not form part of the Convention and have not been signed. Furthermore, they do not have an organic character as do, for example, the explanatory Reports of the conventions of the Council of Europe, and they refer only to certain articles or individual clauses of the 1997 Bribery Convention.

The weight of these Commentaries in interpreting the Convention is debatable. In this author's opinion, they are not "preparatory documents", to which one can have recourse as a supplementary interpretation tool pursuant to Article 32 of the Vienna Convention on the Law of Treaties of 1969, which codified traditional international law in this area. Instead, they provide a significant element of the "context" within which the 1997 Bribery Convention was drafted, for interpretation pursuant to Article 31 of the Vienna Convention. Article 31 mentions as "context" any agreement relating to a treaty that is entered into by all the parties in connection with the conclusion of the treaty. One must doubt whether the Commentaries can really be considered to be such an agreement "in simplified form", for the simple reason that the contracting parties specifically intended not to insert the content of the Commentaries into the Convention. The "context" is not limited to such an agreement, however, and the Commentaries provide guidance in determining the scope of the Convention in the event of doubt, although this would not constitute an authentic and conclusive interpretation. Various countries (*e.g.* Korea) have in fact relied on the Commentaries in drafting implementing legislation for the Convention.

General Features of the 1997 Bribery Convention

The 1997 Bribery Convention's principal characteristic is a novelty. The industrialised countries, home of most large multinational firms, have bound themselves to prevent and repress bribery by their companies. They will do so by criminalising "active" corruption (bribery) of other countries' officials, whether or not those countries are signatories of the Convention. Furthermore, they do so independently of the applicability and enforcement of criminal laws in the latter countries on the "passive" corruption (taking bribes) of their officials. The contracting states thus intend to accept neither the corruption of these foreign officials nor any tolerance of such behaviour by their governments. They simply note, then work around, the reality that pursuing the officials themselves would raise unsolvable jurisdictional issues and open them to the criticism of interfering with the sovereignty of other states.[3]

This approach also arises from economic and trade concerns. It seeks to avoid distortion of international competition by corrupt practices considered inadmissible. It tries to guarantee a "level playing field", *i.e.* to assure common rules for companies of different origins in international markets. Making criminal rules uniform is not common, especially when the initiative comes from a group of leading countries rather than from a multilateral institution. It demonstrates a new orientation in the multilateral regulation of international trade in general, notwithstanding precedents such as co-operation in the fight against money laundering. The 1997 Bribery Convention, open for adherence by other countries as indicated by Article 13 (2) and provided for in the Recommendation of 1997, may represent a model for new initiatives.

Another general characteristic of the Convention closely follows the model of the classic penal law conventions, such as those of the Council of Europe or measures against terrorism, in defining the offence, the jurisdictional basis, the secondary rules and the organisation of mutual co-operation between Member states in matters of assistance and extradition. The 1997 Bribery Convention distances itself from the traditional model in other respects, however. First, its norms are not self-executing. The rule providing for the criminalisation of the corruption of foreign public officials, provided by Article 1, will generally require reformulation for introduction into the criminal legislation of the Member states. Rules on the extent and type of sanctions, jurisdiction and statutes of limitations receive no exhaustive formulation, but rather indicate the fundamental content, which national implementing rules will have to respect.

This approach was not fortuitous. The negotiators had to take note that different criteria inspired the criminal systems of different states on a number of crucial matters, such as the subjection of legal persons to criminal law, the extension of jurisdictional competence on the basis of the nationality of the person charged or, on the contrary, solely on a territorial basis, and the obligatory or discretionary character of criminal prosecution. Given the Convention's method, stated in the preamble, of combating the evil through equivalent national measures, the signatories can fulfil their obligations by having recourse to different measures dependent on their legislative structures, on the condition that they adequately attain the prescribed result.[4]

Second, the Convention also contains non-criminal rules; aimed at both transparency and prevention, they specify requirements for corporate accounting and auditing. Third, it gives a multilateral, supervisory role to the OECD Group. The Group will promote and monitor full implementation of the Convention through periodic examinations of measures adopted by the signatories and their concrete application. This mechanism replaces the dispute-settlement procedures often present in criminal conventions. It provides a more flexible and efficient way to ensure the respect of reciprocal commitments and, in general, the realisation of the Convention's objectives. It aims, emphatically, not just at introducing criminal rules into national legislation, but more specifically at deterring, preventing and combating international corruption through effective, co-ordinated national measures.

The Offence of Active Bribery and the Responsibility of Companies

The Convention contains in Article 1 the obligation to establish the corruption of foreign public officials as an *offence* in the same manner as domestic law criminalises the corruption of national officials. Accompanying preventive and repressive rules may require the update of laws relating to internal corruption as well. In conformity with the non-self-executing approach of the Convention, the Commentaries specify that signatories can implement the undertaking through different means. The basis could be a law punishing corruption in general, an extension of the penal code's offence of corruption of national public agents, or recourse to *ad hoc* provisions, such as the US FCPA.

Article 1 (1) of the text defines the offence as "the act of offering, promising or giving an undue advantage, whether pecuniary or not, to a foreign public official, for that official or for a third party, in order for him to act or to refrain from acting in relation to the performance of official duties, in order to obtain or retain business or other improper advantage in the conduct of international business".[5] Thus, a bribe can consist of a gift as well as a sum of money. It is irrelevant, moreover, whether the bribe goes to a third party (such as a relative, an institution or a political party), provided that it is the *quid pro quo* for the improper conduct of the public official.

On the basis of Article 1 (2), complicity (participation) and incitement to corruption also constitute criminal offences. They include "authorisation". When, for example, a parent company authorises a foreign subsidiary to pay a bribe, this act will lead to the exercise of jurisdictional competence and application of criminal law against the parent and/or any of its responsible managers.

Article 1 (3) defines a *foreign public official* as any person in a foreign country, who holds a legislative, administrative or judicial office, or who exercises a public function, including a public agency or enterprise, and any official of an international organisation. This wide definition combines subjective qualifications with the objective exercise of public functions in a manner similar to that of numerous national criminal legal systems. It aims to take into account that the framework within which the state directly exercises economic functions varies from one country to another, and that the current trend towards privatisation entrusts the private sector with public functions.

The extension of the offence to the behaviour of managers of private companies controlled by the state gave rise to considerable discussion, and it was not possible to insert supplemental specifications in the text. The Commentary, however, specifies that a company is deemed "public" if the state can exercise a dominant influence on it, through any of the different means available. It also specifies that the responsible person in such a company does exercise a public function, unless the company operates as a private company, on a normal commercial basis and without state support.

Each signatory state must punish the offence by "effective, proportionate and dissuasive criminal penalties", including imprisonment, equivalent to those provided for the corruption of national public officials. Other punitive measures, such as seizure and confiscation of the bribe and of the proceeds of the bribery, are to be applied.[6]

Articles 2 and 3 address the author of the offence and the central question of the responsibility of companies that bribe or benefit from it, given that only certain legal systems recognise the criminal responsibility of firms. The Convention does not impose on them an obligation to introduce the concept of criminal responsibility of legal persons, an innovation that would have had a far wider reach. Such countries have committed themselves to introduce effective, proportionate and dissuasive non-criminal (essentially pecuniary) sanctions. This should limit the risk of divergence between countries where companies are subject to criminal law and countries where they are not. Introducing even non-criminal sanctions applicable to companies where such a system generally does not exist might entail substantive legislative changes. Two other questions also arise: that of jurisdictional competence in such non-criminal, administrative matters, and that of the level of the penalties. Non-pecuniary sanctions, such as exclusion from participation in invitations to tender, or the deprivation of directors of their functions even when they are guilty simply of a lack of due diligence, could have more effect than criminal sanctions applied only to responsible managers.[7]

Jurisdictional Criteria

Another delicate point involves the criteria for determining *jurisdiction*. It was debated at great length throughout the negotiation, in a search for a balance between the obligations of the different signatory states as well as balanced and effective enforcement. Predominantly civil-law countries such as France, Germany and Italy consider the nationality of the defendant to be a criterion in determining jurisdiction; given certain conditions, they can prosecute offences committed by their nationals abroad. Conversely, the United States, the United Kingdom and other common-law countries exercise jurisdiction over criminal matters on a purely territorial basis.[8] Article 4 of the Convention requires states to prosecute the offence by applying the legal criteria traditional to their own systems. The necessary balance in the way corruption is punished should come through non-criminal penalties, which may also be imposed in regimes of strict territorial criminal jurisdiction, in all cases where companies commit bribery. That such bribes are promised or paid abroad through an intermediary, or through subsidiaries not under the management of home-country nationals, would not avoid prosecution.

Application of Legislation against Money Laundering

The reference to *money-laundering* legislation in Article 7 of the Convention bears crucially on successful enforcement as well as the prevention of bribery by making the hiding of bribes and their proceeds more risky and difficult. Money laundering involves transferring funds gained in criminal activities, or meant to commit crime, through international financial channels (banks and other intermediaries), hiding their origin in the process, with the complicity of the institutions, trustees, professionals and others involved. Anti-laundering legislation developed first to combat drug trafficking. It has been progressively extended in the 1990s to the transfer of proceeds of other serious crimes, as advocated internationally both under the auspices of a G7 Task Force operating within the OECD (the Financial Action Task Force – FATF) and within the UN. Measures agreed by all main industrialised countries, to which a few others have adhered, include more than criminal-law sanctions and mutual co-operation. They entail, crucially, the obligation of banks and similar institutions not to carry out suspicious deals (such as large cash transactions) and to report them secretly to police, supervisory authorities or prosecutors.

Where domestic corruption is a basis for the application of money-laundering legislation (currently the case in several countries and becoming so in several others), Article 7 of the Convention requires the application of the same rules to corruption of foreign public officials; it thus prescribes "national treatment". This point is fundamental to the effective application of the Convention. It is well known that bribes of high-ranking foreign officials are paid "from abroad to abroad", through banking channels and financial intermediaries in third countries, usually off-shore financial centres protected by bank secrecy and hostile to international collaboration. These payments hitherto did not entail money laundering, because transnational corruption was not a crime. Things are now changing. With the adherence to the 1997 Bribery Convention of financial centres like Luxembourg and Switzerland, among others, local regulations against money-laundering, including reporting and disclosure obligations, and seizure and confiscation of the funds, will apply when an offence of corrupting a foreign public official is at issue. Participating in such dubious financial transactions will incur the risk of criminal responsibility.

The Commentary to the Convention explains that this refers to the bribe both before the payment is made (*i.e.* funds earmarked for the illicit payment) and after the money has moved and become available to the corrupt beneficiary. This is a significant specification. As the Convention incriminates only active corruption (promising or giving a bribe), it was important to specify that the transfer of funds by the beneficiary after they are obtained (typically from the official to a bank) does not exempt the transaction from the rules against money laundering. The money remains the result of the offence.

Non-Penal Obligations for Accounting and Financial Statements

The provisions of Article 8, which deals with company accounting, assume fundamental importance. Their great practical and certainly innovative dimensions go beyond the penal framework and take on a predominantly preventive role. This Article prescribes that, in order to combat international corruption effectively:

1. *... each Party shall take such measures as may be necessary, within the framework of its laws and regulations regarding the maintenance of books and records, financial statement disclosures, and accounting and auditing standards, to prohibit the establishment of off-the-books or inadequately identified transactions, the recording of non-existent expenditures, the entry of liabilities with incorrect identification of their object, as well as the use of false documents, by companies subject to those laws and regulations, for the purpose of bribing foreign public officials or of hiding such bribery.*

2. *Each Party shall provide effective, proportionate and dissuasive civil, administrative or criminal penalties for such omissions and falsifications in respect of the books, records, accounts, and financial statements of such companies.*

These obligations already exist in national legislation, as well as in the generally accepted accounting principles applicable to large companies or listed corporations. The Group had discovered this when it made enquiries and commissioned studies between 1994 and 1997 in order fully to grasp the issue. National legislation and practices require large companies, and certainly those listed on stock exchanges, to maintain proper books and financial records. Entries and other records must be complete, accurate, detailed and systematic, listing correctly all payments made and received as well as their nature, including those related to international transactions and payments to agents and other intermediaries. Those records are generally subject to internal and external audit, and sanctions. Even criminal sanctions are imposed in some cases for record-keeping violations.

Nevertheless, practical difficulties impede detecting suspect payments in a company's records and accounts, and finding irregularities may be quite difficult. Illegal payments normally are disguised, often as commercial commissions or fees. Auditors do not look at every transaction. They generally check whether adequate procedures and internal controls are in place and applied. Moreover, they organise their work to discover errors, omissions and irregularities substantial enough to have a "material" impact on the financial statements. Not all incorrect payments, even of large amounts, will be discovered under this approach. Finally, auditors usually do not have to disclose the results of their investigations to public authorities, except in regulated industries such as banks and insurance companies. The duty of confidentiality may even prevent them from doing so. Irregularities may have to be disclosed only to the management (which may be responsible for them), or to some committee of the board.

The purpose of Article 8 is to reinforce the preventive function of accounting requirements and of controls on them, in order to avoid the diversion of large sums of money from company accounts for "grand" corruption abroad, which appeared from investigations in various countries. It should result in a re-examination by competent national authorities of the effectiveness of the internal accounting and audit controls in place. It also is relevant, as the Commentary recalls, to the consideration of potential liabilities in financial statements, and to the discharge of their duties by auditors. Put more bluntly, with the entry into force of the Convention auditors will be liable if they have not detected corruption by properly examining a company's books and records.

The proper implementation of these obligations does not concern only non-criminal pecuniary sanctions as regards accounting, balance sheets and the auditing standards that apply (a matter which, in the European Community, is included mostly within the competence of the Commission). Article 8 (2) indeed requires the application of criminal sanctions for grave omissions, such as forgery, falsification and fraud.

Mutual Assistance and Extradition

Effective *mutual assistance* is fundamental, given the frequent use of international financial channels to effect and hide transnational bribery. Article 9 on mutual international judicial assistance lays down an obligation for signatory states reciprocally to provide prompt and effective legal assistance, for non-criminal as well as criminal procedures. It requires them to keep requesting authorities informed of the implementation of any demand for judicial assistance, such as searches, transmission of documents or depositions of witnesses. This binding commitment will certainly have value for prosecutors and judges, who often are disappointed by a lack of collaboration by other states and by delays in getting information and documents. Provisions on co-operation are completed by the usual rules on extradition, which include an obligation for countries that refuse to extradite others' nationals to prosecute them directly [Article 10 (3)].[9]

The Convention also contains innovative norms on some general issues important for effective implementation. Article 5 (on enforcement) aims at limiting the risk that the Convention be applied unequally in the different contracting states because prosecution is discretionary in many of them. It provides that, if prosecution has a discretionary character, considerations of national economic interest, international political relations, or the identity of natural or legal persons involved shall not influence it.

According to Article 9 (1), requests for assistance, such as investigations, taking of witnesses and transmission of documents, must be dealt with promptly and the requesting authority must be informed, if such is the case, of the need to furnish additional elements and documents. This specification seems appropriate; rogatory commissions in corruption cases often get "stuck" in certain countries, thus frustrating effective prosecution in the requesting country when the entire documentation, banking documents in particular, is located abroad. In the same spirit, Article 9 (3) excludes the refusal of assistance in criminal matters solely on the basis of banking secrecy. Article 10 (4) envisages that the "dual" incrimination requirement, often prescribed in the country to which an extradition request is addressed, is considered to be fulfilled when the corruption for which it is requested falls within the definition of corruption in that country. To facilitate the mutual co-operation decisive for prompt and effective prosecution, Article 11 anticipates the possibility of direct notification between the designated competent authorities of the contracting states, rather than notification through diplomatic channels.

Entry into Force and Enlargement of the Number of Participants

Among the *final* provisions of the Convention, that regarding its coming into force became the object of lengthy negotiation, to ensure that the Convention enter into force as nearly simultaneously as possible in the most important OECD countries. The European Union countries, especially (in conformity with their "second common position"), and Japan wanted assurance that the main exporting countries would be parties as of the date of entry into force, so that no companies of any of them would be put at a competitive disadvantage. The agreed mechanism provided that the Convention would enter into force before 31 December 1998 only when the largest exporters among the ten largest OECD members (determined in accordance with statistics annexed) had ratified it. Thereafter the Convention would enter into force for any ratifying country. In fact, on 17 December 1998, just one year after signature, these conditions were met, thanks to the deposit of their ratifications by Japan, Germany, the United States, the United Kingdom, and Canada, besides a few other countries. The Convention entered into force 60 days thereafter in accordance with Article 15 (1), on 15 February 1999. By June 2000, 21 signatory countries had deposited their ratifications.

The Convention is also open to non-OECD countries, whose adhesion was invited by the Council in its Recommendation of 23 May 1997 and again by the signatory states on signature. States that wish to adhere must first gain admission to the OECD Working Group on Bribery in International Business Transactions, so that they can subscribe to the more general commitments to the fight against corruption listed in the Recommendation, and participate in the control mechanism managed by the Group.

Some countries outside the OECD have formally applied to join the Working Group, and others have made informal inquiries to the OECD Secretariat. The Working Group has debated guidelines for future enlargement. The first criteria would be those laid down by the OECD for non-member participation in any committee of the Organisation, namely that the applicant be a "major player", at least in the specific field, and that there be "mutual benefits" in its participation. The Working Group has proposed that, additionally, an applicant country should be "able and willing" to participate in its anti-bribery activity. The Group will assess this on the basis of answers to a questionnaire concerning national laws and policies, to be discussed with the applicant. Initial participation could be as an "observer", to be followed, one hopes, by full membership and adhesion to the Convention (see Chapter ten).

Implementing the 1997 Recommendation

The 1997 Bribery Convention is the most important result of the OECD Members' joint fight against international bribery, but by no means the only one. The 1997 Recommendation of the Council provided for other activities by Members individually and within the OECD, with monitoring by the Working Group. Notwithstanding the priority given to the Convention's conclusion, ratification and implementation, both the Working Group and other OECD bodies take care that other commitments do not fall into oblivion. There are of course different degrees of attention and effectiveness, especially as an OECD Recommendation does not contain binding commitments, but the OECD has a good record in affecting policy through recommendations. Member countries do take them into account when crafting their policies and enacting legislation in any field, to carry out the common objectives that these instruments express. OECD recommendations have more relevance than similar instruments of other forums, because a follow-up procedure backs them. It involves close monitoring by competent bodies of the OECD through national reporting, examination of the reports and comparative evaluation for further action.

The 1997 Recommendation on Combating Bribery (Annex II), which built upon that of 1994, recommended that member countries "take effective measures to deter, prevent and combat" transnational bribery in a number of areas:

- Criminal legislation, which is covered by the Convention negotiated pursuant to the Recommendation.

- Taxation, in order to eliminate any indirect support of bribery.

- Company and business accounting and audit rules and procedures.

- Banking, financial and other relevant provisions, to ensure that adequate records are kept and made available for inspection and investigation.

- Public subsidies, licenses, government-procurement contracts or other public advantages that could be denied as sanctions for bribery in appropriate cases.

- Civil, commercial and administrative law to make bribery illegal.[10]

- International co-operation in general.

The Recommendation gives specific guidance in several of these areas, and it has led to further initiatives. On the denial of tax deductibility of bribes, for example, countries that allowed this deduction, in some cases for international contracts, have explicitly terminated it, either in their legislation enforcing the 1997 Convention or in connection with it. Belgium, France and Germany deserve note here (see also Chapter four and Annex III).

Article 8 of the Convention deals specifically with accounting standards and controls, but the Recommendation focuses additionally on the roles of both internal and external auditors. It advocates that competent legislation and professional practice address effectively the need to deter bribery by closing loopholes in accounting standards, and for effective controls and reporting.

Further current initiatives concern public procurement, another sensitive area. Corruption in international procurement funded by aid from OECD donor countries is especially worrisome. This kind of bribery raises criminal and good-governance issues, plus concerns about the maintenance of fair competition. It also implies misuse of public funds (taxpayer money) meant to alleviate the misery of the poorest countries. OECD bodies such as the Export Credits and Guarantees Group (ECGG) and the Development Assistance Committee (DAC) have tackled the issue, to insert antibribery clauses in relevant instruments and contracts, and to exclude from participation in such programmes any supplier found to be involved in bribery (see Chapter five). Individual countries have reported in the Working Group's initial monitoring phase in 1999 that public-procurement procedures, both for domestic public works and supplies and for those officially funded in third countries, provide increasingly for undertakings by bidders to abstain from improper practices, and for exclusion from further participation when bribery occurs.

This important overall approach to enforcing anti-bribery policies short of criminal law action receives widespread support. The World Bank announced in 1999 that it would exclude from participation in competitive procurement and bids financed with its funds any supplier independently determined to have resorted to bribes. The Bank announced shortly thereafter that a few companies had in fact been declared ineligible for this reason.

The Effects of Enforcement and Monitoring on International Business

The potential effectiveness of legal and enforcement action against transnational bribery has often aroused perplexity, to say the least. This is unexplored territory, as economic crime takes on a global scale whereas states traditionally have tended to act in a dispersed, fragmented way. In assessing the effectiveness of the Convention, therefore, particular attention must focus on the newly created mechanism of constant monitoring and follow-up entrusted to the Working Group by Article 12.

This mechanism will use the tested OECD "peer pressure" technique – a procedure of mutual, plenary review by the Group of national implementation measures and practices. The Group will systematically monitor the contracting states' respect for the obligations to which they have subscribed, and the effectiveness of each in applying the Convention to combat transnational bribery. The mechanism provides an important mutual assurance that commitment of all the signatories to render their territories off-limits to such practices will in fact be carried out. The Working Group has already started with Phase One of the monitoring process, the review of participants' implementing legislation, to be completed by the OECD Ministerial meeting of June 2000. Phase Two will involve a detailed review of implementation practice, including visits to the national judicial and administrative authorities entrusted with enforcement.

From the point of view of business, having recourse to bribery of officials of foreign countries has become a dangerous activity in OECD countries: enterprises here run a real risk of prosecution and incrimination. Yet the direct peril of criminal incrimination is not the only factor to take into account when evaluating the impact of the Convention on the conduct of international business. Both the side aspects of criminal law and spillover effects on the competitive climate need taking into account.

The side aspects arise because successful transnational bribery implies reliance on a network of intermediaries, such as agents, lawyers, fiduciaries and banks, to divert funds from corporate accounts, set up offshore companies and transfer bribes and their proceeds across national borders while hiding their illegal origin. With the new legal framework in place in major countries, professionals will be wary of supplying their services for operations that now involve white-collar criminality. Serious banks will deny their financial channels to bribe-related transfers. Serious financial operators will not and should not take money-laundering reporting obligations lightly. Effective international co-operation under the Convention and under anti-money-laundering instruments will make illegal operations involving bribery highly risky and visible. Recent scandals involving Russian and Indonesian banks, companies and politicians, show that secrecy in this respect has become more difficult.

The Convention may also become a relevant instrument for international competition. Until now a company with reason to believe that it had lost a foreign deal due to corruption by a competitor had no direct means of redress, especially without full evidence, as is normally the case. In the political and legal setting of many countries where corruption is widespread, bribery involving top officials and politicians, those involved in the awarding of big contracts to foreign enterprises, would not receive serious investigation. The home country of the affected company could not do much to protect it since bribing a foreign public official was not an offence in the country of the bribing competitor. For the same reason, a claim for damages based on unfair competition would, as a rule, be pointless; the company that had lost the deal could not satisfy the burden of proof, which in civil litigation falls on the claimant.

An example from a recent International Bar Association conference in Barcelona shows how matters have changed. A session on the 1997 Bribery Convention attracted a world-wide crowd of lawyers eager to update themselves. It considered the following hypothetical case. A large public contract has just been awarded to a German company in a Latin American country known for widespread public-sector corruption. The international press then reports suspicions of bribery as a decisive element in the awarding of the contract. A US company that competed unsuccessfully asks its legal advisor what avenue of redress it may pursue.

Before the entry into force of the Convention, the US company could only have complained to the US authorities, which in turn could only have used the information (as they indeed did in the past) to address public opinion in OECD countries. Now – and even if in the country concerned serious investigation of the politicians and high officials involved looks improbable – the US firm could approach the competent German prosecutor, who would open an investigation *ex officio* or based on preliminary information from the firm. US law-enforcement authorities could also start investigations and seek mutual assistance from the German authorities, or refer the case to them if no sufficient US territorial link to establish jurisdiction could be shown. Other OECD countries, such as Switzerland, could be approached directly or by the authorities of Germany or the United States if there were suspicions of laundering the bribe money through their banks.

The digging out of documents from corporate files and accounts, as well as from OECD-based banks, and the gathering of oral testimony, formerly impossible burdens on the claimant, would now become the task of the investigating authorities, using coercion if necessary. Moreover, based on the result of the criminal investigation, the US company could attack its competitor in German (or possibly even US) civil courts, claiming damages from the loss of the deal due to an illegal activity. This avenue, financially interesting for the US company, would also remain open if criminal prosecution should ultimately be unsuccessful because, for instance, of a lack of German jurisdiction over those liable. This could occur if the bribery was organised and carried out by a non-German manager of the Latin American subsidiary of the German firm.

Even in such a case the German parent could be subject in Germany to non-criminal liability, and therefore to pecuniary and possibly also non-pecuniary administrative sanctions, for lack of proper internal organisation and control (including control over its foreign subsidiaries) in disregard of corporate law. On the other hand, if the parent company did have adequate internal systems and controls, and if the bribery occurred without its knowledge, it might be able in its turn to claim civil damages from an untrustworthy manager who had endangered its reputation.

The possible consequences of the investigation in law and fact would not necessarily stop even here. The German enterprise and/or its shareholders might sue the auditors for lack of due diligence in not having detected the bribery. The related criminal investigations in the signatory countries of the Convention, and the accompanying publicity, might force the reluctant authorities of the country of the corrupt official(s) to investigate and prosecute all those responsible for passive corruption in their government. A few such cases and scandals would surely attract wide national and international press coverage. This would contribute to better behaviour by enterprises, and encourage better governance as well as more respect for anti-bribery standards in the conduct of global business.

Notes

1. Countries that are not OECD Members but are members of the Group, participated in the negotiations and signed the Convention are Argentina, Brazil, Bulgaria, Chile and Slovakia.

2. During this last phase of the negotiations, the Council of the European Union adopted, for the first time in history, two common positions under Art. K3 of the Maastricht Treaty that the member States followed during the negotiations pursuant to Art. K5. The first, more general position is dated 6 October 1997 (ECOJ, 1997*b*). The second, of 13 November 1997 (ECOJ, 1997*c*), defines the positions "which the member States intend to support" in the framework of the OECD and Council of Europe negotiations on different important points, especially to ensure that the texts being prepared correspond to the principles introduced in the framework of the Union. During the OECD negotiation, the question arose of how the delegations of EU member States could maintain the degree of flexibility required in the negotiations to conclude a treaty when they were tied by a common position, unanimously adopted and officially published in the *Official Journal*.

3. The fight against corruption in countries that benefit from international multilateral assistance is now being pursued through other means, such as making any aid and assistance conditional upon the reorganisation of their administration in accordance with the principles of "good governance". See World Bank (1997). For the European context, see EC Commission (1997).

4. In this perspective, the Convention does not admit any reservations, although this exclusion is mentioned only in the preamble and not in the operative part.

5. The United States has not managed to obtain the support of the other Member countries for the extension of criminalisation to include the corrupt financing of political parties, a specific case regulated differently in different countries, and not everywhere the object of criminal sanctions. If the granting of a pecuniary advantage to a political party or its officers is the vehicle for a corruption in the true sense of the word, however, it will clearly fall under the Convention. The matter remains on the agenda of the Working Group.

6. The text does not define "international business transactions", which must be interpreted broadly. Furthermore, according to Art. 1 (1) corruption must occur "with a view to obtaining or *retaining* business or other *improper advantage* in the conduct of international business". The text therefore not only covers bribery in transboundary export operations, procurement or investment, but also in contracts and related business, even if it arises only at a later stage (for instance, bribery by an established foreign investor to escape or reduce taxation).

7. The European Union Convention addresses this question differently in its Art. 6 relating to the "criminal responsibility of company directors". The criminal responsibility of directors or others responsible for acts of corruption "committed by persons subject to their authorities or for the benefit of the company" is provided for.

8. In enforcing the 1997 Bribery Convention, the United States has amended the FCPA, adding the nationality link to territorial jurisdiction, so that US citizens and companies outside the country are now subject to the prohibition of bribing foreign public officials.

9. The Working Group held a session in 1996 and again in 1999 and 2000 with prosecutors of several countries (such as France, Korea, Switzerland and Italy), to learn about the practical difficulties they encounter in investigating bribery cases with an international dimension. A direct result of these contacts is Art. 9.3 of the Convention: "A party shall not decline to render mutual assistance for criminal matters within the scope of this Convention on the ground of bank secrecy".

10. The Council of Europe opened for signature at the end of 1999 a civil-law convention against bribery. Under it, contracts providing for bribes shall be null and void, and contracts obtained through bribery shall be voidable.

Bibliography

BERNASCONI, P. (1996),
"La confisca e la punibilità del riciclaggio del provento della corruzione di pubblici funzionari", *Riv. trim. diritto penale dell'economia*, 1996, p. 539.

CAVALERIE, P. (1998),
"La Convention OCDE du 17 Décembre 1997 sur la lutte contre la corruption d'agents publics étrangers dans les transactions commerciales internationales", *Ann. Français Droit Int.*, 1998, p. 609.

CCI (1992),
Les commission illicites, Publ. 480/2.

ECOJ (*Official Journal of the European Commission*) (1997*a*),
C.195, 25 June, European Union Convention on Combating Corruption of 26 May 1997.

ECOJ (1997*b*),
L.279, 13 October, European Union common position of 6 October 1997.

ECOJ (1997*c*),
L.320, 21 November, European Union common position of 13 November 1997.

EUROPEAN COMMISSION (1997),
Une politique de l'Union contre la corruption, Document COM(97)192, 21 May.

PIERROS, P. and C. HUDSON (1998),
"The Hard Graft of Tackling Corruption in International Business Transactions, Progress in International Co-operation and the OECD Convention", *Journal of World Trade*, 1998, vol. 2, p. 77.

PARISI, N. (1996),
La cooperazione giuridica internazionale nella lotta alla corruzione, Milano

PIETH, M. (1998),
"The Prevention of Money Laundering: A Comparative Analysis", *European Journal of Crime, Criminal Law and Criminal Justice*, p. 159.

PIETH, M. and P. EIGEN (Eds) (1998),
Korruption im internationalen Geschäftsverkehr, Neuwied, Kriftel, Luchterhand Verlag.

SACERDOTI, G. (1998),
"La Convenzione OCSE del 1997 sulla lotta contro la corruzione", *Rivista italiana di diritto e procedura penale,* p. 1349

SACERDOTI, G. (1999),
"La Convention de l'OCDE sur la lutte contre la corruption", *"Journal droit des affaires internationales",* No. 1, p. 3

YANNACA-SMALL, C. (1994)
"Les paiements illicites dans le commerce international et les actions enterprises pour les combattre", *Annuaire Français du Droit International,* p. 792.

UNITED NATIONS (1998),
Financial Havens, Banking Secrecy and Money Laundering, New York, UN Office for Drug Control and Crime Prevention.

WORLD BANK (1997),
Helping Countries to Combat Corruption, Washington, World Bank.

ZEDALIS, R. (1998),
"How Does the New OECD Convention on Bribery Stack Up Against the Foreign Corrupt Practices Act?", *Journal of World Trade Law,* 1998, Vol. 3, p. 167.

Chapter 3

From Ideal to Reality:
Making the New Global Standard Stick

by

Mark Pieth*

Introduction

Why will the OECD initiative succeed where many others have failed?
Businessmen regularly ask this and similar questions when discussing OECD's
work on corruption. Officials in turn, even in a more formal setting, inquire what
assurances the OECD can give that their country will not be the only one to implement the new anti-corruption programme to the letter.

One must take these questions very seriously. Only ten years ago, the prospects
of doing anything significant against global corruption looked very bleak indeed.
Few experienced observers would have believed that in 1997 Ministers of
34 countries, representing collectively over 70% of world exports and over 90% of
foreign direct investment, would sit around a table and pledge their countries to do
all in their power to prevent and repress the bribery of foreign public officials in
international business. Why are even sceptical diplomats now confident that significant advances in reducing corruption, one of the world's most serious and difficult
problems, are at hand? The question goes to the heart of the OECD initiative. What
motor drives this dynamic process? What mechanisms of "soft law" make the
OECD initiative and others look like anything but a "soft" option?

The Significance of the OECD Initiative Against Corruption

The significance of the OECD's anti-corruption programme could be summarised in three points: First, it will immediately reduce the flow of corrupt

---

* Mark Pieth is Professor of Criminal and Criminology Law at the University of Basel, Switzerland
  and Chairman of the OECD Working Group on Bribery in International Business Transactions.

payments. Second, it has had a catalytic effect and promoted dramatic policy change over the last ten years. Third, it could become a test case for developing standards of global governance.

Reducing the Flow of Corrupt Payments

The OECD's work on corruption has been the first multilateral initiative to attempt seriously to reduce corrupt payments globally. It ended an era of mutual finger pointing between countries of the North and the South, which inhibited all progress in the reduction of corruption. It basically demonstrates the willingness of industrialised states to act collectively *and* unilaterally to put an end to large corruption payments into countries of both the North and the South. That has an immediate effect in promoting good governance and fair trading conditions. The approach addresses itself primarily to companies in the North and it fosters the development of adequate compliance schemes against corruption by the private sector. For the non-compliant, it has serious, very tough criminal and non-criminal sanctions in store, which should make corruption economically unattractive.

Catalytic Effect

The OECD initiative, especially in the years between 1989 and 1994 leading up to its first Recommendation, has generated confidence that corruption need not be accepted as an inevitable fact of life. Many other organisations and fora picked up the issue or had a new look at some of their older instruments. The Council of Europe began work on the topic regionally following a summit of Ministers of Justice in Malta in 1994. The OAS equally began to draft its Convention against corruption in 1994 on the basis of an initiative by Venezuela. The ICC (International Chamber of Commerce) resumed work on its 1977 Rules of Conduct, and mandated a special Working Group to reconsider the text. The leading NGO on the prevention of corruption, Transparency International, was itself founded in 1993. The UN picked up the topic and many of the principles contained in other documents shortly after, with the General Assembly declarations of 1996. No direct, causal link ties the work of the OECD to these more recent initiatives. Yet the bold statement by OECD Members in 1994 of their commitment to combat corruption effectively undoubtedly had a catalytic effect on the work of international governmental organisations, the private sector and civil society in general.

A Test for Developing Structures of Global Governance?

The OECD work is a first in international law. It has used relatively newly developed methods of "soft law", borrowed from techniques for promoting and monitoring human-rights standards since the 1970s and more recently from the so-called Task Forces on transnational economic and organised crime,[1] combined with methods applied in accession procedures to international organisations. With these tools, the Organisation generated a technique to draft, implement and monitor legal standards across the world in a very short time. The refinement of the 1994 standards took until March 1997, but the transformation from "soft" to "hard" law in the 1997 Bribery Convention on Combating Bribery of Foreign Public Officials in International Business Transactions (Annex I) required barely a few more months, to end 1997. The pace accelerated further. The 1997 Bribery Convention entered into force in February 1999, after six of the major countries ratified it. By February 2000, 20 countries had ratified and implemented their legislation, with some others to follow shortly.

Beyond its breathtaking and unheard-of speed, the OECD process – together with the work done on money laundering, which has influenced the OECD procedures in many respects – has become regarded as a model technique to secure adequate implementation of standards. Potentially, the initiative could offer an example in a much more fundamental sense. It has been driven largely by the urge to open and liberalise world markets. Combating corruption and strengthening notions of fairness or a level playing field in trade contribute to the establishment of global standards. In this sense, the process could serve as a template for building dams against the wild stream of economic globalisation when it generates noxious effects. It thus can promote global governance in areas where national action alone can no longer adequately prevent risks. The future will show whether this approach could apply in such areas as the prevention of child labour, safeguarding climatic conditions and other major challenges to humanity.

Developing a Common Standard

The current standards of the OECD and associated countries[2] to prevent and combat transnational and commercial bribery are enshrined in the two key instruments, the Revised Recommendation of May 1997[3] (Annex II) and the 1997 Bribery Convention.[4] Whereas the 1997 Recommendation contains the entire programme as agreed by participant countries[5] so far, the Convention focuses on one specific issue, the criminalising of bribery of foreign public officials in a commercial framework.[6] The outside observer may find it strange that parts of the programme remain in a "soft law" status, while others are set in a legally more binding instrument. This merely mirrors the particular process OECD has gone through over the last few years.

From "Soft Law" To A Convention

It is not generally known that work on corruption in the OECD reaches back more than two decades into the 1980s. The first policy statement – in rather general terms – appeared in the OECD Guidelines for Multinational Enterprises of 1976.[7] This text, primarily defining standards for companies, was of course written under very different conditions, when the conflict over the role of MNEs and their adverse effects on the newly decolonised nations grew evident in the late 1970s.

The actual initiative for governmental action against corrupt payments dates from 1989, when the United States made a new attempt to promote criminalisation of foreign corrupt practices world-wide and suggested work on an anti-corruption instrument in the OECD. The UN had abandoned its efforts ten years previously, when preparation of a convention ran into serious political problems. In 1989, the United States was still the only country in the world criminalising transnational bribery and enforcing its FCPA legislation of 1977. Its own private sector perceived it as putting US industry at a trade disadvantage.

However, the time was ripe for another reason as well. With the opening of the East in Europe and general economic globalisation progressing fast, the chances of a collective approach became far greater in the 1990s. Nevertheless, work in the OECD took until 1994 to produce a first policy instrument for adoption by Ministers and publication. This 1994 Recommendation[8] had all the advantages and disadvantages of genuine "soft law". Bold statements could be made[9] without immediate legal obligations to act. It contained a "shopping list" of items for further examination. Its real value, in fact, lay in its initiation of a dynamic process of close-up examinations of these items (especially criminal law, tax treatment, accounting provisions and rules on public procurement) over the next three years.

This stage was crucial, because it built awareness that concerted action could benefit all participants, at the same time as it gave the issues a concrete profile. It marked the first major step from unilateralism towards collective action. This phase of in-depth, detailed work led to yet another "soft law" instrument, written in far more concrete and prescriptive language, the Revised Recommendation of 1997. Its most notable feature provided for a follow-up procedure for monitoring progress in implementing the Recommendation by Member states.

The moment had come when a group of Member countries no longer wished to continue the harmonisation process on a mere "soft law" basis, because they felt that in such a highly sensitive area terms needed definition as clearly as possible. They proposed a binding agreement. This request originally met with some resistance, because the rest of the Group feared that the dynamic process could be stalled by a move too early into binding law.

The compromise that governs the current phase of work relies on two elements. The first is the 1997 Bribery Convention, which defines illegal behaviour and establishes a tough set of sanctions – and thereby indirectly influences non-penal sanctions and preventive measures defined in the Recommendation. Second, Ministers tried to maintain momentum by insisting on a tight timetable, a stringent monitoring mechanism and an outreach programme, both to invite more countries to participate and to link with other organisations working on corruption. Substantive work continues on the basis of the "soft-law" method. The main risk of the approach adopted lies not in substantive disagreement but in overburdening the institution.

The "Soft-Law" Method

The OECD has particular experience in the area of "soft law". Much of its work leads to politically but not legally binding Recommendations.[10] Consequently, one of the most essential, normal working principles of the Organisation involves decision by unanimity. Other organisations, at least in their subsidiary bodies, allow for majority voting or use a qualified-majority principle. While this seems a rather formal issue, it has tremendous consequences for the working atmosphere and methodology. It may be easier to advance by majority decisions, but they risk serious difficulties at a higher, political level of the body. In the OECD, most of the politically touchy issues are addressed in the subsidiary bodies from the start. Working on the basis of unanimity implies a specific style, which for the OECD typically means negotiation among peers. Among peers it is wise to be subtle, but one can also be very frank – and peer pressure to go along with the Group can be substantial; it is the correlate to the unanimity principle.

Very direct questions may be asked, and with all its respect for diplomatic culture the OECD does not shy away from dissent. Unanimity also means that arguments have a chance for consideration on their merits rather than merely on the political and economic clout of the speaker. Power play does occur, of course, and sometimes things can get rough, especially when countries use the media to support their points in a crucial phase of negotiation. Politically, participants are adept in the methods of forming alliances to prevent hegemony. In specific areas – especially within the monitoring mechanism – there are clear rules of fairness, a formalised procedure for adopting reports and strict confidentiality before final decisions by the OECD Council. These rules are fundamental to the peer-review approach, because organised public censure by the highest body of the Organisation is the main sanction for slow or insufficient compliance.

Aside from procedures and the "style of the house", reasons inherent to the issue itself allowed for the extremely rapid progress towards a Convention, once the general outlines had been concluded in the 1997 Recommendation. Even if some countries may have doubted the possibility of bringing about a radical policy change on transnational corruption in such a short time and on a world-wide scale, a consensus developed among the Parties over the years of preparation that competition would greatly benefit from a strict no-corruption pact. Beyond the fair-trade agenda, the position of everybody doing business abroad will profit from a drastic reduction of large illicit payments into any country. Apart from companies' no longer having to compete on irrational markets for bribery, finding an objective, uncorrupted judiciary helps to reduce uncertainties. Citizens of the countries affected and investors alike will benefit from the promotion of the rule of law, from better economic and social conditions, and ultimately from democracy.

Monitoring the Legal Implementation

Given the Parties' overarching common interest, the main difficulty in constructing an anti-bribery instrument that would be operational in a reasonable time involved creating a standard that would respect the fundamental legal structures and principles of the Parties, but at the same time would allow insistence on compliance. The theory behind the approach chosen in the 1997 Bribery Convention is called "functional equivalence".

Functional Equivalence

Paragraph two of the Official Commentaries to the 1997 Bribery Convention states:

> This Convention seeks to assure a functional equivalence among the measures taken by the Parties to sanction bribery of foreign public officials, without requiring uniformity or changes in fundamental principles of the Party's legal system. [11]

The Convention borrows a principle from comparative law and further develops it. The functional approach of comparison draws attention to the overall working of systems rather than individual institutions. It assumes that each legal system has its own logic, one not necessarily determined by the legal texts alone. Practices and informal rules have relevance in this approach, as do other aspects of the legal system that take over ancillary functions. Therefore the focus of comparison, in terms of functional equivalence, should lie on the overall effects produced by a country's legal system rather than the individual rules. The paragraphs below give a few examples taken from the monitoring of the 1997 Bribery Convention. For some issues the Convention itself provides alternatives; for others it merely leaves the necessary leeway.

Confiscation. Article 3, paragraph 3 of the Convention requires Parties to take appropriate measures to ensure that bribery and the proceeds of bribes as defined in the Treaty, or their value, be subject to seizure and confiscation *"... or that monetary sanctions of comparable effect are applicable"*. Here the Convention demonstrates its flexibility. European Countries have introduced sweeping confiscation laws, following the Vienna Convention of 1988 on illicit trafficking in drugs[12] and the Council of Europe Convention 141 on Money Laundering, Search, Seizure and Confiscation.[13] The United States and Korea would attempt to achieve a similar result with a large fine. To a legal expert, the two options have no equivalence at all, because confiscation depends upon the provenance of the funds from crime, and fines are defined according to the culpability of the offender. Whereas in principle all ill-gotten gains are to be forfeited, the fine is delicately calibrated on the degree of culpability. In the OECD context, both approaches are explicitly acceptable if their effects are comparable. This is certainly the case where a simple, objective pro-portionality to the earnings is used as the criterion. Where, the discretion of judges in lieu of confiscation is very wide, however, comparability will have to be further examined. The OECD Working Group on Bribery in International Business Transactions (The OECD Working Group) frequently reserves its right to pronounce itself on the efficiency of such a sanction in practice during a second round of eval-uations, as described below.

Definition of the act of corruption. In a similar way, the 1997 Bribery Con-vention indicates acceptable alternatives in defining corruption as a *quid pro quo*. When describing the *pro quo*, the goal of the briber, it refers to an approach found in many laws, such as the French, British or US legislation. A bribe is paid *"... in order that the official act or refrain from acting in relation to the performance of official duties. ..."* (Article 1, paragraph 1). Commentary No. 3, however, offers as an alternative the requirement of a real or at least envisaged "breach of duty". This variation is acceptable *"... provided that it was understood that every public offi-cial had a duty to exercise judgement or discretion impartially and this was an "autonomous" definition not requiring proof of the law of the particular official's country."* This is the approach adopted by countries like Norway, Germany, Switzerland and Austria.

The significance of this distinction might not be immediately evident. Acceptability of a breach-of-duty concept allows a country to evade all those tedious discussions on *de minimis* rules (facilitation payments, *bona fide* expenditures). By definition, mere "grease payments" are excluded. This approach offers a simple concept to distinguish genuine corruption from gratuities and other forms of petty corruption.

Corporate liability. The 1997 Bribery Convention gives far less direction on the highly relevant issue of corporate liability. Article 2 asks countries to introduce the "responsibility of legal persons". Article 3, paragraph 2 indicates, however, that non-criminal sanctions against a corporation are also acceptable, provided that they include monetary sanctions and that they are, overall, "effective, proportionate and dissuasive".

Experts will see it as evident that the alternative (criminal versus administrative liability) is not the real problem, except where countries find it difficult to accord legal assistance to administrative proceedings abroad. The far more relevant issue is the approach to responsibility. Do we talk about strict or vicarious liability? Do we hold a company liable for the misconduct of its employees or for an insufficient compliance structure? The many other relevant questions in this area include the issue of adequate sanctions. Clearly, the OECD Working Group was not in a position to unify criminal law in the divergent systems represented by its Parties. While it drew a line here in order to conclude the Convention on time, however, it clearly left room for further work on the basis of a horizontal analysis after the country reviews.

"Functional equivalence" is therefore the key principle in evaluating countries' approaches. Given the demanding nature of such a comparison, there is a danger of concentrating just on issues that seem easy to operationalise. The Convention touches upon the statutes of limitation and penalties provided for by the individual countries.[14] Some authors have already made their own comparisons of the maximum prison sentences for transnational bribery. This author, however, would advise against a simplistic reading of the concept of equivalence. Although severe penalties are outward signs of offence seriousness, for instance, maximum provisions are rarely used in practice. What the Convention demands is that every country takes transnational bribery to be as serious an offence as domestic corruption. Its basic approach respects countries' own sanctioning cultures. In searching for a principle that respects local sanctioning traditions, one should also compare the sanction for transnational bribery with that for other comparably serious offences, *e.g.* theft, fraud and embezzlement internally, before simply contrasting the figures in an international comparison.

Sanction should be consistent with the central norms of criminal law in every Member state. Thus, a maximum of one year of imprisonment for transnational bribery would seem very low if the maximum for domestic corruption, theft or fraud were five years in the same country. More difficult is the situation where a whole cultural area (*e.g.* the Nordic States in Europe) has a much lower level of maxima, where theft, for example, can be punished with a two-year maximum of imprisonment. The OECD should not upset the entire system of "ordinal proportionality" just because countries make different use of criminal law.

The Monitoring Procedure

"Country evaluations", which are formal, systematic, detailed reviews and judgements by the entire Membership of aspects of each Member country's policies and their implementation, are an essential, highly developed part of the OECD's operations. Many committees and other subsidiary bodies of the Organisation use the technique. In drafting its own procedural rules,[15] the OECD Working Group has drawn from this experience, especially OECD accession procedures and the evaluation methods used by the FATF on money laundering.[16]

The first monitoring phase, currently under way, concentrates on the legal implementation of the 1997 Bribery Convention and the Recommendation. The evaluation is based again on the OECD peer-review principle. The OECD Secretariat drafts descriptive texts on the basis of countries' answers to a questionnaire as well as legal materials submitted by the countries. The OECD Working Group designates two examining countries, chosen from a rotational list, to give the Group their opinion on the standard of implementation. The procedures assure a thorough exchange between these examiners and the examined country before the actual hearing in the Group. They provide for written representations by the country evaluated and a pre-meeting of examiners and country experts to answer questions, clarify misunderstandings and develop a focus for the Group's discussion of specific topics.

The OECD Working Group holds two hearings per country on two consecutive days. In the first, the Group discusses questions raised by the examiners and the answers given by the country. During the evening of this first day, the examiners draft a short evaluative text to be attached to the report itself. They immediately test the text with the examined country on the same evening. The second hearing, on the following day, concentrates on this evaluation, which is modified if necessary, then adopted verbatim by the Group, with the country under examination asked to abstain from voting. To secure fair treatment, unanimity of the rest of the Group is requested, and the examined country has the right to express a dissenting opinion in the report. The evaluation is appended to the descriptive part of the report, which is itself amended on the basis of the discussions and adopted in a written procedure. After an intensive one-year round, all finalised laws were examined and the Ministerial Council received all the reports for formal adoption. They were published in June 2000. The procedure is open to participation by members of civil society who can, and have, contributed written comments; the evaluation schedule is published on the internet and all submissions are distributed and included in the procedure.

Will Laws also be Applied?

What are the guarantees that enacted legislation will actually be applied? Legislation sometimes run the risk of remaining a dead letter. It would be all too easy to write strict laws, then to ignore them as "tedious". The rationalisations for such non-enforcement are familiar. Corrupt acts frequently take place abroad and evidence may be difficult to come by, especially where the government of the person bribed does not favour investigation, even of only the briber, into dealings that might show it or the leading Party in a negative light.

The second phase of monitoring, directed at the application of the implementing legislation, will most likely start in 2000/2001. It will include on-site visits of examination teams, which will look for structures in place capable of dealing with this type of case, sufficient resources available, personnel trained etc. There may already be first cases to prove that the system is working, although there may be many good reasons for the absence of trials. Another indicator of the seriousness of implementation could be the extent to which companies domiciled in Party states have introduced compliance structures. More broadly, the second phase of monitoring will focus not only on the 1997 Bribery Convention but also on the other issues covered by the Recommendations, especially tax treatment of bribes and accounting rules. Once again, the results will be published at regular intervals.

Planning the Future

Completing Work on Criminal Law

The OECD work on corruption is a process, and peer review is not the only means to keep the dynamic alive. During negotiation of the Convention, Parties agreed to give closer attention to a series of issues touched upon in the text of the 1997 Bribery Convention but needing further clarification. Because they relate to the coverage of criminal law, they attempt to finalise the "first storey" of an anti-corruption structure. While criminal law is not the only approach to corruption, it is crucial because it defines the illegal act and has a strong preventive effect. These outstanding matters are commonly referred to as "the five issues":

- Adding

  - *Foreign Political Party officials and Parties* as well as

  - *Candidates* to the scope of beneficiaries beyond public officials has especially had further discussion. The OECD saw no immediate necessity to enlarge the scope of the 1997 Bribery Convention, because such beneficiaries would be partly covered by the existing text and most countries already cover a further segment in their national legislation. Nevertheless, the general topic of *recipients* needs further examination soon, in the light of practice. Possible lacunae have been examined on several occasions.

- The issue of *bribery through foreign subsidiaries* is a similar piece of possibly unfinished business. The 1997 Bribery Convention and domestic law in most countries already cover various cases of such bribery. For the time being, the OECD Working Group has recommended that corporations extend their due diligence and compliance concepts to their foreign subsidiaries.

- A very delicate issue which other fora, most notably the UN, the EU and the BIS have especially targeted involves the abuse of *offshore financial havens*, to prepare corruption, handle bribery payments and launder corruption money.[17]

- The broader issue of *corruption-money laundering* is the last of the five. The 1997 Bribery Convention addresses it (Article 7), but some uncertainty remains on whether the agreed standard requires the extension of the anti-laundering concepts of criminal and prudential law to include active bribery of foreign officials as a predicate offence. At least some countries have taken the position that the coverage is not mandatory. Therefore a further discussion of this topic is necessary. The issue of money management related to bribery is in fact much wider. It starts with preparative acts to create so-called "slush funds" – *caisses de guerre*, used in all sorts of ways ranging from illegally financing one's own Party to corrupting foreign officials. Next, covert transactions themselves need focus. Finally, corruption-money laundering goes beyond the bribe itself to how it is used to obscure the whereabouts of the profits.

A "Second Storey" on the OECD's Structure?

The Recommendation, as the "founding document" of OECD action against corruption in international business transactions, mentions a series of non-penal sanctions. Some items have been addressed in greater detail in the Recommendation itself, notably tax treatment, accounting and auditing, as well as sanctions in public-procurement procedures. These topics too form part of the evaluation process.

Other issues have not yet been concretised to the same level of detail, like *civil law sanctions* or *sanctions in export credits*. The private sector has continuously asked that two further issues, *solicitation of bribes* and *private bribery*, go onto the OECD's Working Group's agenda. Intensive deliberations have taken place including contacts in sub-groups.[18] These talks showed that private corruption especially needs some very profound analysis before it reaches the level of policy debate in the Group.[19]

The Group's mandates both to monitor and to extend the issues on the agenda illustrate the heavy workload that it faces. The list of new issues also indicates the kinds of strategic decisions in store. Parties must decide on the best and most effective procedures, sort out which parts of the global problem of corruption should be covered by the Organisation and determine how to co-operate with other forums.

Final Remarks

Why should this initiative work, where others have failed? The answer now seems relatively simple. The Parties to the OECD instruments – as the pace of implementation shows – have firmly committed themselves to reducing corruption. The peer process that drives monitoring, the review of the programme and further work has developed into a very strong motivating force indeed. So far, the OECD has succeeded by restricting itself to a clearly defined goal, and by creating an economic interdependency among countries that forced them to act mutually, in their own interests. Members of the private sector voice anxieties about the OECD process, yet companies' primary task will be to implement the preventive concepts internally. The role of an international organisation cannot at this stage go beyond establishing a common framework of rules among countries and insisting on their implementation. To give them meaning in everyday life becomes the task of governments and companies alike.

Furthermore, remember that in this aspect of its work, the OECD, focusing on the supply side of corruption, necessarily has adopted a restrictive approach dealing so far exclusively with the active corruption of foreign public officials. The recipients of bribes will have to be taken to court by the "victim" states. To secure mutual legal assistance among countries, regional organisations, especially the Organisation of American States, the Council of Europe and the European Union, have developed instruments of legal harmonisation.[20] They are typically broader in approach than the OECD's texts, especially in defining standards on active and passive domestic bribery. Some go beyond the bribery of officials to include private-to-private bribery, and some even include trafficking in influence. In some situations, this broad reach has created impediments to rapid and equal implementation.

Beyond the harmonisation of concepts in criminal, civil or administrative law, both the multilateral development banks and bilateral donors have deep involvement in preventing corruption in their own aid-funded contracts. In a wider framework, they work actively to promote good governance. Finally, the UN, the widest forum, is reconsidering action against corruption, especially in its work against transnational economic crime.

Notes

1. Most notably the Financial Action Task Force on money laundering and the Chemical Action Task Force on precursor chemicals used in the production of drugs.

2. Additionally to the 29 OECD Members, five non-OECD states are Parties to the anti-bribery initiative, namely Argentina, Brazil, Bulgaria, Chile and the Slovak Republic.

3. *Revised Recommendation of the Council on Combating Bribery in International Business Transactions*, 23 May 1997.

4. *Convention on Combating Bribery of Foreign Public Officials in International Business Transactions*, 21 November 1997, signed on 19 December 1997, in force since 15 February 1999.

5. Including such issues as tax treatment of bribes, accounting and auditing rules, and public procurement procedures. The details of the instruments are described in Chapter 2 by Prof. Giorgio Sacerdoti of Bocconi University, Milan, who as Vice-Chairman of the Working Group contributed decisively to the elaboration of the standards.

6. This context is defined by the mandate of the Organisation. Other forums (*e.g.* the Council of Europe) may have a wider approach.

7. OEDC *Guidelines for Multinational Enterprises*, first adopted in 1976, newest edition in 1997, currently again under revision.

8. *Recommendation of the Council on Bribery in International Business Transactions*, 27 May 1994.

9. *E.g.* "... *that countries take effective measures to deter, prevent and combat the bribery of foreign public officials...*" (Para. I, Recommendation 1994).

10. Article 5 of the OECD Convention of 28 October 1961. See also Articles 18-20 of the Procedural Order of 1961.

11. See Commentary No. 2, in *Commentaries on the Convention on Combating Bribery of Foreign Public Officials in International Business Transactions*.

12. *United Nations Convention Against Illicit Traffic in Narcotic Drugs and Psychotropic Substances*, Vienna, 1988.

13. *Convention on Laundering, Search, Seizure and Confiscation of the Proceeds from Crime*, 8 November 1990.

14. For such an approach, see, for example, GAREIS, Robert J. (1999), *International Trade Corruption Monitor* (ITCM), April, p. A-1025.

15. In addition to, and essentially outside the detailed, country-by-country monitoring system described here, the Working Group conducts a "tour de table" at least four times a year, during which all countries report their progress on legislation implementing the anti-bribery standards. This information is published on the internet immediately following the meetings.

16. The FATF actually is a G7 group, which meets at the OECD premises and is serviced in part (with G7 funding) by the same Directorate of the OECD Secretariat as the Working Group.

17. M. *Thierry Francq* of the French Ministry of Finance chaired a full day's meeting of prosecutors of various countries on the dangers of off-shore havens in financing corruption as well as laundering bribes and the gains from bribe-affected contracts. A follow-up meeting has been held on 29 February 2000.

18. Sub-groups have held joint meetings with representatives of the private sector. The group on solicitation was chaired by Mr. Puk van der Linde of the Dutch Ministry of Economy. That on private to private corruption was chaired by Mr. Mark Jones of the UK Department of Trade and Industry.

19. Further work on this topic has already been completed in a regional setting, both in the Council of Europe and the European Union.

20. Pieth, Mark (1999) in *The International Trade Corruption Monitor*, Winter.

Chapter 4

No More Tax Breaks for Bribes

by
Martine Millet-Einbinder[*]

Background to the OECD Recommendation on Tax Deductibility

The payment of bribes in international business transactions raises serious moral and political concerns and exacts a heavy economic cost, hindering the development of international trade and investment by increasing transaction costs and distorting competitive conditions. The tax treatment of bribes may add to this distortion.

In June 1994, the Committee on Fiscal Affairs (CFA), the main tax-policy body of the OECD, initiated a review of Member countries' tax legislation in order to identify any provisions that may indirectly encourage the bribery of foreign officials. It agreed that where such provisions exist and where changes would effectively discourage the corruption of foreign officials, tax administrations should be encouraged to make them. In the review, the CFA first assessed the effects of the deductibility and non-deductibility of bribes to foreign officials. This examination led the CFA to consider whether a deduction for such bribes should be either disallowed or subjected to disclosure conditions.

In April 1996, on the proposal of the CFA, the OECD Council adopted a Recommendation on the Tax Deductibility of Bribes to Foreign Public Officials (Annex III). This Recommendation calls on Member countries that allow the deductibility of such bribes to re-examine it with the intention of denying such deductibility. The Council recognised that the trend to treat bribes to foreign public officials as illegal might facilitate such action. The Recommendation instructs the

---

[*] Martine Millet-Einbinder is Principal Administrator in the Fiscal Affairs Unit of the OECD Directorate for Financial, Fiscal and Enterprise Affairs.

CFA to monitor its implementation and to promote it in its contacts with non-member countries. It received reinforcement from the Revised Recommendation of the Council on Combating Bribery in International Business Transactions adopted on 23 May 1997 (Annex II), which urges the prompt implementation by Member countries of the 1996 Tax Recommendation. In 1996, the CFA also considered whether the cross-border exchanges of tax information under international tax treaties or other agreements could be used to discover and prosecute illegal bribery; discussion on this issue continues.

Denying Deductibility

The CFA examined the arguments traditionally put forward in favour of deductibility of bribes paid to foreign officials:

* According to a basic tax principle, all expenses associated with earning or obtaining taxable income should be taken into account for tax purposes, either as deductible expenses or as capitalised expenditures, provided the payments are properly documented. A documented current expense should be denied only if the tax administration concludes that there is an insufficient nexus between the expense and the realisation of income (which in practice is frequently the case). General tax principles will admit exceptions to this rule for certain legal expenses such as gifts and entertainment expenses, as well as for certain payments that are illegal under domestic law. It is under this rubric that deductions are disallowed for bribes paid to domestic public officials in most but not all Member countries. Illegality did not generally extend to bribes paid to foreign officials.

* Although non-deductibility would change the effective cost of a bribe, it would be an ineffective deterrent against bribery of foreign officials: either a smaller amount could be paid or the payer would bear a higher cost. The CFA felt that this argument took too narrow a view and that it ignored the signal that deductibility sends to enterprises.

* Non-deductibility may make it more difficult to obtain information about bribes. The CFA accepted that, in theory, tax deductibility may encourage the payer of a bribe to disclose the name of the bribe recipient, but it felt that in practice taxpayers will be reluctant to identify a bribe just to gain the benefit of a deduction, and would usually disguise the payment as a commission. In addition, information concerning the beneficiary may, in any case, be confined within the tax administration.

* The identification of a bribe is not easy for a tax inspector. Confronted with the problem during a tax audit, he will generally have difficulty asserting that "com-

missions" are *de facto* bribes benefiting foreign public officials and as such criminal and therefore non-deductible. The CFA accepted that detection could be difficult, but saw this as an opportunity for countries to work together.

The CFA felt that these arguments did not outweigh the need to promote good governance and discourage bribery of foreign public officials. It also considered that disallowing the tax deductibility of bribes serves as a strong and politically visible symbol of the common international commitment to combat bribery, especially if combined with its criminalisation. Limitations on the deductibility of bribes can be considered as consistent with the treatment of other expenses of a similar nature, such as extortion payments, entertainment expenses, gifts and certain categories of expenses deemed as abusive or illegal.

Exchange of Information

Two forms of information exchange are relevant to bribery of foreign public officials. In a domestic context, can tax authorities pass information on bribery to the judicial authorities or are they required to do so? That is a matter of domestic law. In an international context, is there a possibility of exchange of information, either spontaneously or on request, between judicial authorities or between tax authorities of different countries? Such exchanges will be effective only insofar as the information can reach the judicial authorities of the recipient country. Most OECD countries that receive the tax disclosure may not hitherto have been able to prosecute because bribes to foreign officials were not illegal. If such bribes were illegal in the country of the payer, as is rapidly becoming the case (see the preceding two chapters), the disclosure would lead directly to prosecution. It seems highly unlikely that a payer would risk criminal prosecution by disclosing a bribe just to gain a tax deduction. The payer might, however, try to claim a deduction by disguising the payment as a consultancy or marketing fee, which may happen even where the bribe is not a criminal offence for the payer.

How can information obtained in the country of the payer get transmitted to the country of the official who has been bribed? One approach would provide a way for the tax administration in the first country to transmit the information about a bribe or a suspected bribe to its own judicial authority, which then could pass the information to its counterpart in the recipient country under the framework of international judicial assistance. This approach would likely require amendments to secrecy laws concerning the circumstances in which tax administrations may transmit information to judicial authorities. Countries that do not consider the active corruption of a foreign public official a crime may consider such amendments as too broad.

Another possibility would allow the information to be transmitted from one tax administration to the other pursuant to tax treaties or other tax information-exchange agreements. Once the information is in the hands of the tax administration of the country of the bribe recipient, it may be easier to pass it to the judicial authorities for use in a criminal prosecution. The receipt of a bribe by a domestic official is a crime in all countries, without regard to whether the briber is a resident or a foreigner. Because the information relates to illegal activities, in many countries a disclosure could be made by the domestic tax administration to the domestic judicial authority.

This approach raises two issues. First, does authorisation for the exchange of information exist? Second, would the international authorisation for the exchange preclude use of the information for other than tax purposes (*i.e.*, for a criminal prosecution), even where such use would be allowed under domestic law?

Both of these issues relate to Article 26 of the OECD Model Tax Convention on Income and on Capital (the "Model Convention"). Article 26 sets forth provisions for the exchange of information between tax administrations. First, information exchanged must relate to taxes imposed on behalf of the contracting States. Second, the country receiving the information may disclose it "only to persons or authorities concerned with the assessment or collection of, the enforcement or prosecution in respect of, or the determination of appeals in relation to the taxes imposed on behalf of the contracting States."

The first statement would seem to allow the transmittal of information concerning bribes on the basis that tax evasion may be involved, as the illegality of the bribes in the country of receipt would make the reporting of the bribe very unlikely. The Commentary to the Article suggests that the exchange could even be spontaneous, if, for example, a country supposes that information on the bribe acquired through certain investigations could be of interest to the recipient country. This type of understanding regarding the interpretation of Article 26 might even be clarified through bilateral agreements or notes between countries.

The second statement is more problematic. The text is definitive in its prohibition on disclosure of tax information to non-tax authorities, with one exception. Both the text and the Commentary acknowledge that the information may be disclosed in court sessions held in public to prosecute for the related tax offence. Once the information is made public in such a fashion, the court proceedings would be a matter of public record and could be used as possible evidence in a non-tax (*i.e.*, criminal) proceeding. The bribed official could defeat this result, however, if, for example, he agreed to a tax assessment for the non-reported bribe without any court proceeding. Moreover, in a tax proceeding the nature of the payment as a bribe would not be of particular relevance, so that critical information about the bribe might not reach the public record.

In light of this limitation in the Model Convention, the CFA suggested that tax administrations (and possibly judicial authorities) might wish to look outside bilateral double-tax conventions to address the issue. They might, for example, consider executing separate agreements for exchange of information on bribe payments (an approach adopted for money laundering), or might add this item to existing information-exchange agreements. This approach could also have the advantage of addressing bribery of officials in countries that have not entered into double tax conventions. The CFA recognised that this option is unlikely to be implemented in the short term, but discussion of the issue continues.

An alternative is to consider modifying bilateral agreements (or perhaps the Model Convention itself) to permit disclosure of information on bribe payments to the judicial authorities of the country whose tax administration has received the information. The CFA felt that the principle of confidentiality of tax information requires that it should not be used for non-tax purposes. Allowing an exception to this principle in the case of bribes might jeopardise voluntary tax compliance.

Implementing the Recommendation on Tax Deductibility

To ensure that countries adopt consistent approaches to the tax treatment of bribes and to permit them to learn from each other ways to overcome the practical difficulties of eliminating deductibility, the CFA set in place the following monitoring procedures, which have been implemented over the past three years:

- Member countries that had completed reviews and adopted new legislation or rules denying the deductibility of bribes to foreign public officials, were asked to report on their experience in the implementation of the new legislation. At a later stage, a system of informal peer reviews will monitor how the new legislation is implemented.

- Member countries which had re-examined tax deductibility were asked to report on how they organised and conducted their reviews, on the results and on the involvement of the business community in the review process.

- Member countries where the deductibility of bribes to foreign public officials was under re-examination were asked to report on the organisation of the review and on the progress made.

- Member countries that had not yet begun to re-examine the tax treatment of bribes to foreign public officials were asked to report on how they plan to implement the Recommendation and set up their reviews, and to provide their timetables.

Countries with experience in denying deductibility were invited to present their legislation, regulations and administrative practices as well as the way the legislation had been presented to their business communities. These experiences proved useful for countries re-examining their laws and rules, and helped the identification of problems or obstacles.

Country Legislation and Practices

Tax Treatment of a Public Official who Receives a Bribe

Most OECD Members treat bribes as taxable income to the recipient. With a few exceptions, taxation is imposed only by the country in which the bribed official is a resident, and not by the country of source. If the government confiscates the bribe as a result of a court decision, the bribe will continue to be taxable to the original recipient in some countries (Austria, Belgium, Canada, Germany, France and Luxembourg), while in others (Denmark, Finland, Ireland, Italy, Norway, Sweden and Switzerland) it will cease to be taxable because it has been confiscated under juridical proceedings. The United Kingdom has no general presumption that an illicit receipt is not taxable, but the actual liability will depend on the facts of the case. If a public official receives a bribe, he will not declare it and it is therefore unlikely that the receipt will be taxed as an emolument of his employment or, separately, as free-standing income.

Tax Treatment of a Person who Pays a Bribe to a Foreign Public Official

The situation in 1996

Member countries' attitudes towards the deductibility of bribes to foreign public officials varied. Most OECD Member countries disallowed a deduction for a bribe paid to a domestic official but only 14 denied the deductibility of bribes to foreign public officials as a general rule and on the following grounds:

- The illicit nature of the bribe in the country of the payer (Canada, United Kingdom and the United States).
- The illicit nature of the bribe for the payer and the recipient (Poland).
- The characterisation of the bribe as an expense not deductible for tax purposes, such as a gift (Czech Republic) or an entertainment expense (Japan).

- Bribes do not qualify as a deductible expense (Finland, Greece, Hungary, Italy, Korea, Mexico, Spain and Turkey).

At that time, some countries (Denmark, Iceland, Norway and Sweden) allowed the deductibility of bribes if they were documented business expenses, but only if they were customary in the recipient countries. In Australia, Austria, Belgium, France, Germany, Ireland, Luxembourg, Netherlands, Portugal, New Zealand and Switzerland bribes to foreign public officials remained in principle deductible like any other business expense. In practice, these countries often disallowed deductions in tax examinations, because of insufficient documentation to substantiate that the expenses were necessary for the realisation of income. More particularly, the deductibility of bribes to foreign officials was generally conditioned upon disclosing the identity of the recipient to the tax authorities, which taxpayers are naturally reluctant to do. Moreover, in certain countries the attitude of tax administrations became stricter after the publication of the 1996 Recommendation. In Denmark, Finland, Ireland and Luxembourg, the tax authorities started to take a harder line in challenging deductibility during tax examinations.

Status in early 2000

The Signatories of the 1997 Bribery Convention have made substantial progress in implementing the 1996 Recommendation: out of the 15 Member countries that didn't deny tax deductibility in 1996, 13 have reviewed their legislation. They now deny the tax deductibility of bribes to foreign public officials. In the remaining two countries (Luxembourg and New Zealand) draft legislation denying deductibility has been submitted to Parliament. Among the non-member signatories of the 1997 Bribery Convention, Argentina, Bulgaria, Brazil and the Slovak Republic legislation already deny the tax deductibility of bribes to foreign public officials.

The CFA will continue to monitor the implementation of the 1996 Recommendation and contribute to the reviews of the Working Group on Bribery. The CFA has also undertaken work to assist in the implementation of legislation denying deductibility. The existence of such legislation is a strong deterrent to bribery, but its practical implementation should not be neglected. The deterrent effect may diminish over time if no effort is made to ensure that taxpayers comply with the law.

Developing best Practices

As legislation denying tax deductibility fell into place in many countries, the CFA decided to pursue work on its implementation with a specific project: to draw up OECD Audit Guidelines for the Detection of Bribes to Foreign Public Officials to assist in the identification of bribes in the course of tax examinations. As a first step, it is discussing domestic measures to facilitate the identification of suspicious payments as well as ways to improve international co-operation in detecting them.

OECD Audit Guidelines for the Detection of Bribes to Foreign Public Officials

Audit guidelines enable tax administrations to educate tax examiners better on the best techniques to use and the facts to look for during examinations likely to lead to the identification of non-deductible bribery payments. They also raise the awareness of tax examiners in the identification of transactions connected with bribery. Since many Member countries are in the process of, or are considering, designing guidelines for tax examiners, it appeared timely to consider the issues that should be addressed in such guidelines. OECD Audit Guidelines for the Detection of Bribes to Foreign Public Officials are being designed on the basis of the principles that they should:

- Be provided by tax administrations as a follow up, either to the introduction of new legislation denying deductibility or to supplement pre-existing legislation if specific guidance has not yet been provided to tax examiners.

- Clearly specify the applicable rules on burden of proof.

- Provide examples enabling tax examiners to identify risk (*i.e.* contracts with foreign or quasi-foreign governments at all levels, important cash transactions, large miscellaneous expenses and recurring payments to persons who are not normal suppliers).

- Include sanitised examples of actual bribery cases.

- Identify business sectors where suspicious payments are more likely to occur.

- Indicate which government agencies are likely to have relevant information.

- Contain guidance on what feedback information to include in the tax examiner's report, which can then be used for input in the next tax audit plan. This information can also be helpful for the design of a database on new trends and techniques, or can be included in updates of tax-auditor manuals.

- Provide clear guidance as to whether under domestic law the tax examiner is under obligation to inform the criminal prosecutor (or is prevented from doing so).

Increasing Exchanges of Information on Bribes and Suspicious Payments

A growing number of countries are concluding agreements to improve exchanges of information that include a specific reference to commissions, fees and similar payments. Because these agreements between competent authorities are generally publicised, this should have a deterrent effect on bribery. A draft Council Recommendation, approved by the CFA, for an *OECD Model Memorandum of Understanding on Automatic Exchange* deals with automatic exchange of various kinds of tax information and makes a special reference to the need to enhance international co-operation to combat bribery of foreign public officials. In its Article 2.n, it states that *"the competent authorities shall endeavour to exchange information on commissions and other similar payments"*. It also recommends that the competent authorities agree to *"intensify exchange of tax information (spontaneous and on request) in the case of the following categories of income: commissions, fees, brokers' fees and other remuneration paid to natural or legal persons"*.

To improve the identification of payments of bribes to foreign public officials in international transactions, the CFA is exploring a number of possibilities such as:

- intensification of spontaneous exchanges and exchanges on request, on commissions, fees and similar payments made to individuals and legal entities, and inclusion of a specific reference to such exchanges in documents or bilateral agreements on information exchange, in order to raise the awareness of tax officials and taxpayers; or

- expansion of the scope of automatic exchange to include commissions, fees and similar payments.

Simultaneous Tax Examinations

Simultaneous tax examinations may provide another tool to identify bribes to foreign public officials. The 1992 OECD Model Agreement to undertake simultaneous tax examinations states that "The main purpose of simultaneous tax examination is *inter alia*: To determine a taxpayer's correct liability in cases where: (…) unreported income, money laundering, kickbacks, bribes, illegal payments, etc. are identified".

Looking ahead

In 1996, the OECD Council called for the CFA to promote the proposals of the Recommendation on the Tax Deductibility of Bribes to Foreign Public Officials in its contacts with non-member countries. The CFA and representatives of Member countries have taken an active part in OECD-sponsored events in Latin America and in Asia (see Chapter Ten), aimed at promoting the relevant OECD instruments to counteract bribery on a global basis. Other global and regional initiatives in the tax area have helped this effort. The United Nations General Assembly adopted in 1998 a Declaration against Corruption and Bribery in International Commercial Transactions, calling for criminalising foreign bribery and denying tax deductibility of bribes. The IMF adopted Guidelines regarding Governance issues in 1997. These guidelines seek to promote greater attention by the IMF to such issues, in particular the tax treatment of bribes. The Criminal Convention on Corruption of the Council of Europe, opened for signature on 27 January 1999, covers the prohibition of the tax-deductibility of bribes. The European Commission adopted in May 1997 a Communication to the Council and the European Parliament on a Union Policy against Corruption. The communication deals with a number of actions and in particular with the elimination of the tax deductibility of bribes. Such collective action can help governments to win the war against bribery on the tax front.

Chapter 5

Cleaning Up Public Procurement

by
William Nicol* *and* **Cynthia Walker****

What is the Problem?

Some of the preceding chapters have touched briefly on corruption in public procurement, noting that it had a prominent place in the thinking of the OECD Working Group on Bribery in International Business Transactions as it developed the Revised Recommendation (Annex II) and the 1997 Bribery Convention (Annex I). The United Nations, the multilateral development banks and other international institutions also give it considerable attention, as will become clear later in this chapter.

Why is this so? Many incentives to bribe public officials can exist outside procurement decisions themselves – to obtain favourable tax treatment, get an import license, move a big shipment quickly through customs, obtain a regulatory decision that will lead to ongoing business and a strong market position, and so forth. The examples are, unfortunately, legion.

Yet an immense class of actual business transactions can include both the strongest temptations to corrupt behaviour and the biggest corrupt deals. These transactions share one defining characteristic: they go forward, or do not, from the decisions of public officials. They include public procurement as it is commonly understood, namely purchases of goods and services by governments themselves or by state-owned firms. Depending on countries' particular institutional arrangements, the degree of official impact on purchasing decisions does not stop, but rather fades along a continuum. One cannot decide with precision where along that continuum transactions stop looking effectively like "public procurement",

---

* William Nicol is Head of Division in the OECD Development Co-operation Directorate.
** Cynthia Walker was Principal Administrator in SIGMA in the OECD Directorate for Public Management Service.

but that is not necessary to show that the phenomenon covers a huge range of business transactions.

Procurement often involves large sums of money spent locally or internationally. Domestic procurement attracts attention among local businessmen and government officials; international purchases bring in goods and services not easily available in the local economy, fostering envy and the wish to divert some of those products and the money for personal use. When corruption occurs in areas and activities supported by aid, it can devalue the reputation and efforts of aid agencies; this is equally true for the abuse of taxpayers' money by public officials.

Public procurement is big business indeed. Estimates place its value within the European Union at about 14% of EU GNP, which probably is typical of the industrial countries in general. The figure can be as high or higher in developing and transition economies, in which spending on public works and infrastructure plays a large role. Despite trends towards privatisation, many countries retain a legacy of relatively great state participation in the economy. The corruption stakes therefore are high, affecting all countries at all stages of development. They call for serious and effective policies, both to punish corruption and to improve public-procurement systems themselves.

During the 1990s, the public became more aware of the costs to society of corruption in public procurement – fewer and lower quality goods and services, inefficient and ineffective government, and dishonesty among both public and private employees. Many countries responded with efforts to raise public knowledge of the harm corruption may cause, in terms of both actual costs and lost opportunities. In part as a result of these efforts, the public has become less tolerant of corruption generally and less willing to pay the indirect and often substantial costs to all citizens that a non-functional and corrupt government implies. Officials in countries where corruption is rampant often find that, instead of obtaining the goods and services they really want, they often have to contend with second or even third choices.

The OECD has been encouraged to contribute to the anti-corruption fight as its Member countries have come to recognise that improvements in public management and governance must be made before the battle against corruption can be won. The aspects of good management and governance that must be the focus of anti-corruption efforts include transparency, prevention techniques, ethical standards, capacity building and effective law enforcement, with sanctions.

The opportunities and incentives for corrupt practices found world-wide emerge from social, political, economic and administrative systems. They include inappropriate roles for the state, bureaucratic approaches to resource allocation, and weak accountability and enforcement. In developing and transition countries, the opportunities for and the acceptance of corruption can be broader than in countries where democracy has been practised for a longer time, and where the rule of law is more deeply rooted and state institutions better developed.[1] This becomes particularly worrisome in countries trying to install a democratic system after decades of non-democratic regimes. Pervasive corruption undermines the credibility of democratic institutions and works against good governance. Where it is tolerated, the state fails to generate credibility and authority.

OECD Member countries know that an effective and credible approach to checking the spread of corruption requires addressing it at all levels of government and business, but especially at the most senior ones. Anti-corruption campaigns will not deliver expected results without sustained, high-level political backing.

Exclusion from Public Procurement as a Sanction of Corrupt Behaviour

OECD Member countries generally have well-developed systems of public procurement.[2] Provisions regulating access to bidding for public contracts vary widely among countries. Most have laws or rules that provide for the denial of access to tender procedures for bidders convicted of certain offences, including bribery. Exclusion from bidding may be governed directly by public-procurement laws or the penal code, or based on regulations and guidelines, such as guidelines relating to gifts. Usually, formal exclusion procedures do not exist, and exclusion is at the discretion of the competent judicial or administrative authority.

The basis for exclusion normally is a criminal conviction. In some countries, however, an indictment for bribery or a reasonable belief that an act or omission has occurred suffices. Other elements of due process, such as standing to bring a suit, the nature of hearings, notification, etc., also vary considerably from country to country. In countries with no laws or regulations specific to government procurement, denial of access to bidding is a matter for procuring departments or agencies. They presumably act on the commercial grounds of lack of confidence in a company's competency, good standing as a contractor or failure to meet pre-qualification criteria. Several Member countries could extend exclusion to the offence of bribery of foreign public officials under various conditions, even before any improvements in scope that they might have enacted pursuant to the Revised Recommendation of 1997 (Annex II).

The most common sanction involves temporary exclusion from bidding. Periods of exclusion vary from a minimum of one month to up to eight years; only a very limited number of countries can impose definitive debarment. Some countries also levy fines. The exclusion penalties generally go against firms; only a few countries apply them to companies' employees as well. No country makes distinctions based on nationality. Foreigners face sanctions on the same basis as nationals.

Regional organisations and other international institutions with public-procurement concerns also have defined approaches to sanctions. The European Union has adopted rules with provisions that enable contracting authorities to exclude firms that engage in misconduct or use corrupt or fraudulent practices. The World Bank has also rules for exclusion from procurement.

The European Community adopted, notably as part of the single-market pro-gramme, various Directives designed to enhance transparency, open up public procurement and guarantee non-discriminatory treatment to suppliers from the European Union. While these Directives make no specific reference to corruption, some include provisions that could apply to corruption cases. The "Public Supplies", "Public Works", and "Public Services" Directives provide that any contractor *"may be excluded from participation in the contract who ... has been convicted of an offence concerning his professional conduct by a judgement which has the force of res judicata ... [or] has been guilty of grave professional miscon-duct proven by any means which the contracting authorities can justify..."*.[3]

Procurement of civil works and goods financed by World Bank loans and International Development Association (IDA) credits is subject to the Bank's *Guidelines for Procurement under IBRD Loans and IDA Credits*. These *Guide-lines*, together with the Bank's standard bidding documents, establish a fair, objec-tive and transparent procurement system. In August 1996, the Guidelines were revised to make them a better instrument to fight corruption in Bank-financed pro-curement. A new section 1.15 was introduced which, *inter alia*, explicitly declares ineligible for Bank-financed contracts firms found to have engaged in corrupt or fraudulent practices in competing for, or executing, Bank-financed contracts. In September 1997, a further amendment accepted, under certain conditions, require-ments that bidders undertake to observe the country's laws against fraud and corruption (section 1.16).

Based on the foregoing information, the OECD Working Group on Bribery in International Business Transactions concluded that the denial of access to public procurement could effectively sanction and deter corruption, including the bribery of foreign public officials. It formulated the standard in section VI of the Revised Recommendation, which states that if Members provide for procurement-related sanctions in cases where companies are found to bribe domestic public officials, they should provide for the same sanctions on enterprises bribing foreign officials in contravention of the Member's national laws. Each country will impose the sanction using its own normal rules and procedures.

Access to Procurement as an Incentive against Corrupt Behaviour

The use of access to procurement as an incentive – the so-called "white list" approach – requires companies which wish to bid for public procurement contracts to certify that they comply with all anti-bribery laws and that they have internal management and accounting practices adequate to ensure compliance with these laws. Contractors must state that no bribe, gift, benefit, or other inducement has been or will be paid directly or indirectly to obtain the contracts; and contracts are terminated if the statements turns out to be, or become false. Self-certification can be reinforced or replaced by third-party certification, by auditors or other independent entities, that the company has in place adequate internal management and accounting practices and controls. One can also include in contracts provisions for liquidated damages, *i.e.* a certain percentage of the amount of the contract to be held back from payments and forfeited if corruption occurs.

Certification approaches are occasionally but not widely used, even in highly developed procurement systems. While they can be useful because they oblige the company's management to focus on the issue of bribery in public procurement, they raise legitimate questions, such as those of potential discrimination and discouragement of bids from small firms. An alternative, which would apply the requirement only to companies selected for contract awards, rather than imposing it as a condition for bidding, may have more promise.

Corruption in Aid-funded Procurement

Because corruption is clandestine, no one can estimate with any degree of confidence its extent in aid-funded procurement, but all agree that its effects are wide-ranging and pervasive. Through years of experience, donors have learned much about the many forms corruption can take in procurement activities. Common practices include bribery, kickbacks, padded commissions, over-invoicing and under-invoicing, overcharging, document falsification, shipping substandard or insufficient quantities of supplies and equipment, and using consultants other than those originally proposed.

Donors have established comprehensive and detailed rules and procedures to safeguard procurement in their aid systems. All have measures to ensure accountability, transparency, and value for money, although the scope and rigour of legislation, regulations, and policy guidelines on procurement differ from country to country. Depending on national law and the donor/recipient aid agreements, donor governments, private executing agencies, and/or recipient agencies or governments follow their own specific rules for aid-funded procurement. Detailed procurement procedures typically apply to all phases of the procurement process (*i.e.* bidding, evaluation, contracting, transport, inspection, invoicing, disbursements, and auditing). These procedures, often set out in loan or project agreements, generally fall within four broad categories:

- Vetting of procurement operators (pre-qualification, two-step bidding).

- Encouraging competition, through advertising requirements, mandatory competitive bidding for goods and services, and publication of contracts awarded.

- Checks and controls, governing participation in and monitoring of bid evaluations, pre- and post-shipment inspections, requirements for verification of signatures and documents, and approval of disbursements against documents, performance benchmarks, audits, etc.

- Surveillance by procurement consultants who follow all or certain steps of the procurement cycle.

Concerted Action by Donors

Aid-funded procurement is more controlled internationally since donors have agreed on the need to reinforce their procedures by introducing specific and clear anti-corruption provisions, thus clearly signalling their intent. In 1995, the OECD Development Assistance Committee (DAC)[4] adopted "Orientations on Good Governance and Participatory Government". This policy document endorsed the need to fight corruption, to improve transparency and accountability in the use of public funds, and to address these issues in a dialogue between donors and recipients of development assistance.

Subsequently, the DAC selected eight developing countries for a pilot study of the fight against corruption through experimentation with country-level processes that start from in-country diagnoses of the problem. Continued monitoring of progress takes place within the eight countries, as well as internationally in consultative-group and round-table meetings. An informal network established in 1998 guides these pilot country studies and pools efforts to ensure that implementation of anti-corruption actions becomes an important factor in determining overall performance and levels of future aid allocations.

To further highlight its intention to tackle corruption, the DAC adopted a Recommendation in 1996 (Annex IV), in which DAC Members agreed to introduce or require anti-corruption provisions governing bilateral aid-funded procurement.

Members took these actions in close collaboration with their partner countries, the multilateral development institutions, and the other efforts within the OECD to fight corruption. The DAC Recommendation subsequently became integrated with the OECD's Revised Recommendation on Combating Bribery in International Business Transactions.

The DAC Recommendation addresses some crucial issues for the effectiveness of anti-corruption actions:

* The scale of the costs to *all* of no or ineffective action.

* Recognition that "it takes two to tango"; the parties to aid-supported procurement must co-operate. This infers no suspicion on either side but serves to reinforce the mutual objectives shared by donors and recipients to combat corruption and maximise the use of scarce aid resources. Indeed, the need for coherence and co-operation extends further, to bilateral and multilateral donors and, in-house, different parts of the OECD in its efforts to fight corruption.

* The need for other, wider initiatives, because the Recommendation addresses only one dimension of the problem, aid-funded procurement.

The Recommendation required the DAC to follow up within 12 months on Members' actions to give it effect. By 1997, all DAC donors reported that they were in full compliance with the Recommendation. Those that previously had no explicit anti-corruption clauses in their procurement documentation now have them. Those that already had such clauses or equivalent procedures have taken steps to ensure that they align fully with the scope and intent of the Recommendation. Many donors have further strengthened their existing procedures. The DAC intends to assess experience with the impact of the Recommendation by December 2000.

Anti-corruption Clause in Aid-funded Procurement

In preparation of the 1996 Recommendation, the OECD Development Co-operation Directorate drafted the following anti-corruption clause to assist DAC Members' in their efforts to draft their country's own anti-corruption clause:

No offer, gift or payment, consideration or benefit of any kind, which would or could be construed as an illegal or corrupt practice, has or will be made, either directly or indirectly, as an inducement or reward for the award or execution of this contract. Any such practice will be grounds for mis-procurement.

All donors could not be invited to adopt identical provisions because of important differences in the forms and modalities of their policies and programmes, as well as the wide range of operating rules on aid-funded procurement. Nevertheless, the clauses they have now introduced have important common elements consistent with the proposed DAC anti-corruption clause. They all:

- Give a clear signal that corruption will not be tolerated.

- Cover the spirit, language and scope of the DAC anti-corruption clause, and in some cases strengthen and/or go beyond it.

- Cover all bilaterally funded procurement contracts and address all parties to them (donor/recipient governments and/or their agents) and all relevant documentation (*e.g.* contracts, agreements and memoranda of understanding).

These very focused actions by DAC Members target only one dimension of the broader problem of corruption in development programmes. Nevertheless, they have a number of merits. The objective, aid-funded procurement, is an important area of DAC Members' development programmes. Tangible and immediate actions send a clear signal of donors' intentions to deal concretely with corruption. This helps establish credibility, trust and mutual interest for subsequent dialogues with development partners. The measures reflect the need to act, albeit partially, with a sense of urgency. The next step is to assess their impact and take the further actions required.

Reforming Public-procurement Systems in Transition Countries

Since 1992, the SIGMA Programme[5] has counselled transition countries on the reform of their core management systems of government, including the civil service, state budget and financial control, external audit, administrative oversight, policy co-ordination, and regulatory practices. These are the essential underpinnings of a reliable and efficient administration. SIGMA has played an active role in helping these countries to create effective and efficient public procurement systems characterised by accountability and transparency. In addition to providing advice and information, it has helped to raise awareness of the benefits of setting up such systems. SIGMA's operations, therefore, link directly with the OECD's anti-corruption and anti-bribery objectives across the range of government operations, including public procurement.

Experience has shown that a properly constructed procurement system, underpinned by appropriate legislation and regulations, helps to eliminate corruption in procurement administered under national rules, whether financed with domestic resources or with foreign-aid funds. It also obtains more goods and services directly meeting the needs of the end users, for less money and with speedier delivery. SIGMA counsels on the adoption of appropriate legislation, and helps to train both public and private staff. More generally, it assists the transformation of centralised government-purchasing systems into more decentralised ones that are open and ensure accountability and non-corruptibility to their clients, the citizens of their countries.

Virtually all the central and eastern European countries have applied for membership in the European Union or are otherwise seeking closer relations with the EU. SIGMA helps the candidate countries fit their procurement systems to the EU's procurement requirements. It provides information about systems proven successful in other countries that have gone through similar transitions. Over the past 30 years, the European Commission has drawn up public procurement Directives to encourage competition and allow firms to compete on an equal footing for contracts from public and private entities. Since the approval of the first procurement Directive in 1970, both their number and amendments to them have increased. In some areas the Directives impose obligations on how public procurement should be regulated in EU Member States. In others, the issues are considered a national concern as long as public procurement laws or regulations adhere to the basic principles of the Rome Treaty on non-discrimination, equal treatment and mutual recognition.

SIGMA offers transition countries access to an international network of experienced public-administration practitioners, information about public procurement systems in other countries, experts in anti-corruption in procurement and technical knowledge in the procurement field. It tries to nurture lasting relationships with those responsible for public procurement reform in transition countries. It regularly sends experts to assist them with the practical actions needed to establish procurement systems that work effectively and efficiently, and, in the process, contribute to the broader objectives of good governance and corruption-free operations.

Step-by-step Reform

SIGMA has taken a three-step approach. It advises countries on how to:

- *Draft laws and secondary legislation* setting up viable procurement systems in line with the EC Directives on procurement.

- *Develop and teach training courses for trainers*, aimed at both officials who award contracts and business people who bid for and carry them out.

- *Encourage cross-border sharing* of knowledge and experience in public procurement and resultant reduction of corruption through international conferences and the development of databases and websites.

Legislation Drafting. SIGMA's partner countries frequently ask it to assist in drafting legislation. In response, it typically organises a visit to the country by its staff and recruited experts. They explain good procurement practices, promote understanding of the needs and reasons for new legislation, assist with the overall planning and either participate in legislative drafting or provide comments on drafts which officials have prepared.

Most of the early legislation in central and eastern European countries was based not on the EC Directives on procurement, but rather on a model law on procurement prepared by the United Nations Commission on International Trade Law (UNCITRAL) in the early 1990s. This model law emerged from several years' work by a large team of consultants and advisers; it forms a good basis and organisational structure for a procurement law. Despite its merits, it is aimed at all countries and not specifically potential EU Members, who must include the requirements stated in the EC Directives in their procurement legislation. Thus, the countries with which SIGMA works must amend their laws or draft entirely new ones to bring them into line with the EC Directives. With support from and close consultation with the European Commission Directorate-General responsible for the EC procurement Directives, SIGMA points out what is required. It will soon make available a summary table outlining the key differences between UNCITRAL-inspired legislation and EC Directives, to facilitate harmonisation of procurement laws with those in force in EU Member States.

Beyond providing detailed advice on the legal aspects of drafting procurement legislation, SIGMA recommends methods and operations that have proved effective at promoting transparent and functional procurement systems in other countries. For example, it advises on the size of central government procurement units, an important factor because those too small will be unable to perform the tasks necessary in good procurement systems, while those initially too large may have too many staff members without adequate backgrounds and training.[6]

Training Procurement Officials. A procurement system will fail without sufficient training of its staff. Consequently, SIGMA has also provided practical advice on how to set up good training programmes. In 1996, it and the International Training Centre of the ILO in Turin (Italy) published the *Public Procurement Manual*, a basic guide for procurement officials. They later revised it and added a nine-volume set of training materials based on the EC Directives. After testing and revision, they published the series during the summer of 1999 as *Training of Trainers in Public Procurement.* This package comprises brief lecture notes, overheads, case studies, and tests based on the materials. A grant from the European Training Foundation has made the series available as a CD-ROM distance-learning course.

Sharing Information and Experience. SIGMA produces other publications, including the newsletter *Public Management Forum* (*PMF*), which appears six times a year. *PMF* often features articles on procurement. In 1997, SIGMA published its *Policy Brief No. 3 – Public Procurement*, which outlines in just six pages the main actions to create a good public procurement system.[7] SIGMA also participates in and organises many meetings and conferences for practitioners. In May 1999, SIGMA and the OECD Directorate for Financial, Fiscal and Enterprise Affairs notably held a workshop in Istanbul, Turkey on building a public procurement system, for procurement officers from central and eastern European and CIS countries.[8]

Other International Initiatives to Ensure Integrity in Procurement Actions

European Bank for Reconstruction and Development (EBRD) agreements relating to the procurement of goods and services include a number of covenants and procedures which combine to create a transparent environment that reduces the potential for misuse of the proceeds of Bank loans. The EBRD's supervision and disbursement procedures for public operations aim to ensure that disbursement relates directly to contract performance. The Bank's procurement rules and procedures, reinforced by contract conditions, provide grounds for termination or default if any bribe, gift or commission is given as an inducement for the award of a contract. Any staff member who suspects that a transaction in which the Bank is participating involves "illegal payments or an illegal scheme or arrangement" is required to inform the General Counsel.

The UNCITRAL Model Law (mentioned briefly above) on Procurement of Goods, Construction and Services, adopted in the early 1990s, sets out a number of rules of conduct for suppliers and contractors to grant fair competition and prevent procedural abuses. It ensures transparency and accountability of the procurement process with record-keeping requirements, disclosure provisions, public accessibility of laws and regulations concerning procurement, foreign-language and publication requirements regarding prequalification and solicitation documents, and public notification of procurement contract awards. Its standards also provide that the procuring entity must reject any offer accompanied by inducements of any kind (monetary or otherwise), and that rejection of the tender be noted in the procurement-proceedings record and promptly communicated to the supplier or contractor.

The World Bank, in addition to its guidelines to help ensure economic and efficient procurement under bank-financed projects, has started programmes financed through grants from the Bank's institutional development fund to help countries establish or improve public procurement systems. The programmes:

* Assist countries in drafting public procurement laws and regulations where they do not exist, based on the UNCITRAL model law.

* Help countries establish central procurement authorities, regulatory bodies or agencies to supervise the implementation of procurement laws and regulations, and to prepare standard tender documents to be used for construction, goods or services contracts using public funds.

Transparency International (TI) is the major NGO in the anti-corruption field. It proposes strengthening normal procurement rules by the addition of two elements: the timeliness of actions and the involvement of outsiders in procurement procedures to hamper the creation of insider relationships during decision-making and implementation.[9]

In parallel with the agreement establishing the World Trade Organisation (WTO), a revised Government Procurement Agreement (GPA) was signed to bring government procurement under internationally agreed rules. The revised GPA, which builds on a first pluri-lateral agreement going back to 1981, entered into force on 1 January 1996. Its aim is to further liberalise and expand world trade by eliminating discrimination against goods or services of foreign suppliers and to enhance transparency of public procurement laws and practices. It does not explicitly address corrupt practices, but provides implicit constraints through strengthened provisions for transparency of the tendering process. WTO Ministers, at their December 1996 meeting in Singapore, agreed that the "Member countries should support the initiative in the WTO to conduct a study on transparency in government procurement practices, taking into account national policies, and, based on this study, to develop elements for inclusion in an appropriate agreement".

Procurement in the Broader Context of Governance and Donor Support

A few last words are in order on the theme, covered earlier in this chapter, of how the relationships and policies of aid donors and recipients can affect honesty in public procurement. The theme itself really forms part of a larger whole, the subject of good governance. The significant, specific actions taken by the OECD Member countries and other donors to promote accountable and transparent procurement systems, by themselves, will certainly not suffice to deal with systemic and pervasive corruption in procurement. Reducing corruption without simultaneously promoting integrity throughout public administrations could be a strategy for failure; procurement does not take place in a vacuum separate from other government activities. Moreover, support for integrity is barren without support for the general economic and institutional development of recipient countries, as donors clearly perceive. Poverty; sharp income disparities; poor administrative structures; weak judicial, legislative and regulatory frameworks; inadequate education; and cultural and social value systems that condone corrupt practices all give rise to corruption. Specific measures by donors to tighten procurement procedures will have greater effect to the extent that recipient-country attitudes, policies and institutions evolve.

In addition to encouraging economic development, donor and recipient governments must also stress the benefits of procurement systems that are not corrupt. When governments do not promote the benefits, citizens see no reason to change the system. Donor programmes and activities also need to operate in ways that respect and encourage strong local commitment, participation, capacity development and ownership. In the 1990s, good governance and its corollary, participatory development, served as focal aspects of development assistance.[10]

Donors' procurement transactions themselves can help set an example of transparent procurement and contribute to:

- Establishing or reinforcing mechanisms in developing and transition countries to reduce the opportunities for corrupt practices.

- Strengthening the human and institutional capacity for establishing and implementing transparency, accountability standards and anti-corruption programmes in the public and private sectors.

- Reducing the potential for diversion of funds implicit in the various kinds of aid packages.

- Assessing the efficiency of financial control and external audit procedures in place in donor and recipient countries to ensure honesty in procurement and in the use of aid funds generally.

- Supporting and encouraging all involved, including the media and society at large, in exposing corrupt procurement practices.

- Sharing with partner countries the results of intra-OECD anti-corruption work and propagating best practices beyond the specific field of aid procurement.

Conclusion

Real progress towards curbing corruption can occur only to the extent that overall development progress takes place as well. Yet policies for economic development and the struggle against corruption go together. Public procurement systems that are corrupt and not transparent force citizens to pay more for fewer, lower-quality goods and services, and frustrate economic progress. If public procurement were fair and honest, adhering to internationally accepted principles, such would not be the case, and citizens could see the benefits of uncorrupted systems. Non-transparent procurement systems sustain inefficient and ineffective governments and undermine the rule of law, democracy and their benefits. When governments – donor and recipient alike – do not promote the benefits of uncorrupted procurement systems, citizens see no reason to challenge the minority that benefits from corruption at society's expense.

Notes

1. See, *e.g.*, Transparency International's "Corruption Perception Index", *http://www.transparency.org/*.

2. The information in this section is based on a 1996-1997 review which drew on responses of many Member countries to a questionnaire on the subject.

3. Article 20 for Council Directive 93/36/EEC (Public Supplies), Article 24 for Council Directive 93/37/EEC (Public Works) and Article 29 of Council Directive 92/50/EEC (Public Services).

4. The DAC membership comprises 22 OECD Member countries as well as the Commission of the European Communities.

5. SIGMA ("Support for Improvement in Governance and Management") is a joint initiative of the European Union and the OECD, principally financed by the EU's Phare Programme. The initiative operates within the OECD's Public Management Service (PUMA), and supports 13 countries in building modern systems of public administration: Albania, Bosnia-Herzegovina, Bulgaria, Czech Republic, Estonia, Former Yugoslav Republic of Macedonia, Hungary, Latvia, Lithuania, Poland, Romania, Slovakia and Slovenia. See also Chapter eleven on SIGMA's anti-corruption activities.

6. The units will generally have responsibility for:

   • Setting national procurement policy.
   • Preparing explanatory booklets detailing how to work with the procurement law.
   • Preparing drafts of acts, regulations and other secondary legislation about procurement, and collecting statistics and general information about procurement advertising, signed contracts, and complaints.
   • Compiling lists of trained and experienced arbitrators.
   • Preparing training and awareness programmes for both the public and private sectors.
   • Drafting model contracts, general conditions and standard procedures, disseminating them throughout the country, and publishing a public procurement bulletin announcing future tenders and the results of past tenders.

7. See RODLAUER, MARKUS (1995), "An IMF View on Government Purchasing: A Good Procurement Law is Good for the Economy", *Public Management Forum*, Vol. I, No. 3; CERNIGOJ, PETER (1996), "Public Procurement in Slovenia", *PMF*, Vol. II, No. 4; GÓRECKI, PIOTR-NILS (1998), "Development of the Polish Public Procurement System", *PMF*, Vol. IV, No. 2; NADAL, JEAN-PHILIPPE (1998), "Instituting Complaints Procedures for Public Procurement", *PMF*, Vol. IV, No. 2; PARUPS, EDVINS (1998), "Latvia on the Way to a Modern Procurement System", *PMF*, Vol. IV, No. 2; WESTRING, GOSTA (1998), "The International Legal Context for Public Procurement in Central and Eastern European Governments", *PMF*, Vol. IV, No. 2; and OECD, SIGMA (1997), *Public Procurement* – SIGMA Policy Brief No. 3. Paris, OECD.

8. The four-day programme, supported by USAID, highlighted six key steps taken by countries which have made a successful transition to an effective public procurement system:

   - Obtaining support from the highest political levels.
   - Educating the general public about the advantages of the new system.
   - Encouraging co-operation between the public and private sectors.
   - Obtaining good technical procurement training.
   - Passing effective procurement legislation.
   - Establishing a central procurement office to form national procurement policy and to draft supplemental legislation and training programmes.

9. See Chapter seventeen of this book devoted to anti-corruption activities of civil-society groups, and TI in particular.

10. See OECD (1995), *Participatory Development and Good Governance*, Development Co-operation Guidelines Series, Paris, OECD.

Chapter 6

A Sea Change in Anti-corruption Efforts[1]

by
Tom Delare*

The Change of Attitude

The global struggle against corruption and the narrower attack on international bribery are in a particularly dynamic phase. After years in which concern about corrupt business practices remained a quixotic American pursuit, the international community has taken up the issue as well. A horizontal comparison of the formal anti-corruption instruments and declarations indicates that the 1997 Convention on Combating Bribery of Foreign Public Officials in International Business Transactions (Annex I) retains its status as the most effective anti-corruption effort currently available – based on its advanced state of implementation, ongoing monitoring and global reach. The flurry of anti-corruption declarations may be the most obvious signal that a change of attitude toward the problem of global corruption has taken place, although the concrete result of this declarative embrace is still uncertain. The ebbing of the global economic crisis of 1997-1999 and stabilisation of politics in the transition economies calls for renewed efforts to maintain commitment to anti-corruption actions. The 1997 Bribery Convention appears to be the most appropriate mechanism for preserving momentum in anti-corruption efforts.

The US Perspective: Foreign Corrupt Practices Act Through the Asian Economic Crisis

US concerns about the corrosive impact of international business bribery are long standing, but broader international interest and a flourishing of anti-corruption instruments are new phenomena. From the US perspective, it has been a long

---

* Tom Delare is Deputy Director of the Office of Investment Affairs, U.S. Department of State.

struggle to bring the issues of corruption and, more specifically, international commercial bribery to this point of general concern. How did we move from a quixotic US preoccupation, based on little appreciated moral arguments and a unique political situation? In the briefest terms, we probably owe a great deal to the fall of the Wall, troubles of the *baht* and some new contributions from the dismal science of economics.

The Foreign Corrupt Practices Act (FCPA) was enacted under the Carter Administration more than 20 years ago, in 1977. In large measure, the provisions of the Act foreshadowed the present 1997 Bribery Convention in establishing substantial and dissuasive penalties for persons and corporations making payments to foreign government officials, political parties and candidates in order to retain or obtain business. At least since 1988, originally acting according to the authority of the Omnibus Trade Act of that year, the United States has energetically striven to internationalise this anti-corruption effort.

It is an interesting point that the original motivations for unilateral US action were moral and political, while economic bases for an attack on corruption remained undeveloped. It is safe to say that the moral argument reflected a general distaste among much of the American public about US firms making impermissible contributions to US political campaigns and, using the same payment methods, funnelling money to foreign governments.[2] The political argument also related to a desire to avoid or mitigate negative foreign reactions to perceptions of US meddling in their domestic affairs. The end of the Vietnam War a few years earlier had left a US public less inclined to tolerate interference abroad by business interests or government. In addition, the Carter Administration came into office promising a new and more ethical standard of conduct.

The translation of popular distaste into practical international action has depended, naturally enough, on the support of a US business community anxious to level a playing field that had suddenly tilted against them. Thus, the moral and political argument became joined with the practicalities of business – a potent combination.

The negotiation of the OECD Recommendations and the 1997 Bribery Convention followed a course well outlined elsewhere in this volume, with political support for a sustained attack on the problem of international bribery gradually developing. However, a supporting academic consensus also emerged, as described in this volume by Professor Cartier-Bresson, about the negative consequences of corruption on economic growth and rational resource allocation. The broadening international effort now taking shape in a variety of regional pacts, changed policies in international financial institutions, altered conditionality in national assistance programs and the like – all point toward a new understanding of the corrosive aspects of corruption.

Apart from pressure brought to bear by the United States, it is arguable that the international community's new-found interest in the problem of corruption also was decisively linked to two clearly identifiable events. Certainly, the end of the Cold War offered an opportunity to domestic reformers. In a number of countries, they suddenly found themselves unconstrained by the limiting debate of East-West politics and were able to raise the profile of corruption issues. As the reality of confrontation between antagonistic political systems began to fade and then disappeared altogether, the consequences of shaking hidebound and sometimes corrupt domestic political institutions to their roots seemed like a viable option. A new politics emerged, most prominently in Italy and Korea, but also throughout Latin America and in portions of Africa, where reform assumed new importance.

Finally, the international economic crisis beginning with the collapse of the Thai *baht* in July 1997 and lasting through much of 1999 had a particularly catalytic and beneficial effect in the anti-corruption area. While the crisis was largely an example of macroeconomic failure, its rolling impact on countries in Asia, Latin America and Eastern Europe usefully served to show the negative consequences of the lack of good governance in public and private decision-making.

The international anti-corruption effort has seen adoption of a number of new efforts that have leapfrogged some of the traditional anti-corruption undertakings. Thus, we see new focus on anti-corruption programs by the World Bank[3] and other international lending institutions. In a surprising evolution, the Organisation for Security and Co-operation in Europe (OSCE), formerly a primary agency for bridging the political divide between East and West Europe and focusing attention on human rights, has been active in pursuing a variety of democratisation, good governance and anti-corruption measures in the transition states of Eastern Europe and Central Asia. The end of war in the Balkans has been translated into investment and anti-corruption compacts that aim at a wholesale remaking of economic and political structures in the area. The Global Coalition for Africa has been animated by the fact that key political leaderships, notably in South Africa and Nigeria, are ready to assume leadership roles in combating corruption. Equally important to an emerging generation of African leaders has been the realisation that corruption is a real and substantial drag on economic development.

A Broadening International Effort: Horizontal Comparison

The 1997 Bribery Convention is the most effective instrument currently available for curbing international corruption. Yet the instrument has a relatively limited reach and does not even have seniority among the various conventions. That honour goes to the Inter-American Convention Against Corruption, the instrument of the Organisation of American States (OAS), which was opened for signature in March 1996. Enthusiasm for the instrument negotiated under the auspices of the OECD is largely pragmatic. Partly owing to a broadly homogeneous OECD membership, it has been possible to push forward with a relatively tight anti-corruption agreement with specific commitments, to secure ratification from an unparalleled number of parties and to seek rough equivalence in implementation via a vigorous peer review. All these factors combine to produce an instrument that is setting new global norms for private and public governance. Moreover, an emphasis also should be paid to another aspect of the global reach of the 1997 Bribery Convention. The other major anti-corruption instruments have been, despite involvement by one or more "out of area" participants, essentially regional. Only the 1997 Bribery Convention, with signatories representing five continents and an accession policy that may open the door to an even more diverse geographic representation, is truly global.[4]

While the 1997 Bribery Convention may be a pacesetter, it will remain one of many anti-corruption efforts.[5] A horizontal comparison of major anti-corruption activity should include, in addition to the 1997 Bribery Convention, the Criminal Law Convention of the Council of Europe (CoE), the Inter-American Convention Against Corruption of the OAS, the various treaties of the European Union directed against corruption, the Global Coalition for Africa, and the Global Forum Against Corruption. The sheer number and variety of these activities has produced confusion, even among *cognoscenti*. How do the various initiatives differ from one another? Is there a binding instrument or is the effort hortatory? Which states are covered? Is there a transnational reach? Are there "opt out" clauses? Is a peer review system in place? If not endless, such questions are exceedingly numerous.

To place the 1997 Bribery Convention in context and to attempt a better understanding of the global anti-corruption effort, a basic typology would be useful. To begin with, a division between legally binding instruments and hortatory declarations seems appropriate. While the former have specificity and, presumably, a measurable impact, the latter are no less important. Particularly among transition economies and developing states, they offer vehicles to raise the awareness of the corruption problem and may, in fact, evolve into more binding commitments. Among binding instruments, comparisons suggest themselves according to geographic coverage, type of corruption treated and system of enforcement. To simplify the horizontal comparison, a table follows for convention-style instruments.[6]

Three major items differentiate the concrete initiatives. First, as suggested above, only the 1997 Bribery Convention has a truly global reach. The other instruments

Anti-corruption Initiatives
Conventions and Protocols (as of January 2000)

	1997 Bribery Convention	Inter-American Convention Against Corruption (OAS)	CoE Criminal Law Convention	European Union
Basic Information				
Type of initiative	Convention	Convention	Convention	Convention and Protocols
Entry into Force?	15 Feb. 99	6 Mar. 97	No	No
Opened for signature	17 Dec. 97	29 Mar. 96	27 Jan. 99	
Signatories/Parties*	34/20**	26/17	31/1	15 signatories
Bribery Covered				
Supply Side				Conventions and
Foreign/Domestic	Foreign Only	Foreign and Domestic	Foreign and Domestic	Protocols call for the
Public/Private	Public Only	Public Only	Public and Private	criminalisation of
Purposes Covered	Obtain/retain international business	Domestic – Any Purpose Foreign – Any economic or commercial transaction	Any Purpose	certain types of active (supply) and passive (demand) bribery of EU or member state officials.
Demand Side				
Foreign/Domestic	Not Covered	Domestic Only	Foreign and Domestic	
Public/Private	Not Covered	Public Only	Public and Private	
Purposes Covered		Any Purpose	Any Purpose	
Monitoring				
System in Place?	Yes	No	Yes	
Status?	Ongoing	Considering Mechanism	Monitoring Beginning	No regularised system in place.
Peer Review?	Yes	No	Yes	

* Parties are countries that have signed and ratified the respective instruments.
** See Annex I, Appendix B for parties to the 1997 Bribery Convention.

have retained a regional focus, despite a sometimes broad membership (the OAS Convention encompasses, for example, North and South America) and the inclusion of one or more "out of area" participants. In terms of bribes "covered", this is most evident in the conventions and protocols adopted by the EU that call for the criminalisation of certain types of passive and active bribery. These initiatives appear to apply only to the bribery of EU or member state officials.[7]

Second, the 1997 Bribery Convention is the most limited in terms of coverage of activity. Thus, its focus on the supply side of bribery is exceeded by the coverage of both supply and demand by the Conventions of the CoE and OAS. However, the CoE Convention permits parties to enter numerous "opt out" reservations that could inhibit the emergence of a uniform, high-standards approach to corruption issues.

Finally, and perhaps most importantly, is the matter of monitoring. The 1997 Bribery Convention provides a mechanism, detailed elsewhere in this volume, for the monitoring of both implementation of the Convention by ratifying states and its enforcement by them. The first stage of implementation monitoring is well past the halfway point (implementing legislation of 21 states examined as of April 2000) and active discussions aimed at initiation of enforcement reviews are underway. While the CoE Convention specifies a similar mutual evaluation process, the Group of States Against Corruption (GRECO) monitoring system is only in its beginning stages. No country evaluations have been completed and the process will initially focus on declarative principles rather than concrete implementing measures. The OAS is considering a mechanism for monitoring, but at this point, the organisation is still engaged in soliciting and collating basic information about legal regimes from member states. If we make the reasonable assumption that monitoring is a *sine qua non* of convention effectiveness, the 1997 Bribery Convention stands out at this point in time.

On the declaration side, a conceptual breakdown is harder to achieve. Many of the significant initiatives are new and evolving, and they cover a broad spectrum of conduct and activity. The Global Forum Against Corruption, sponsored by Vice President Gore in February 1999, attracted attendees from 90 countries to Washington. While raising the profile of the anti-corruption effort, with particular emphasis on law enforcement, the Forum also produced "Twenty Guiding Principles" that appear to be gaining broader currency internationally. A follow-on Forum will be hosted by the Netherlands in early 2001. Also in February 1999, the Global Coalition for Africa (GCA) saw eleven African participants endorse twenty-five anti-corruption principles. The efforts of the African states were met with particularly warm applause, as they appeared to represent a sea change in African attitudes toward corruption. Importantly, the link between corruption and lagging economic development appears to have been broadly recognised.

Conclusion: Looking at the Future

The ratification of the 1997 Bribery Convention has moved at a remarkably brisk pace by international standards. At the same time, progress has been made, albeit at a slower speed, on the other major anti-corruption conventions. Moreover, satisfaction should be taken in the proliferation of anti-corruption declarations. They appear to represent the acceptance of new norms of global behaviour, a valuation of good governance and recognition of the growing academic consensus about the debilitating impact of corruption on economic growth and socially responsible resource allocation.

Yet satisfaction has to be tempered with a realistic appreciation of the tasks ahead. In this regard, it is worth recalling that a major impetus was given to the global anti-corruption effort by the economic crisis of 1997-99. As the crisis has ebbed and economic growth has restarted, some of the force behind broad-based economic reform and the anti-corruption agenda also has weakened. At the same time, the liberating impulse generated by the end of the Cold War has largely dissipated. Politics has become more routine and reform has lost some of its lustre.

Yet the need for robust anti-corruption mechanisms has not diminished. Given the leading role played by the 1997 Bribery Convention to date, it is not unreasonable to see it as the instrument most likely to maintain international interest in the anti-corruption effort and to set enforcement norms for the other conventions. Unlike the other binding instruments, the 1997 Bribery Convention is well into its implementation phase. While a substantial number of ratifying parties do have deficiencies in their implementing legislation, it is clear that a start can be made toward active enforcement.

An action agenda supportive of robust implementation and enforcement of the 1997 Bribery Convention would be politically helpful and could include the following activities on the part of signatory and ratifying states:

- mutual support aimed at the elimination of implementation deficiencies identified by the Working Group;

- initiation of public affairs activities to support education in Convention obligations and to build support for active enforcement;

- encouragement of states lagging in implementation via bilateral and multilateral contacts;

- launching of Phase II reviews of Convention enforcement to test implementation regimes in practice and create additional pressure on lagging ratifiers.

It is incumbent upon the parties to the Convention to join in an effort to strengthen the working of the agreement. Otherwise, there is the real risk that the Convention will become one more meaningless, but well-intentioned document.

Notes

1. The views expressed here are solely those of the author and do not necessarily reflect the views of the Department of State or the US Government.

2. For an accessible overview of the origins of the FCPA, particularly the impact of Watergate and revelations about corporate financial misbehaviour, see Judge Stanley Sporkin, *The Worldwide Banning of Schmiergeld: A Look at the Foreign Corrupt Practices Act on Its Twentieth Birthday*. The Northwestern Journal of International Law and Business, Winter 1998.

3. The new literature on governance and corruption indicators issuing from the World Bank has been particularly influential among policymakers in Washington. The ability to broadly qualify varieties of corruption and estimate their relative severity in a given country has produced new attempts to maximise the impact of scarce assistance resources and target them on critical needs in key countries. The recent work of Daniel Kaufmann and his collaborators, for example, is already regarded as seminal. A relatively early analysis of corruption surveys, using data from Albania, Latvia and Georgia, is typified by Kaufmann, *et al.*, *New Frontiers in Diagnosing and Combating Corruption*, PREM notes, No. 7, October 1998, available on the World Bank website. A comprehensive presentation of governance, its measurement and consequences for development appears in Kaufmann, *et al.*, "Governance Matters", October 1999, also available on the World Bank website.

4. Neglected here as it is currently under negotiation is the United Nations Convention Against Transnational Organised Crime. It should criminalise the bribery of domestic public officials by an organised crime group. In addition, the pending completion of this Convention, it is expected that the UN Crime Commission will recommend to the UNGA that it adopt a comprehensive global anti-corruption convention.

5. Accession policy recently adopted by the OECD Bribery Working Group explicitly recognises the value of regional anti-corruption efforts. Given relatively strict economic and infrastructure requirements for admission to the Working Group or accession to the 1997 Bribery Convention, it is likely that many applicants for accession will be directed to appropriate regional anti-corruption bodies.

6. Thanks to Michael Tracton for compiling the information appearing in chart form and in producing an earlier version of the presentation.

7. Relevant EU protocols and conventions are outlined in a paper prepared by Claire A. Daams of Basel University for the 9th International Anti-Corruption Conference in Durban, South Africa, October 10-15, 1999. See "Regional Initiatives: European Union against Corruption".

Chapter 7

The Promise and the Reality: Monitoring Compliance with the Convention

by
Enery Quinones[*]

Expression of a Common Will

The date is 21 November 1997. It is five a.m. at the OECD's headquarters in Paris. There is great excitement as thirty-four countries finally reach agreement on the draft text of a treaty laying the foundations for one of the first, co-ordinated, and most significant steps to combat international bribery. In less than one month, the draft text will be unanimously adopted and signed by the governments of the countries that took part in the negotiations. This unprecedented move will then become legally binding in international law on 15 February 1999 with the entry into force of the Convention on Combating Bribery of Foreign Public Officials in International Business Transactions (see Annex I).

Since then, the 1997 Bribery Convention has enjoyed resounding success. Often hailed as a landmark in international legal relations, it has contributed to the recent sense of euphoria surrounding the international fight against bribery and corruption, where many are persuaded that the "good guys" have finally gained the upper-hand. Thirty-four of the world's major trading and investment countries bound themselves together in a mutual willingness to bring to an end one of the most pernicious forms of bribery. They agreed to adopt national laws making it a crime to bribe foreign public officials, injecting for the first time in international business transactions a sense of morality and fairness. How far have they come in bringing into reality the promise of that November morning?

---

[*] Enery Quinones is Head of the Anti-Corruption Unit in the OECD Directorate for Financial, Fiscal and Enterprise Affairs.

Earlier chapters in this book, notably those of Professor Sacerdoti and Professor Pieth, described the difficult negotiations and legal hurdles that had to be surmounted before reaching an agreement and provided in-depth analysis of the Convention's main obligations. This chapter looks at the promise and the reality of the 1997 Bribery Convention. On the basis of the first results of monitoring countries' commitments under the Convention[1], the chapter will assess whether, and to what extent, countries have met their pledge to outlaw bribery in international business transactions.

Where Do We Stand

Status of Ratification

The Convention was signed by all 29 OECD Member countries and by five non-members (Argentina, Brazil, Bulgaria, Chile, and the Slovak Republic). It is the responsibility of the Working Group to regularly survey countries' progress in ratifying and implementing the Convention and to report to OECD Ministers[2]. As of 21 June 2000, the following countries had ratified the Convention and their implementing legislation had been examined by the Working Group, including: Australia, Austria, Belgium, Bulgaria, Canada, Czech Republic, Finland, Germany, Greece, Hungary, Iceland, Japan, Korea, Mexico, Norway, Slovak Republic, Spain, Sweden, Switzerland, United Kingdom, and the United States (see Annex I, appendix B). Denmark and France have enacted implementing legislation but have not yet been examined.

The remaining countries, which are in varying stages of their legislative process, are fully committed to ratifying and implementing the Convention. Many countries have implementing legislation in Parliament and are expected to complete the necessary legislative action so they can deposit their instruments of ratification by the end of the year (Ireland, Italy, Netherlands, New Zealand, Luxembourg). In other countries, implementing legislation has not yet been submitted to Parliament (Argentina, Brazil, Chile, Poland, Portugal, and Turkey). The approval of ratification bills is complete in Poland, Portugal and Turkey. For Argentina, Brazil and Chile, ratification has to precede submission of implementing legislation and in these countries, the necessary steps towards ratification have been taken.

Results of Phase 1 Monitoring

The following analysis summaries the findings of the twenty-one countries evaluated so far. These are generic observations, focusing on specific issues that will need to be studied in more depth. For individual country evaluations, the reader

© OECD 2000

should consult the country specific reports on the OECD web site (*www.oecd.org/ daf/nocorruption/*).

General findings

Ministers commended countries for their efforts to ensure that legislation to implement the Convention in national law was in conformity with the Convention. Overall, this objective has been realised and in the great majority of countries there is, at present, compliance with the Convention's obligations. Despite this positive assessment, there are serious concerns about deficiencies and potential gaps in some cases. It is clear that for almost all countries reviewed, specific issues will need addressing. These issues are not, however, all of the same magnitude of importance. In several instances, specific recommendations for remedial action have been made wherever potential loopholes or gaps were observed, or where the provisions fell below the standards set by the Convention. In other cases, the issues will need further study possibly in a broader, or horizontal context that potentially could affect implementation of the Convention.

Elements of the bribery offence

In certain cases, loopholes or provisions that could present potential for misuse were identified. These include: exceptions to the scope of application of the offence of bribery of foreign public officials which were not foreseen by the Convention and defences which go beyond general defences in penal codes and which could be used to circumvent liability by a defendant. In these cases, immediate remedial action has been recommended. In certain countries, there was a lack of coverage of certain elements of the offence or the addition of a requirement not found in the Convention. It will be necessary to determine whether, in practice, these elements affect the application of the Convention and they will be carefully monitored in the Phase 2 examinations for the countries concerned.

Some inconsistencies were observed in the treatment of elements of the offence that could lead in some cases to an uneven application of the Convention. For example, the Convention contains an autonomous definition of the "foreign public officials" that should be covered. Some countries did not include an express definition, relying on direct applicability of the Convention in internal law. In others, there was a lack of clarity as to the coverage of the foreign public official provision. In one or two cases, countries referred directly to the national definition of the public official of the foreign country, which clearly diverges from the standards of the Convention and could affect implementation. These issues will be followed-up either on a horizontal basis, or as part of the monitoring of the country concerned in Phase 2.

© OECD 2000

Effectiveness of sanctions

In general, countries implemented the obligation to sanction the bribery of foreign public officials by effective, proportionate, and dissuasive criminal sanctions in ways that were logically consistent in the context of a country's penal system. Nevertheless a general question of the level of sanctions for natural persons (imprisonment and monetary fines) and monetary fines for legal persons will need to be evaluated at a later stage once other countries have been examined.

In some cases, the sanctions provided were too low in comparison to sanctions for similar criminal offences in the same country, such as theft, fraud, or embezzlement. Sanctions that are too low may also impact adversely on a country's ability to provide effective mutual legal assistance and extradition in accordance with the Convention. The countries concerned have been asked to reconsider the level of sanctions with a view to increasing them. The same could be said for countries where there are discrepancies between the sanctions provided for bribery of foreign public officials and bribery of domestic officials, a discrepancy which would fall short of the requirements of the Convention.

There are other issues which warrant closer study including the implementation by certain countries of Article 3.3 of the Convention on seizure and confiscation. The question was raised with respect to more than one country about the non-confiscation of the proceeds of bribery, and the unavailability of confiscation where the assets generated by the foreign bribery offence are no longer available. Other topics include the interpretation of the Convention in respect of the obligation for confiscation of the bribe when it is still in the possession of the briber and the discretionary power to confiscate property equivalent in value to a bribe that has been converted into another form.

Responsibility of legal persons

One of the thorniest and potentially complicated areas for further examination is Article 2 of the Convention dealing with the responsibility of legal persons. At present, some countries do not adequately provide for either criminal or non-criminal responsibility of legal persons. While the absence of criminal liability of legal persons, per se, is not an issue of non-compliance, there is concern that in some countries that do not recognise corporate criminal liability, the non-criminal sanctions were either lacking or very limited. In such cases, it is doubtful whether those countries have met the standards of the Convention that obliges Parties to ensure that legal persons are subject to effective, proportionate, and dissuasive non-criminal sanctions. Those countries that are considering introducing legislative amendments that would impose criminal liability were requested to do so as soon as possible. For others, this matter will need to be reviewed again in the Phase 2 evaluations to determine whether the non-criminal sanctions are effective.

Effectiveness of jurisdiction

The Convention requires countries to establish broad territorial jurisdiction over the bribery of a foreign public official. In addition, Parties that have the ability to establish nationality jurisdiction are required to take such measures as necessary to establish its jurisdiction in respect of bribery of foreign public officials according to the same legal principles. As a general matter, countries are obliged to review whether their current basis for jurisdiction is effective in the fight against the bribery of foreign public officials and to take remedial steps where it is not.

In a few cases, countries that establish nationality jurisdiction condition its application to the requirement that the country where the act of bribery was committed also criminalises bribery of foreign public officials (dual criminality). A few countries require certain conditions for the establishment of territorial jurisdiction, such as the requirement of governmental authority in order to prosecute cases of foreign bribery. These requirements might affect implementation of the Convention and it will be necessary to monitor them in Phase 2.

Enforcement

Countries are obliged to investigate and prosecute bribery of foreign public officials in accordance with their rules and principles. However, the Convention recognises the fundamental nature of national regimes of prosecutorial discretion. In order to protect the independence of prosecution, such discretion should not be subject to improper influence by concerns of a political nature. In carrying out the evaluations it came to light that in a few cases the prosecution of foreign bribery is subject to a requirement that such prosecutions be in the public interest. Whether the application of this requirement is an obstacle for effective implementation of the Convention will be examined in Phase 2.

Statute of limitations

According to the Convention, any statute of limitations applicable to the foreign bribery offence should allow for an adequate period of time for investigation and prosecution. The evaluations show that the range of statutes varies between 2 years and no limitation at all. Most countries were in the middle range of about 5 years with many countries also providing for the possibility of extending it under certain conditions. In one or two cases where it was determined that the statute was too low, the country concerned was asked to consider increasing it. Given the nature of the offence and the difficulty that might arise in investigating it, this issue will likely require a more in-depth review as to the adequacy of the length of the statute of limitations to be determined by a horizontal analysis for all countries.

What Happens Next

Completion of Phase 1 examinations and launching of Phase 2

The 13 countries that have not yet been examined in Phase 1 will be reviewed as soon as they have adopted implementing legislation and deposited their instrument of ratification of the Convention. For those that have been examined, the countries concerned are giving serious consideration to the recommendations for improving compliance with the Convention. Some have already taken the necessary legislative steps to amend legislation taking account of the recommendations made by the Working Group. Most countries have signalled their willingness to abide by these recommendations and it is up to the Working Group to ensure that effective measures are taken to remedy deficiencies.

It is expected that Phase 2 can begin by early 2001. Phase 2 will entail a more in-depth analysis to assess each country's structures to enforce the laws implementing the Convention and its application of the laws and rules in practice. It will also monitor more fully implementation of the non-criminal aspects of the 1997 Revised Recommendation. Phase 2 examinations will likely be conducted over a five to seven year period.

Critical Analysis of Issues Identified in Phase 1

In conducting the Phase 1 monitoring, several issues relating to the implementation of the Convention were identified as requiring further analysis. These issues are significant in that they potentially impact on the implementation of the Convention.

Some of these issues are of a general nature, such as the applicability of the Convention to a country's internal law where it has represented that the Convention will effectively compensate for possible loopholes in the offence or the lack of a definition of "foreign public official" in its implementing legislation as well as questions of interpretation of certain provisions of the Convention.

The Working Group will turn its attention to how countries have implemented Article 2 of the Convention requiring the establishment of the liability of legal persons, including assessing the comparative effectiveness of non-criminal liability and the different thresholds for criminal and non-criminal liability. It will also be necessary to analyse the overall effectiveness of the level of sanctions for natural and legal persons. This would involve evaluating the comparability between the sanctions in each country for foreign and domestic bribery as well as the sanctions for similar offences such as theft, fraud and embezzlement.

The issue of the basis of jurisdiction provided for by countries in their implementing legislation is also one of critical importance for the effectiveness of the Convention. The Working Group will be particularly attentive to the conditions required for the establishment of jurisdiction, such as government authorisation and dual criminality and/or reciprocity. Other issues mentioned previously include the adequacy of the statue of limitations and how effectively countries are able to comply with the obligations to provide mutual legal assistance for the purpose of investigating and prosecuting offences under the scope of the Convention.

Examination of further issues relating to corruption[3]

Adoption of the 1997 Bribery Convention is not the end of the road. In fact, it may be considered one step, albeit an important one, in the on-going effort to combat bribery in its different forms and manifestations. The countries that negotiated the Bribery Convention were aware that not all issues had been completely resolved by the Convention. They identified five issues which, in their view, justified further examination including: bribery acts in relation to foreign political parties, advantages promised or given to any person in anticipation of that person becoming a foreign public official, making bribery of foreign public officials a serious crime which triggers application of money laundering legislation, the role of foreign subsidiaries in bribery transactions and the role of offshore centres in bribery transactions.

The Working Group has done extensive work on issues relating to offshore financial centres as a result of several international initiatives in this area. Other issues relating to corruption particularly bribery in relation to political parties, or candidates, and the role of foreign subsidiaries in bribery transactions will be addressed in the coming months. Consultations with the private sector, trade unions, and civil society will focus on carrying forward proposals made to deal with the solicitation of bribes, whistle-blowing, and measures to secure greater compliance with the accounting provisions of the Convention and the 1997 Recommendation. Consideration will be given to the possibility of broadening the scope of the Convention to cover bribery that takes place between private agents (no public officials involved) upon completion of a study being conducted by the International Chamber of Commerce.[4]

End of the Honeymoon?

Not everyone welcomed the 1997 Bribery Convention with open arms. There were sceptics who questioned whether in fact the Convention would ever make a real dent in the level of bribery and corruption especially whenever important international commercial interests were at stake. Governments, however, were eager to gain public recognition and credit for joining the Convention and pledged that companies, enterprises, and individuals engaging in international business transactions would abide by the new rules or face criminal prosecution for any transgressions.

Civil society had long advocated such an agreement and was ready to give all parties concerned the benefit of the doubt. A year and a half after the Convention's entry into force, it cannot fail to notice that 11 countries have yet to provide for the implementation of the Convention in their national law, which means that they still do not have the legislative authority to punish those who act with impunity against the spirit of the Convention. The public can form its own opinion about a particular country's performance as the reviews of each country's legislation and, subsequently, the seriousness with which it applies its laws, are made publicly available. Countries that do not comply with recommendations to correct deficiencies or close potential loopholes or countries that appear to be lax in enforcing their laws, will be asked to account for their failure to take action.

The press continues to uncover almost daily allegations of corruption as well as instances of companies constituting illegal slush funds to pay bribes to foreign officials. Transparency International has published for the first time a Bribe Payers Perception Index[5] in which some OECD countries, signatories to the Convention, are listed. The monitoring mechanism described in this chapter can be a very powerful tool in ensuring that all countries abide by their legal obligations. More importantly, strong and continued political will is needed to give life to this important agreement which is so far the only remedy to the illness that has pervaded much of our commercial relations for many years.

The good will that accompanied the 1997 Bribery Convention will not last *ad infinitum*. Perceptions that countries are not living up to their obligations under the Convention will inevitably weaken the agreement and lead to erosion of public confidence. Countries must make renewed efforts to adopt appropriate legislation, correct deficiencies, and show determination and will to prosecute cases in accordance with the Convention. Recuperating the momentum and enthusiasm of that initial accomplishment will go far to ensuring that it is not yet the end of the honeymoon.

Notes

1. See Chapter 3, *infra*.
2. The Report to Ministers on the Implementation of the 1997 Bribery Convention can be found on the OECD web site: *www.oecd.org/daf/nocorruption/report.htm*.
3. See also chapter 3, *infra*.
4. See chapter 13, *infra*.
5. See chapter 17, *infra*.

II

PREVENTION AS THE BEST REMEDY

As the Member countries of the OECD worked increasingly on anti-corruption issues, they came to realise both the complexities of the subject and its pervasive presence affecting many areas of the Organisation's work. A comprehensive approach to fight corruption requires measures to help prevent corruption from occurring, as well as measures to sanction it when it does.

This Part of the book explores three separate but related areas aimed at discouraging bribery and corruption:

- improving ethical conduct in the public service of the Member countries themselves, thus targeting the supply as well as the demand sides of the corruption market;

- combating money laundering (whose relevance to bribery in international business quickly became apparent);

- improving international corporate governance standards and increasing financial transparency, as essential weapons in the fight against corruption.

Chapter 8

Public Sector Ethics: an Infrastructure

by

János Bertók*

Targeting both the Demand and Supply Sides of the Corruption Market

OECD anti-corruption activity addresses the problem from the supply side – the implementation of the 1997 Bribery Convention – as well as the demand side – through work on public service ethics. The work of the OECD Public Management Committee (PUMA) on ethics and corruption prevention supports Member countries in their efforts to improve their systems of governance and public-sector management. It aims to help governments monitor the broader public-service environment in order to maintain effective frameworks for promoting integrity and preventing corruption on the part of public officials. The OECD work on public ethics sees corruption as more than individual criminal acts. It results from systemic failure and is a management problem, manifested by low-quality legislation and weak public institutions that do not enforce laws, and – even more – fail to provide adequate control, oversight and transparency. Underlying the OECD's contribution is the conviction that the state has a role in preventing corruption as complex as the phenomenon of corruption itself, and that it needs a combination of interrelated mechanisms – such as adequate control, guidance and management – for success. Drawing on the experience of its Member countries, the OECD has identified the institutions, systems, tools, and conditions that governments use to promote ethics in the public sector – the necessary elements and functions of a sound *ethics infrastructure*. Furthermore, the OECD has delineated a checklist and a set of principles to provide guidance for public managers on how to review their ethics-management systems.

This work led to the adoption by the OECD Council in April 1998 of the "Recommendation on Improving Ethical Conduct in the Public Service" (Annex V),

---

* János Bertók is Administrator in the OECD Directorate for Public Management Service.

which is built upon these ethics-management principles. At the request of OECD Ministers, PUMA prepared a report on the implementation of the recommendation for the June 2000 Ministerial Council meeting.

Ethics: why so Critical Today?

The public service confronts difficult challenges and pressures. An apparent decline in public confidence in government presents an important political challenge for both OECD and non-member countries. Public servants face new and different objectives and conflicts of interest due to reforms in the public sector, such as devolution of responsibility and greater managerial discretion, the changing relationship between the public and private sectors, and increased reliance on market mechanisms. Other factors are limited resources, which lead to downsizing and restructuring, and globalisation, which increases contacts with different ethical and cultural norms and results in a change in society's perception of the role of the public service. Nevertheless, the reliability of public institutions and the credibility of public officials have remained vital factors of good governance. Overall, integrity and ethics – high standards of conduct in the public service – have become key factors in the quality of government.[1]

From Challenges...

One of the major challenges has resulted from the adoption of private management methods. Public managers face a radically changing environment in countries that have introduced and managed substantial reforms in the public sector in the last one or two decades. The first reforms involved rethinking what should constitute the core business of government and what could, or should, be provided by private enterprise or the voluntary sector to increase the cost efficiency of public administration and broaden the choices available to citizens. Governments have moved progressively to make public functions contestable, and a number of those previously performed by the public service are being commercialised, privatised or outsourced.

Moreover, significant progress has been made towards devolved public management, giving additional powers to managers. Devolution has reduced central regulations and control, providing flexibility to manage people and resources creatively in ways tailored to match particular business plans and to achieve the outcomes sought by government. Opening the administration also has meant more recruitment from the private sector to management positions. Yet these reforms have had unintended impacts on traditional public-service values.

The increased use of private sector methods enhanced the efficiency and effectiveness of public service, but led to a fragmentation of traditional working cultures, standards and ways of operating. This new situation requires public servants accountable for the use of their discretionary powers yet continuing to adhere to an updated framework of values. The balance between devolution and accountability has central importance in achieving a well-performing, professional public service. As traditional central regulation and control get reduced, the role of values and the public-interest concepts that they embrace becomes increasingly significant, both as a guide for behaviour and as a common reference point and unifying thread for the public service. Mechanisms for safeguarding values need upgrading to protect the public interest in new and current situations.

Furthermore, countries in transition and emerging economies have had to face a rapidly changing political, social and economic environment. The result has transformed fundamental social values, the legislative framework and the make-up of institutions, all of which have contributed to uncertainty about expected behaviour in the public service.

... to Strategies for Supporting Good Governance

PUMA's work was driven by the recognition that preventing corruption should be as complex as corruption itself. Corruption is not a cause but a result of systemic failure. PUMA conducted two surveys to determine the factors influencing ethical behaviour in the public service. Its analysis used a holistic approach and invented the notion of the ethics infrastructure as a cornerstone for a comprehensive strategy. The key issue addressed in the first report (OECD, 1996) is how public servants can be given support in observing the highest standards of integrity and ethics in a rapidly changing public-sector environment, without undermining the main thrust of management reforms, which aim to enhance efficiency and effectiveness. All OECD countries included in this first study[2] employ a range of tools and processes to regulate against undesirable behaviour and to provide incentives for good conduct. Yet there is no single method for constructing an ethics infrastructure in the public service. Rather, a combination of incentives and sanctions is needed to encourage professional standards of conduct. The following paragraphs outline the key elements.

Political Commitment. In the absence of sustained political commitment to ethical behaviour, efforts to encourage it will be in vain. Attempts to improve public-sector ethics in OECD countries have emanated from the highest political levels. Examples include the Korean Government's approval in August 1999 of a comprehensive anti-corruption strategy and programme requested by the President, the

The Ethics Infrastructure*

A well-functioning ethics infrastructure encourages high standards of behaviour. Its elements provide separate, important building blocks, but they should be complementary and mutually reinforcing. They must interact to achieve the necessary synergy for a coherent and integrated infrastructure. They can be categorised according to the main functions they serve – guidance, management and control – although different elements may serve more than one function. The ideal mix of these functions will depend on the cultural, political and administrative milieu.

Guidance comes from strong commitment by political leaders, statements of values such as codes of conduct, and professional socialisation activities such as education and training.

Management can be co-ordinated by a special body or an existing central management agency, and realised through public-service conditions as well as management policies and practices.

Control depends primarily on a legal framework enabling independent investigation and prosecution, effective accountability and control mechanisms, transparency, public involvement and scrutiny.

---

* See also the Background Note to the OECD Recommendation on Improving Ethical Conduct in the Public Service at *http://www.oecd.org/puma/gvrnance/ethics/index.htm.*

Government Programme to Fight Against Corruption adopted by the Czech Republic in February 1999, the most recent integrity measures sponsored by the Minister of the Interior in the Netherlands in 1999, and the creation and work of the Committee on Standards in Public Life set up in 1994 by the Prime Minister in the United Kingdom. Political leaders also serve as important role models, and they should set a positive example.

Workable Codes of Conduct. Codes of conduct play a vital role in stating expected standards of behaviour, particularly in OECD governments that have reduced the rules applying to public servants and adopted more "managerial" styles. Some countries (*e.g.* Australia, New Zealand) chose a broad public-service code of conduct from which individual agencies design purpose-built codes to reflect their particular objectives and missions. In other countries (*e.g.* Netherlands, Norway), codes are all agency-based.

Professional Socialisation Mechanisms. The contents of codes of conduct or even legal provisions remain simply words on paper, if not adequately communicated and inculcated. Public servants learn and adopt ethical norms, standards of conduct, and public service values through socialisation mechanisms. Training (induction and ongoing) is an essential element to raise ethics awareness and develop skills for solving ethical dilemmas; good role models (especially managers) also serve this purpose. Ethics now constitutes an integral part of the initial training of future managers in Belgium, while all senior entrants to the civil service in the United Kingdom focus on ethics issues in their mandatory induction training.

Ethics Co-ordinating Bodies take various forms, such as parliamentary committees, central agencies, or specially created entities. They also assume various functions. France's permanent anti-corruption investigation commission and the New South Wales Independent Commission Against Corruption in Australia are "watchdogs" with investigative powers. Norway's Department of Public Administration and New Zealand's State Services Commission serve as "general promoters" of public-sector ethics. The United States Office of Government Ethics and the Canadian Ethics Counsellor are "counsellors and advisors". The Committee on Standards in Public Life in the United Kingdom is a "permanent ethics workshop". The existence of a co-ordinating body should not, however, absolve departments and managers of the responsibility for ensuring ethical conduct within their jurisdictions.

Supportive Public Service Conditions. High standards of ethical conduct expected of public officials are one side of the coin. The other side is a package, which provides decent working and living conditions for the "servants of the public". It consists of such basic elements as sufficient job security, reasonable promotion and career prospects, fair remuneration or social appreciation. Fair and impartial human-resources management policies can ensure that selection and promotion in the public sector are based on general professional requirements, and that other factors, such as political considerations, get minimised. If public servants feel underpaid, overworked and insecure, they are less likely to embrace initiatives to improve performance, including ethics.

Effective Legal Framework. The legal framework provides the "teeth" of the overall ethics infrastructure. Laws and regulations define basic standards of behaviour and enforce them through systems of investigation and prosecution. In reviewing its legal framework, a country must check that existing criminal codes and civil-service laws, conflict-of-interest statutes and other relevant regulations are clear and consistent. Recent efforts include the Japanese law on the ethics of public servants, the country's first such legislation (passed in August 1999 and taking effect in

April 2000). This law requires the Cabinet to establish a new code of conduct as government order which bans public servants from receiving gifts and/or entertainment from private companies under their jurisdiction. Furthermore, senior officials in the central government will be required to report gifts or entertainment worth more than 5 000 yen, with some in higher positions required to report their stock transactions and income as well. Poland recently adopted a law requiring all public officials to declare their financial assets, property and business capital.

Efficient Accountability Mechanisms. Accountability mechanisms should encourage ethical behaviour by making unethical activities hard to commit and easy to detect. They set guidelines for government activities, for checking on results and for verifying that due process has been observed. They include internal administrative procedures (*e.g.* requirements that activities or requests be recorded in writing), comprehensive processes such as audits and evaluations of agency performance, or new forms of procedures, such as whistleblowing, which can encourage public servants to expose wrongdoing committed by others or to say no when asked to do something inappropriate. They might also be external to the public service, like oversight mechanisms in parliamentary committees.

Active Civic Society. Ethics is everybody's responsibility, including that of assertive media, which through their probing and reporting help citizens to watch over the actions of public officials. Freedom-of-information laws, such as those adopted by the majority of OECD countries in the last three decades and drafts under consideration in Switzerland and the United Kingdom, can institutionalise and support public awareness and responsiveness.

Two Main Approaches

Governments take two general approaches to the task of improving ethical conduct in the public service. One – *compliance-based ethics management* – focuses on strict compliance with procedures, control mechanisms and detailed rules, which define what public servants should avoid, what they should do, and how they should do it. The other – *integrity-based ethics management* – founded on aspirations, relies on incentives and encourages good behaviour rather than policing and punishing errors and wrongdoing. International trends in ethics management reveal common directions despite political, administrative and cultural diversity across countries.

Two international meetings, a symposium followed immediately by a seminar, held in November 1997 in Paris,[3] revealed a shared consensus on the elements of the ethics infrastructure and the need for a tool to help review the functionality of ethics-management systems. The symposium, a landmark meeting on public ethics, brought together over 130 senior participants and observers from OECD countries, central and eastern European countries, and international organisations. The discussion underlined the strong complementarity between traditional compliance-based systems and integrity-based techniques in promoting ethical behaviour. It found that regulations are essential but not sufficient for maintaining integrity without supporting guidance and incentives.

In 1997-98 a further survey in 15 countries revealed that governments have the greatest concern in areas where the private sector comes into contact with public officials exercising discretion. The most common measures employed against corruption in the public sector include criminal and other legal sanctions, increasingly supplemented by greater transparency (conflict-of-interest regulations and disclosure policies) and control. Methods for evaluating the effectiveness of anti-corruption measures are less well defined and largely take the form of reporting or periodic inspection.[4]

Improving Ethical Conduct in the Public Service

Considering these findings and analyses, OECD countries have recognised the role that sound domestic governance plays in effective action against corruption and made a commitment to improve the elements of their national ethics-management systems. In the Recommendation adopted by the OECD Council in April 1998, Member countries expressed their commitment to regularly review policies, procedures, practices and institutions encouraging high standards of conduct and preventing misconduct as well as countering corruption. As a strategic tool, they developed and agreed on a reference checklist – a set of twelve principles for managing ethics in the public service – to support governments in their reviews of ethics-management systems. Through this instrument, the Council recommended six actions:

1. Develop and regularly review policies, procedures, practices and institutions influencing ethical conduct in the public service.

2. Promote government action to maintain high standards of conduct and counter corruption in the public sector.

3. Incorporate the ethical dimension into management frameworks to ensure management practices consistent with the values and principles of public service.

4. Judiciously combine ideal-based and rule-based aspects of ethics management systems.

5. Assess the effects of public-management reforms on public-service ethical conduct.

6. Use as a reference the Principles for Managing Ethics in the Public Service to ensure high standards of ethical conduct.

The Council also instructed the PUMA Committee to analyse information provided by Member countries on how they apply the twelve principles and support them in improving conduct in the public service (*e.g.* by facilitating information-sharing and disseminating promising practices). The Council also requested that the Committee prepare a report for spring 2000 examining Member-country practices that have proved effective.

The twelve principles identify the functions of guidance, management or control against which to check public ethics-management systems. They draw on the experience of OECD countries and reflect shared views of sound ethics management. Together, they give managers an instrument to review policies and practices for identifying, communicating, inculcating, monitoring and rewarding ethical conduct, as well as for reporting, detecting, investigating, prosecuting and punishing misconduct. Briefly, they are:[5]

Ethical standards for public service should be clear. Public servants need to know the basic principles and standards they are expected to apply to their work and where the boundaries of acceptable behaviour lie. A concise, well-publicised statement of core ethical standards and principles that guide public service, for example in the form of a code of conduct, can accomplish this by creating a shared understanding across government and within the broader community.

Ethical standards should be reflected in the legal framework, which is the basis for communicating the minimal obligatory standards and principles of behaviour for every public servant. Laws and regulations could state the fundamental values of public service and should provide the framework for guidance, investigation, disciplinary action and prosecution.

Ethical guidance should be available to public servants. Professional socialisation should contribute to the development of the judgement and skills necessary to enable public servants to apply ethical principles in concrete circumstances. Training facilitates ethics awareness and can develop essential skills for ethical analysis and moral reasoning. Impartial advice can help create an environment that makes public servants more willing to confront and resolve ethical tensions and problems. Guidance and internal consultation mechanisms should be made available to help public servants apply basic ethical standards in the workplace.

Public servants should know their rights and obligations when exposing wrongdoing. These rights and obligations should include clear rules and procedures for officials to follow, and a formal chain of responsibility. Public servants also need to know what protection will be available to them if they expose actual or suspected wrongdoing.

© OECD 2000

Political commitments should reinforce the ethical conduct of public servants. Political leaders are responsible for maintaining a high standard of propriety in the discharge of their official duties. They demonstrate their commitment by example and by taking action possible only at the political level. Such actions can include creating legislative and institutional arrangements that reinforce ethical behaviour and initiate sanctions against wrongdoing, providing adequate support and resources for ethics-related activities throughout government and avoiding the exploitation of ethics rules and laws for political purposes.

The decision-making process should be transparent and open to scrutiny. The public has the right to know how public institutions apply the power and resources entrusted to them. Transparent and democratic processes, oversight by the legislature and access to public information should facilitate public scrutiny. Measures such as disclosure systems and a recognised role for active and independent media should further enhance transparency.

Clear guidelines should govern interaction between the public and private sectors. Clear rules defining ethical standards should guide the behaviour of public servants in dealing with the private sector, in public procurement, outsourcing or public-employment conditions, for example. Increasing interaction between the public and private sectors demands more attention to public-service values and requiring external partners to respect those values.

Managers should demonstrate and promote ethical conduct. An organisational environment that encourages high standards of conduct by providing appropriate incentives for ethical behaviour, such as adequate working conditions and effective performance assessment, has a direct impact on the daily practice of public-service values and ethical standards. Managers have an important role in providing consistent leadership and serving as role models in their professional relationships with political leaders, other public servants and citizens.

Management policies, procedures and practices should promote ethical conduct. Management actions should demonstrate an organisation's commitment to ethical standards. It is not sufficient for governments to have only rule-based or compliance-based structures. Compliance systems alone can inadvertently encourage some public servants simply to function on the edge of misconduct, arguing that if they do not violate the law they act ethically. Government policy should not only delineate the minimal standards below which a government official's actions will not be tolerated, but also clearly articulate a set of values to which public employees should aspire.

Public-service conditions and human-resource management should promote ethical conduct. Public-service employment conditions – career prospects, personal development, adequate remuneration and human-resource management policies – should create an environment conducive to ethical behaviour. Consistently using basic principles such as merit in the daily process of recruitment and promotion helps to ensure that the public service operates with integrity.

The public service should have adequate accountability mechanisms. Public servants should be accountable for their actions to their superiors and to the public. Accountability should focus both on compliance with rules and ethical principles and on achievement of results. Accountability mechanisms can be internal to an agency as well as government-wide, or provided by civil society. Mechanisms promoting it can provide adequate controls while allowing for appropriately flexible management.

Appropriate procedures and sanctions should exist to deal with misconduct. Mechanisms for the detection and independent investigation of wrongdoing form a necessary part of an ethics infrastructure. They require reliable procedures and resources for monitoring, reporting and investigating breaches of public service rules, as well as commensurate administrative or disciplinary sanctions to discourage misconduct. Managers should exercise appropriate judgement in using these mechanisms when action must be taken.

Finding the Right Balance

The challenge for governments is to find a correct balance between the two major ethics-management approaches, including what elements warrant the greatest attention for adequate sequencing. Integrity policy should not be considered as a separate and distinct activity, but rather as an integral part of all management systems. It would be inconsistent to marry a strict and centralised, compliance-based ethics-management framework with devolved, results-based management systems. Similarly, it would be inconsistent to combine a general management system based on rules and processes with an ethics framework built on the unenforceable aspirations and incentives of an integrity-based ethics regime. Naturally, countries should draw their own conclusions considering their political and administrative traditions. Recent trends in public management suggest that countries realise the need for consistency. The latest initiatives show three main tendencies:

- Countries focus primarily on checking for gaps in existing ethics infrastructures and reinforcing where necessary, rather than completely overhauling their systems. Many of these reviews have resulted in measures to strengthen both the aspirational and the compliance sides of the ethics regime. Norway, for example, has introduced new rules to close loopholes in contract management while reiterating basic values and developing a training programme on moral reasoning.

- Countries with highly managerial, results-based public services place a great deal of emphasis on refocusing ethics management in relation to overall public-management reform, to emphasise the guidance and management aspects and to redefine the nature of accountability. In 1998 the Australian government amended its Public Service Regulations to incorporate an ethical framework including the Australian Public Service Values, Code of Conduct, whistle-blowing protection and the Public Service Commissioner's annual State of the Service report. The ethical framework is also included in the Public Service Bill 1999.

- A number of countries, such as Korea, Mexico, Portugal or Spain, concentrate their main efforts on putting ethics frameworks in place as part of the modernisation of public administration. For countries in transition in Central and Eastern Europe, the process of creating an ethics infrastructure from the ground up is a critical part of the development of their democratic systems of government.

Further Work to Help Reassure Integrity

Maintaining integrity remains a fundamental condition for governments to provide a trustworthy and effective framework for the economic and social life of their citizens. Countering corruption and promoting public integrity will remain critical components of sustained economic development generally and of a successful transition to a market economy in particular. PUMA's report to the OECD Council of spring 2000 is based on a survey of all OECD Member countries. Its analysis will support strategy design by encouraging policy-makers to consider the experiences of other countries in a comparative way and by providing information on trends, models and concrete, innovative solutions – in their respective national contexts – to assist organisational learning. The report presents – for the first time – directly observable comprehensive data on integrity measures of all Member countries and put them in context by providing information on the surrounding political-administrative and social environments. Among others, the following areas, which also are basic components of good governance, are discussed:

- Clear and understandable core values and legal frameworks, including both substantive and procedural legal provisions.

- Institutions supporting the formulation and implementation of policy objectives and guaranteeing the appropriate application principles and legal rules based on core public-service values.

- Management techniques to ensure the unambiguous application of rules and values, make the best use of resources to accomplish the missions of public institutions and meet public expectations.

- The report identifies major challenges, driving forces, emerging issues, such as whistleblowing, prevention measures to avoid conflict of interest situations, especially the recent trends in disclosure policy, and analyses lessons learned.

Furthermore, a set of country-specific studies helps with the preparation and introduction of national ethics and anti-corruption measures. These in-depth studies, grounded in the cultural and political-administrative milieu of each country, will look for countries' strengths and weaknesses in the selected areas. The analysis will serve as a diagnostic tool for checking that ethics and anti-corruption systems are present and effectively working, and assisting the review and update of institutions.

No single method suffices to construct a sound ethics infrastructure in the public service. A combination of incentives and sanctions must encourage professional standards of conduct. Countries have learned from shared experiences and found individual solutions to their own problems. Ensuring synergy among policies and practices already in place requires constant effort, co-ordination and co-operation, with the involvement of all stakeholders.

Notes

1. For further information on the types of ethical tensions in the public service see PUMA (1997), "Managing Government Ethics", PUMA Policy Brief, Paris, OECD, February, also available on the Internet at *http://www.oecd.org/puma/gvrnance/ethics/index.htm*.

2. Australia, Finland, Mexico, Netherlands, New Zealand, Norway, Portugal, the United Kingdom and the United States. The individual country reports are available on the OECD Home Page on the Internet at *http://www.oecd.org/puma/gvrnance/ethics/index.htm*.

3. OECD Symposium on Ethics in the Public Sector: Challenges and Opportunities for OECD Countries, 3-4 November 1997, and SIGMA multi-country Seminar on Normative and Institutional Structures Supporting Public Service Ethics, 5 November 1997. Information on the symposium, including the programme, issues paper and background papers, is available on the Internet at *http://www.oecd.org/puma/gvrnance/ethics/index.htm*.

4. The survey and accompanying analysis appear in OECD (1999), Public Sector Corruption, Paris. The publication also reports on recent trends in corruption prevention, areas of concern, and new initiatives. The executive summary is available on the Internet at *http://www.oecd.org/puma/gvrnance/ethics/index.htm*.

5. See OECD (1998), "Principles for Managing Ethics in the Public Service", PUMA Policy Brief No. 4, Paris, May, also available on the Internet at *http://www.oecd.org/puma/gvrnance/ethics/index.htm*.

Chapter 9

Money Laundering and Corruption: Two Sides of the Same Coin

by

John Carlson*

Because individuals or groups engage in corruption, organised crime, drug trafficking and many other forms of serious criminality primarily to generate profits for themselves, they must find ways to use and benefit from them without attracting attention to the underlying criminal activity. Money laundering is the processing of the criminal proceeds to disguise their illegal origins.

Corruption, Organised Crime and Money Laundering

Corruption, organised crime and money laundering are closely linked. Profit motivates corruption for both individuals receiving bribes and the persons or companies offering them. Similarly, the very existence of organised crime is predicated on making money, whether from drugs trafficking, illegal arms sales, smuggling, vice or other illegal activities. As well as creating profits directly, bribery provides an important tool for organised criminals; it enables them to continue their money-making activities without the intervention of law-enforcement or other government authorities. Where bribery of a foreign public official is a criminal offence, the criminal who receives corrupt payments usually has to launder the money before he can obtain any benefit from it. The same motivation clearly applies for organised crime. Failure to launder the proceeds of crime considerably increases the criminal's risk of detection, prosecution and confiscation of the proceeds.

International efforts to prevent and punish money laundering aim to deny criminals the ability to launder their illicit gains, to identify and prosecute them

---

* John Carlson is Administrator in the Financial Action Task Force.

and to confiscate illegal benefits. The underlying principle is that if a criminal cannot benefit from his actions he will not want to take the risks involved. Similarly, effective mechanisms to counter money laundering undoubtedly form an essential component of any anti-corruption strategy. Bribery will be significantly discouraged if the person or company that bribes a foreign public official faces prosecution and then deprivation of any profit gained. Important and integral to any action taken against such persons or companies is the need for effective and efficient international mutual legal assistance. In order to take legal or regulatory action against the criminals, one must often seek evidence and other types of assistance from foreign jurisdictions. A sound international system must ensure that countries become parties to relevant international agreements, and put in place the legislation necessary to enable such assistance.

How does money laundering occur? Traditionally the process has three stages, although criminals not uncommonly use only one or two of them. In the initial or placement stage, the launderer introduces his illegal funds into the financial system by making many small cash deposits into bank accounts, purchasing money orders, or moving the monies to the financial systems of countries with fewer controls. Once the funds have entered the financial system, the second or layering stage involves financial transactions intended to remove the connection between the funds and their original placement. This stage can involve the movement of the monies through several locations, often in different jurisdictions; conversion of the funds into different currencies; or the use of business entities to disguise the transfers as payments for goods or services, thus giving them a legitimate appearance. Finally, having successfully processed and disguised the origin of the criminal profits, the launderer can then move to integrate the funds back into the legitimate economy by investing in real estate, luxury vehicles, business ventures or further criminal activity.

The Importance of Acting Against Money Laundering

Money laundering activity is not normally recorded in economic statistics, but rough estimates provide an idea of the scale of the problem. The IMF, for example, has estimated aggregate global money laundering at somewhere between 2% and 5% of the world's gross domestic product. Using 1996 data, this would indicate a range between US$590 billion and US$1.5 trillion. The problem therefore is clearly massive, and the flow of criminal funds raises serious problems for financial institutions, governments and society as a whole. Some institutions or jurisdictions may still have the old-fashioned view that the sources of deposits do not matter because benefits derive from receiving them, but this view is dangerously misguided.

The integrity of financial markets depends heavily on both the reality and the perception that high legal, professional and ethical standards apply. If criminal funds get laundered through a financial institution – because of corruption or because employees turn a blind eye to their criminal origin in order to increase profits – the reputations of financial institutions could suffer serious damage. This could affect the willingness of customers and other institutions to deal with them, and result in action by the regulatory authorities.

A country that allows itself to be misused by money launderers also faces potentially serious negative economic consequences. Studies by the IMF have shown that money laundering can lead to inexplicable changes in money demand, increased prudential risks for the safety and soundness of the banking sector, a contaminating effect on legal financial transactions and increased volatility of international capital flows and exchange rates. It could also bring reduced foreign direct investment if the country's commercial and financial sectors are perceived as subject to the control and influence of organised crime.

A failure to make efforts to counter money laundering also incurs a significant social cost. Money laundering and organised crime are integrally linked. Criminal organisations will use their profits to infiltrate or acquire control of legitimate businesses and to bribe individuals and governments. Over time, this can seriously weaken the moral and ethical standards of society and even damage the principles underlying democracy. Money laundering is an extension of the criminal activity that generated it, and all societies strive to a greater or lesser extent to eliminate crime.

International Efforts to Combat Money Laundering

The driving force behind the initial efforts to combat money laundering stemmed from international efforts to stem the drug trade. They resulted in the first international convention which recognised drug-money laundering as an issue in its own right – the 1988 United Nations Convention against Illicit Traffic in Narcotic Drugs and Psychotropic Substances (the 1988 Vienna Convention). In 1989 the Heads of State of the G7 and the President of the European Commission recognised the broad nature of the threats and resolved to create a Financial Action Task Force on Money Laundering (FATF) that would assess the results achieved and consider necessary additional measures.

The Financial Action Task Force and the Forty Recommendations

The FATF, an inter-governmental body, develops and promotes policies to combat money laundering. A multi-disciplinary body – essential in dealing with money laundering – it brings together the policy-making power of legal, financial and law-enforcement experts. FATF membership currently embraces 26 countries and two international organisations,[1] and includes the major financial-centre countries of Europe, North America and Asia. The FATF Secretariat is located at the OECD Directorate of Financial, Fiscal and Enterprise Affairs; although the FATF itself is not a part of the Organisation, the FATF Secretariat works closely with the part of the OECD tasked with combating bribery and corruption in international business transactions.

The scope of the FATF's Forty Recommendations[2] – the measures the Task Force have agreed to implement and encourage all countries to adopt – reflects the need to cover all relevant aspects of the fight against money laundering. Originally drawn up in 1990, the Recommendations were revised in 1996 to take account of experience gained over the six years and reflect changes that had occurred in the money-laundering problem. They do not constitute a binding international convention, but they do provide comprehensive principles for action. Countries are encouraged to implement them through the monitoring processes described below. These processes and the associated peer-group pressure have operated as an important mechanism for ensuring implementation of effective systems against money laundering.

The Forty Recommendations set out the basic framework for anti-money-laundering efforts and are designed to have universal application. They cover the criminal justice system and law enforcement, the financial system and its regulation, and international co-operation. Some of the major principles that they encompass reveal key imperatives:

- To criminalise the laundering of the proceeds of serious offences.

- To have legislation to trace, freeze and confiscate the proceeds and instrumentalities of crime.

- To require financial institutions to identify their customers, including the beneficial owners of accounts, keep proper records, establish comprehensive internal controls; report suspicious transactions to the proper authorities and generally know their customers.

- To establish mechanisms that provide a clear and effective basis for international co-operation in exchanging information, conducting investigations, mounting prosecutions, extraditing persons charged with serious offences and confiscating the proceeds of crime.

The Work of the Financial Action Task Force

Apart from setting international standards, the FATF works in several different ways to combat money laundering, with the underlying objective of continuing to mobilise international efforts to deepen and widen action. Three principal action plans have been agreed.

Spreading the anti-money laundering message. The FATF tries to promote initiatives in all continents and regions of the globe and to foster establishment of a world-wide network against money laundering. The means to these ends include enlarging the FATF, developing credible and effective FATF-style regional bodies, and continued close co-operation with relevant international organisations or bodies.[3] The FATF began to enlarge its membership when three countries[4] joined as observer members in September 1999; consideration is given to other countries that may wish to join. Similarly active efforts support or foster the development of FATF-style regional bodies in all parts of the world.

Monitoring and suggesting improvements to the anti-money laundering measures in place in FATF member countries. From the outset, FATF members committed to a process of multilateral surveillance and peer review. All members have agreed to monitoring of their implementation of the Forty Recommendations through a two-pronged approach, which includes both an annual self-assessment exercise and a more detailed, mutual evaluation process under which each member receives an on-site examination by selected evaluators from three different countries of the Task Force. This provides a comprehensive and objective assessment of the extent to which each country has moved forward, and highlights areas that require further progress. Two complete rounds of mutual evaluations have taken place. The most recent focussed on the effectiveness of anti-money-laundering systems, identified deficiencies and suggested improvements. The mutual evaluation, a core procedure of the FATF, has been responsible for a significant part of increasing progress in many countries.

Reviewing money-laundering trends. In another major, continuing task, the FATF monitors global developments in money-laundering trends, methods, techniques and counter-measures. This annual review has charted the increasing sophistication, complexity and professionalism of the process; it is essential for identifying and describing developments in money laundering, and for refining counter-measures. It not only analyses existing techniques but also seeks to identify the areas of new risk that could arise from, for example, new technologies or the extension of money laundering beyond the financial sector. The annual FATF report on such trends provides governments and the financial sector with a valuable tool, which helps them determine the nature of the threat, the risks they must deal with and the preventive action they can take.

Other International Initiatives

Concerted international action to combat money laundering dates only from the late 1980s. Before that time, most countries did not treat money laundering as an offence and had no preventive measures in place. The 1988 Vienna Convention was the first significant step. Among other things, it requires countries to make drug-money laundering an offence and to enact laws that allow confiscation of the proceeds of drug trafficking. More than 150 States now are party to that Convention. At about the same time, the Basle Committee on Banking Regulations and Supervisory Practices issued a statement of principles, which laid out guidelines for good practice in the financial sector. Both these initiatives provided the starting point from which further measures developed, particularly on a regional basis.

In 1990 the Council of Europe Convention on Laundering, Search, Seizure and Confiscation of the Proceeds of Crime was agreed. Now signed by 39 countries and ratified by 29, it lays out detailed obligations for penal and judicial measures with respect to money laundering, confiscation, international co-operation and procedural matters. Shortly after the Convention and the issuance of the FATF Forty Recommendations, the Council of the European Union agreed on a Directive on Prevention of the use of the Financial System for the Purpose of Money Laundering (91/308/EC). For EU countries and the members of the European Free Trade Area (Norway, Iceland and Liechtenstein), the Directive lays down a set of principles as the basis for a consistent approach across Europe to prevent money laundering in the financial sector.

International initiatives have also appeared in other regions. The Caribbean FATF issued nineteen additional Recommendations in 1990, while the Organisation of American States (OAS), through the Inter-American Drug Abuse Control Commission (CICAD), has issued model regulations which lay out a series of preventive and penal measures. These Regulations originally focussed on the proceeds of drug trafficking, but since 1998 they have been extended to cover the proceeds of serious crimes generally. The Convention on Combating Bribery of Foreign Public Officials in International Business Transactions also recognises the importance of money laundering by requiring it to be made an offence for the purposes of the Convention.

As the 1990s drew to a close, the United Nations became the forum for two further important initiatives. The first was a political declaration and action plan aimed at combating money laundering, agreed in 1998. The second, currently under negotiation, is a draft Convention against Transnational Organised Crime. It will contain a range of measures, including two articles that require states to introduce penal and preventive measures to combat the laundering of the proceeds of serious offences.

Given the range of international instruments in effect or in negotiation, it becomes clearly apparent that international standards for dealing with money laundering are already well established. Although the instruments vary in geographic scope or subject matter, taken together they provide a solid and comprehensive foundation for action by all countries. The key issue for most countries now is whether the agreed standards have been embedded in national laws and systems. The challenge over coming years will be to ensure, through a range of mechanisms and procedures, that comprehensive and effective implementation takes place, and that results are achieved.

The Future

Considerable progress has already been made in the ten years since the first international efforts to combat money laundering began. FATF member countries now comply fully or partially with a large majority of the FATF Recommendations. Strong efforts have appeared in other regions of the world, such as central and eastern Europe and the Caribbean. Areas of difficulty remain, however, in terms of both the geographical extent of money-laundering counter-measures and their scope. Much further work is required. New money-laundering techniques and trends emerge constantly as criminals seek to move to less regulated countries or sectors. Countries cannot afford to relax their efforts.

All member countries of the FATF have made laundering the proceeds of a range of serious crimes a criminal offence, and this extends to bribery at a national level as a predicate offence in almost all cases. As states parties to the 1997 Bribery Convention fulfil their obligations and pass the necessary legislation, bribery of foreign public officials will also become an offence, and the scope of the predicate offences for money laundering will likely increase to prevent the laundering of bribes in a more comprehensive way. Despite these positive achievements, many countries have found it difficult to prove the offence of money laundering, due to the difficulties of establishing all its elements. It is hard to prove that a defendant knew that the money came from the proceeds of a particular offence. Gathering evidence from a foreign jurisdiction remains too slow or impossible. Whatever the cause, in all countries the situation needs constant review and improvement where necessary.

Almost all states have laws intended to deprive criminals, including persons engaged in bribery, of the proceeds of their offences. Yet a comparison of the IMF estimate of annual global criminal proceeds with the amounts confiscated or for-feited reveals clearly that achievements so far have been limited at best. Many coun-tries need further consideration of laws that enable criminals to be stripped of their ill-gotten gains, and attention to the law-enforcement structures and resources for pursuing this objective.

International co-operation is a vital area frequently cited by national experts as causing considerable difficulties in practice. Most nations have signed the 1988 Vienna Convention, the number of signatories to other conventions or to bilateral agreements steadily increases and many countries have passed the necessary legis-lation, but many practical problems persist. While criminals can freely transfer their illegal proceeds around the world almost instantaneously, it usually takes months, if not years, for law-enforcement and judicial authorities to obtain the required infor-mation, if it can be obtained at all. Many countries or jurisdictions do not co-operate or do so on such a restrictive basis that only limited information becomes available. To acquire needed information or assistance may take so long that it provides the criminal with opportunity not only to escape penal sanctions but also to retain his proceeds. Combating bribery of foreign public officials will by its nature involve international co-operation; although the 1997 Bribery Convention expressly recog-nises this, steps must continue to make co-operation more effective. A number of international forums are now intensifying such efforts.

One of the primary means by which anti-money-laundering systems will be made more comprehensive and effective is the FATF's work in fostering the devel-opment of regional groups seeking to raise the standards of counter-measures. Given the nature of the problem, however, this process alone will not suffice. The FATF is therefore taking action regarding unco-operative countries and territories – jurisdic-tions that offer financial services without appropriate regulation, are protected by strict banking secrecy and do not co-operate in other ways. It has issued a report which lists 25 criteria identifying detrimental rules and practices that obstruct inter-national co-operation against money laundering.

A second stage of the process has now taken place, with four sub-groups reviewing a number of jurisdictions, both within and outside the FATF membership. The factual information on each jurisdiction's regime was analysed with respect to the 25 criteria and draft reports were prepared and sent to the jurisdictions concerned for comment. Once the reports were completed, the FATF considered the degree to which the jurisdictions met or did not meet the 25 criteria. The FATF found that 15 of the analysed jurisdictions had significant deficiencies in their anti-money laundering systems. These results were made public in June 2000. The process of monitoring these jurisdictions and identifying any other potentially non-co-operative ones will continue to be a major focus of FATF work.

It is important that countries improve preventive laws and systems intended to identify and/or stop the laundering of the proceeds of crime through their financial systems. Banks, non-bank financial institutions and other businesses engaged in financial activity play a vital role in preventing money launderers from succeeding. The proper identification of clients and any third parties which stand behind them, as well as the reporting of transactions suspected to be related to crime, are essential measures which can lead to the prevention, identification and punishment of money laundering, bribery and other criminal activity. Trends in FATF countries have shown that as controls in the traditional financial sectors get tightened, criminal money moves to other, less well regulated sectors. The FATF, the European Commission and other international bodies are now working to close these gaps as they become threats, by identifying the problems and putting forward revised measures to counter the risks.

Corruption, organised crime and money laundering pose a serious threat to society. It requires a co-ordinated and co-operative response from all countries. Due to the efforts of many different countries and organisations, increasing international recognition has emerged in many parts of the world, and at the highest levels, that comprehensive steps must be taken both nationally and internationally to counter serious criminality. The FATF and the OECD stand at the forefront in the struggle to combat money laundering and bribery. At the start of the new century, they will continue to work with all concerned countries, organisations and bodies to combat this criminal menace.

Notes

1. Reference in this document to "countries" should be taken to apply equally to "territories" or "jurisdictions". The 28 FATF members are Australia; Austria; Belgium; Canada; Denmark; Finland; France; Germany; Greece; Hong Kong, China; Iceland; Ireland; Italy; Japan; Luxembourg; the Netherlands; New Zealand; Norway; Portugal, Singapore; Spain; Sweden; Switzerland; Turkey; the United Kingdom, the United States; the European Commission and the Gulf Co-operation Council.

2. A copy of the Forty Recommendations and other FATF publications can be obtained from the FATF website (*www.oecd.org/fatf*) or by contacting the FATF Secretariat (fatf.contact@oecd.org).

3. Several organisations and bodies participate in the work of the FATF as observers, and the FATF co-ordinates and co-operates with them to the maximum extent possible to support their initiatives. They include The Asia/Pacific Group on Money Laundering (APG), the Asian Development Bank, the Caribbean Financial Action Task Force (CFATF), the Commonwealth Secretariat, the Council of Europe, the European Bank for Reconstruction and Development, the International Monetary Fund, the Inter-American Development Bank, the Inter-American Drug Abuse Control Commission of the Organisation of American States (OAS/CICAD), Interpol, the International Organisation of Securities Commissions, the Offshore Group of Banking Supervisors (OGBS), the United Nations Office for Drug Control and Crime Prevention (UNODCCP), the World Bank and the World Customs Organisation.

4. Argentina, Brazil and Mexico.

Chapter 10

Sunshine: the Best Disinfectant

by
Aileen Beattie[*] *and* **James Barbour**[**]

Accountants can play a role

The accountancy profession has a special role to play in the global fight against bribery and corruption. Indeed, its external reporting has much to do with good corporate governance in the widest sense. The skills of the qualified accountant make him or her specially qualified to unravel complex criminal schemes. Criminal ingenuity knows almost no bounds, and special skills are required to detect it. The same applies to concealment of criminal activity and the means by which tainted money is disposed of and made to reappear as apparently legitimate – the process of money laundering. Accountancy's contribution derives from its fundamental task, to provide businesses and the public, especially capital markets, with transparent, credible information. The profession assists in developing and ensuring compliance with rules and regulations that prevent dubious accounting practices that might be used to disguise corrupt transactions. Through three recent international initiatives, it has made great strides to improve the quality of financial reporting and audit, as well as to harmonise corporate governance principles and reporting.

Accountancy Issues in the OECD Revised Recommendation on Bribery

The OECD Working Group on Bribery in International Business Transactions believes that accounting, internal controls and external audit can contribute significantly to the fight against bribery of foreign public officials. Proper bookkeeping has a key role because accurate records provide a basis for detecting illegal payments,

---

[*] Aileen Beattie is Director for Accounting and Auditing at the Institute of Chartered Accountants of Scotland.
[**] James Barbour is Assistant Director at the Institute of Chartered Accountants of Scotland. Both authors are associated with the International Federation of Accountants (IFAC).

Definitions

The modern *accountancy profession* comprises practising accountants and those who operate outside practice. Some of the latter work in central and local government or other public agencies. Others work in finance, commerce and industry, often as members of senior corporate management teams. The practising sector offers an increasingly broad spectrum of services, ranging from traditional accounting, audits, tax advice and consultancy to new forms of assurance,* such as environmental audits. In most countries, auditors of limited liability companies, particularly public or listed companies, must be registered and demonstrate appropriate education, training and experience. Maintaining audit registration usually requires ongoing professional development and relevant experience.

Corruption, as legally defined, involves the use of public power for private gain. As such, it does not apply to the private sector. *Bribery* involves an unlawful payment or other inducement for private gain. It can, and does, feature in corruption as the means by which corrupters corrupt officials. The 1999 IFAC paper discussed later in this chapter does not confine itself to corruption in the narrow, legalistic sense, but makes it clear that the accounting profession's duty is to help combat all types of major criminal activity and the means by which the proceeds of crime get concealed. It calls upon the profession to "form a barrier against corruption", defined broadly to include all crimes of dishonesty, such as fraud, embezzlement, tax evasion, bribery and corruption, as well as all means by which the audit trail is obscured and the proceeds of crime concealed.

---

* The term "assurance" is used here and elsewhere in this chapter in the sense of the statements typically made by auditors about the veracity, fairness and conformity with requirements of the statements, reports and the like which they are associated.

and the requirement to keep accurate records, coupled with strong penalties for violations, deters officers and employees of companies from making illegal payments or creating slush funds. The external auditor has a unique opportunity to subject company records to critical analysis and has a clear responsibility to alert management to potentially illegal conduct. Ultimately, the interest of governments is not to prosecute individuals or companies for bribery, but rather to create an environment that will stimulate companies to take the necessary measures to ensure that officers or employees do not engage in it. Strong, internal management controls, in the sense of both accounting controls and broader systems to create an ethical environment and build safeguards into procedures for authorising and supervising payments, form an essential bulwark against corruption.

With the foregoing points in mind, the Working Group agreed to include provisions on Adequate Accounting Requirements, Independent External Audit as well as Internal Company Controls into the 1997 Revised Recommendation on Combating Bribery in International Business Transactions (Annex II). Non penal obligations for the accounting and financial statements are also contained in Article 8 of the 1997 Bribery Convention (Annex I; see also discussion in Chapter two).

Recent Accountancy Initiatives in the Fight Against Corruption

International and individual national accountancy bodies work hard to ensure that information presented to the capital markets is as transparent and credible as possible. Recent financial crises around the world have heightened attention to addressing corruption. The profession recognises its major role in the global effort to fight corruption and bribery. Three recent initiatives by representative international bodies within the profession illustrate this clearly.

In 1999, IFAC issued a key discussion paper on corruption.[1] IFAC speaks on behalf of the international accountancy profession because it brings together 143 professional organisations of accountants in 104 countries, representing more than two million accountants. It is also recognised by major international organisations such as the World Bank, the International Monetary Fund, the OECD and the United Nations. The paper recognises that business management has a critical role in fighting corruption, because it develops and enforces systems of proper corporate governance within individual organisations. Corruption finds it difficult to take root in systems containing proper controls, and in which corporate governance supports such controls and restricts management override. Accountants can help to maintain good corporate governance in many different ways, as internal auditors, in preparing financial statements for external users and as external auditors reporting on the financial statements.

The paper sets out a number of proposals that IFAC wishes to take forward with its member bodies. These bodies should:

* Develop programmes that build collaborative relationships with legislative and regulatory authorities, the legal profession and other groups interested in strengthening the framework for good governance, transparency and accountability, as well as the legal framework, so as to minimise corrupt practices, propose solutions based on model legislation and regulations introduced in other countries, and point out where swift action may be required.

- Work with government to ensure that the requisite definition of corruption is in place, legislation proscribing corrupt acts is prepared, and appropriate means of protection are developed for whistle-blowers.

- Initiate education programmes for accountants and the public to create awareness of the detrimental effects of corruption, thereby motivating public action towards its elimination, through press articles, seminars, continuing professional education and speeches by leaders of the profession.

- Encourage the national media to make corruption a public issue by devoting attention to the types and hazards of corrupt activities and publishing studies of the harm caused by corruption and the various steps that can be taken to prevent or expose it.

- Provide assistance, including technical support, to national and international organisations fighting corruption by publicising their activities, offering assistance in their research and promoting their proposals.

- Encourage practising firms, their clients and governments to adopt codes of conduct setting the "tone at the top", by establishing sound principles of corporate governance that expressly prohibit corrupt activity and provide the benefits flowing from the implementation of internal control systems that help to expose corrupt activities.

- Encourage audit committees expressly to consider whether appropriate policies are in place to prohibit corrupt acts and to require that any such act be reported to them.

- Promote a tax system that is efficient and equitable, to discourage the disparity and burden that leads to corruption, and that does not allow corrupt payments to be deductible from income for tax purposes.

The Fédération des Experts Comptables Européens (FEE) is the profession's European umbrella organisation. It represents accountancy bodies from 22 countries, with a combined membership of over 350 000. In July 1999, FEE (together with associations representing solicitors and barristers) signed the European Commission's *Charter of the European Professional Associations in supporting the fight against organised crime*. This document expresses a commitment by the bodies involved to making an active contribution towards fighting the various forms of organised crime. It has two parts. The first sets out a number of ethical principles and requirements to act with due care. The second requires professional organisations to set up supervisory mechanisms and warning and advisory systems, backed by awareness raising and training.

The Need for Transparent, Credible Information

Efficient capital markets need transparent information about market participants and their transactions. Providing such information increases the quality of decision-making and risk management within the market and decreases the cost of capital. Transparency exists when information on existing conditions, decisions and actions is accessible, visible and understandable to its users. Disclosure provides the information and makes policy decisions known through timely dissemination and openness.

An organisation's annual financial statements make one key element of information available to users. They are transparent when they present a true and fair view of the company's activities, covering both the accounts (normally a balance sheet, profit and loss account and cash flow statement) and associated narrative notes. Accounting standards and company law requirements regulate their content.

Financial statements must be credible as well as transparent. Because the information in them comes from the organisations themselves, its review by an independent third party becomes important. That is the external auditor's role – to give an opinion on the statements and thus provide reasonable assurance that they give a true and fair view and have been prepared in accordance with relevant requirements.

Accounting and auditing requirements vary across countries. Cultural and political differences have led to different forms of reporting in different countries. Yet the increasingly international nature of business has created an urgent need for internationally accepted rules for both financial reporting and the ways in which it is assured. Such international efforts are currently under way, in negotiations between the International Organisation of Securities and Exchange Commissions (IOSCO) and the International Accounting Standards Committee (IASC), on accounting standards, and between IOSCO and the International Federation of Accountants (IFAC), for auditing standards. Both discussions seek comprehensive, core sets of high-quality standards, and their recognition, for cross-border listings.

International Harmonisation of Corporate Governance Principles

Moves are also afoot to improve disclosure of corporate governance practices. In 1995, the International Capital Markets Group (ICMG) published a paper[2] that reflected on governance matters nationally and internationally and made recommendations aimed at those charged with formulating regulations on corporate governance. The report noted that solutions to governance issues had hitherto reacted largely to domestic concerns, and thus mostly reflected local legal, political, social and economic cultures, although it did discern a natural convergence of practices. In this light, it recommended against both prescriptive international regulation of corporate governance and domestic over-regulation and bureaucracy.

The report took a more positive and activist stance on the role of disclosure. In noting that investors must have confidence in the processes of governance adopted by companies, it put forward the view that such confidence should come from transparency of these processes through disclosure, rather than through any attempt to prescribe a universal system of corporate governance rules. At the same time, it supported the development of general principles of corporate governance that countries could use, regardless of their specific cultural and legal frameworks.

The OECD Principles of Corporate Governance

Such general principles are exactly what the OECD produced in 1999.[3] The OECD Principles are non-binding and do not aim at detailed prescriptions for national legislation. Recognising that no single model of corporate governance exists, the Organisation identified common elements that underlie any good system and then built on them, to embrace the different models that do exist and to serve as a reference point. Policy makers can use the Principles as they examine and develop legal and regulatory frameworks for corporate governance that reflect their own economic, social, legal and cultural circumstances. Market participants can use them as they develop their own practices.

The Principles cover five areas, including the rights of shareholders, their equitable treatment, the role of stakeholders, disclosure and transparency and the responsibilities of boards of directors. The broad principle for disclosure and transparency, the subject of this chapter, reads as follows:[4]

The corporate governance framework should ensure that timely and accurate disclosure is made on all material matters regarding the corporation, including the financial situation, performance, ownership and governance of the company.

Four recommendations support this Principle. They cover disclosure itself, reporting standards, audits and information dissemination.

Disclosure. The OECD document stresses the importance of disclosure for the effective functioning of capital markets, noting that insufficient or unclear information may hamper their ability to function, increase the cost of capital and result in poor allocation of resources. Standards of corporate governance disclosure have developed tremendously over the last ten years, driven mainly by corporate failures around the world. The OECD proposes that disclosure should include, but not be limited to, material information on the financial and operating results of the company; company objectives; major share ownership and voting rights; members of the board, key executives and their remuneration; foreseeable material risk factors; material issues regarding employees and other stakeholders; and governance structures and policies.

The company's annual report serves as the main source of information on most of these topics. Although prepared principally for shareholders, it is publicly available for all interested parties. Typically, accountants have focussed on company financial and operating results, but financial reporting is gradually developing to include material risk factors as well. A company's financial statements should comprise, at a minimum, a profit and loss account, a balance sheet, a cash flow statement and a statement of accounting policies and explanatory notes. A current international trend adds to the annual report a financial review by management; it describes and explains in narrative form the main features of the company's financial performance and position, and the main uncertainties that it faces. Increasingly, annual reports also mention governance structures and policies. These disclosures often respond to national initiatives, such as the Viennot Report in France, the Bosch Report in Australia, the Cadbury, Hampel and Turnbull Reports in the United Kingdom and the King Report in South Africa.

High-Quality Standards of Reporting. The quality of information depends on the standards under which it is compiled and disclosed. The OECD Principles support the development of high-quality, internationally recognised standards of accounting, financial and non-financial disclosure and audit. The application of such standards will significantly improve the ability of investors to monitor firms by providing increased reliability and comparability of reporting, plus improved insight into company performance. The IASC leads the way on harmonising financial reporting around the world. Its stated objectives are:

* To formulate and publish in the public interest accounting standards to be observed in the presentation of financial statements, and to promote their world-wide acceptance and observance.

* To work generally for the improvement and harmonisation of regulations, accounting standards and procedures relating to the presentation of financial statements.

International accounting standards tend to stress financial rather than non-financial measurements and disclosures. The accountancy profession recognises, however, that looking at profit alone cannot fully describe a company's performance. Given its expertise in measurement, the profession has an important contribution to make in developing systems of performance assessment that integrate financial and non-financial factors.

For audit, IFAC's International Auditing Practices Committee (IAPC) works to improve the uniformity of auditing practices and related services throughout the world by issuing pronouncements on a variety of audit and attest functions and promoting their acceptance. Its International Standards on Auditing outline basic responsibilities, which help auditors to cope with increasing and changing demands for financial information and guidance in specialised areas. International Auditing Practice Statements promote best practice and provide practical assistance to auditors in implementing the standards. Audit Risk Alerts apprise auditors of the audit implications arising from recent international issues and events.

The Annual Audit carries responsibilities for both auditors and boards of directors. The OECD document states that independent auditors should conduct annual audits in order to provide external and objective assurance on the way in which financial statements have been prepared and presented. Auditors thus bear a heavy ethical burden. Ethical codes are fundamental in the accountancy profession. IFAC's Code of Ethics for Professional Accountants serves as a model for all such codes in national accountancy organisations. It endorses the concepts of objectivity, integrity and professional competence, and highlights how all accountants can attain the highest levels of performance in meeting their responsibilities to the public.

Many misconceptions surround the auditors' role, particularly in relation to fraud and corruption. They must give an opinion on whether the financial statements show a true and fair view of a company's performance and financial position. They thus plan and perform the audit procedures, and evaluate and report the results, recognising that fraud and corruption may materially effect the financial statements. Although not responsible for detecting fraud, they should exercise sufficient scepticism to be aware of it and ensure its detection if it would have a material effect on the financial statements.

The basic responsibility for detecting fraud and corruption is now generally accepted as residing with company management, including the directors. Among the key directors' functions identified by the OECD are:

- Monitoring and managing potential conflicts of interest of management, board members and shareholders, including misuse of corporate assets and abuse in related-party transactions.

- Ensuring the integrity of the corporation's accounting and financial reporting systems, including the independent audit, and that appropriate systems of control are in place, in particular systems for monitoring risk, financial control and compliance with the law.

- Monitoring the effectiveness of the governance practices under which (the firm) operates, and making changes as needed.

In carrying out these responsibilities, directors often find it useful to assign particular responsibilities to an internal audit function. The relevant international body in this area is the Institute of Internal Auditors, which issues standards to cover its members' work. It currently proposes to amend the definition of internal auditing to cover corporate governance, as follows:

> Internal auditing is an independent and objective assurance and consulting activity that is guided by a philosophy of adding value to improve the operations of the organisation. It assists an organisation in accomplishing its objectives by bringing a systematic and disciplined approach to evaluate and improve the effectiveness of the organisation's risk management, control and governance processes...

Channels for disseminating information. The OECD Principles note that these channels can be as important as the information itself, and recommend that they should provide for fair, timely and cost-efficient access to relevant information by users. Technological advances in recent years have made vast amounts of data available reliably and cheaply. Users have become more active and proficient in filtering information with the advent of software that can search and analyse it. One must therefore expect that business reporting will become more user-driven in the future, and the accountancy profession will have to adapt to this changing technological environment. A recent publication by The Institute of Chartered Accountants of Scotland[5] addresses such issues and, based on survey evidence, puts forward for debate a blueprint for business reporting in the future.

Conclusion

The representative bodies within the accountancy profession are now well placed to take an active part in the fight against corruption, but they are not the soldiers on the ground. The IFAC document points this out clearly in its own conclusion:

> "*Ultimately, it is the individual accountant who must carry out his/her responsibility in the anti-corruption campaign. Professional scepticism is necessary when establishing business relationships and in the review of transactions between related parties, especially when they appear to have questionable business sense. Corrupt entities and individuals must realise that accountants constitute a barrier against corruption. Above all, each individual accountant must ensure that his/her own behaviour should reflect an unswerving commitment to truth and honesty in financial reporting.*"

Notes

1. IFAC (1999), The Accountancy Profession and the Fight Against Corruption, New York.
2. ICMG (1995), International Corporate Governance: Who holds the reins?, London.
3. OECD (1999), OECD Principles of Corporate Governance, Paris.
4. OECD (1999), Section IV.
5. Institute of Chartered Accountants of Scotland (1999), Business Reporting: the Inevitable Change, Edinburgh.

III

GLOBALISING THE FIGHT AGAINST CORRUPTION

In developing its anti-corruption initiatives, described in the preceding chapters, OECD has acquired a wide range of experience. The exchange of information with countries not members of the OECD has been an invaluable part of that experience.

This Part of the book examines the active, co-ordinated and indeed often pioneering programmes with non-members that have taken on lives of their own in the global struggle against bribery and corruption.

Chapter 11

Sharing Anti-corruption Values

by

Bart Édes*, Nicola Ehlermann-Cache** *and* **Frédéric Wehrlé*****

Why everybody is concerned

In the last decade or so, OECD Member countries have come to fully appreciate the negative economic and political effects of corruption. Their governments' attitudes have changed fundamentally as a result. They interpret recent financial crises as dramatic examples of the corrosive impact of corruption and weak governance on investment, economic growth, political stability and the development of both market-based economies and democratic political institutions.

In an increasingly interdependent world, the dynamic forces of change, including privatisation and the selling and licensing of economic rights, may themselves create new opportunities for corruption. Corruption has crossed the divide between North and South, leaving as victims in its wake the citizens, institutions and democratic processes in these countries. In the long run, no country can afford the social, political, or economic costs that corruption entails.

That is why international standards on fighting corruption cannot be applied by OECD countries alone. Most countries now loudly proclaim their anti-corruption fervour. The challenge is to move from slogans to action. OECD engages in programmes with other countries to raise awareness of international anti-corruption efforts and the instruments that underpin them, and to share information concerning best practices and successful anti-corruption programmes across countries and

---

*   Bart Édes is Principal Administrator in SIGMA in the OECD Directorate for Public Management Service.
**   Nicola Ehlermann-Cache is Administrator in the Anti-corruption Unit in the OECD Directorate for Financial, Fiscal and Enterprise Affairs.
***   Frédéric Wehrlé is Co-ordinator of Anti-corruption Outreach Activities in the OECD Directorate for Financial, Fiscal and Enterprise Affairs.

across regions. The goal is to increase public support for anti-corruption efforts by bringing together all actors – public and private sector representatives, trade unions, and civil society.

Raising Awareness

As the preceding chapters in this volume demonstrate, OECD governments have developed several undertakings to promote high ethical standards and good governance, and to attack bribery and corruption at the national and international levels.

Regional conferences and seminars provide information about these actions to participants from areas with different levels of economic development and involvement in international trade, and with different interests and understandings of anti-corruption issues. By explaining the consequences and opportunities of anti-bribery instruments, especially those of the OECD, these conferences and seminars aim to appeal to government officials and others to take effective measures to fight bribery and corruption in national administrations and in international business transactions.

A genuine desire is emerging to translate anti-corruption initiatives effectively into national action plans. One key element has been the creation of regional webs. These webs co-ordinate regional exchanges over the Internet which can be followed up by regional meetings. They aim to create links, establish synergies and avoid duplicative initiatives in areas with similar political and economic preoccupations.

So far, the Organisation has provided countries in central and eastern Europe and the Newly Independent States (NIS), Asia, and Latin America with information about measures to sanction bribe givers and to promote public ethics and good governance. These programmes may be extended to wider audiences and other regions, including Africa.

These activities are a co-operative venture in OECD. The OECD Anti-corruption Unit focuses on identifying the best means to fight world-wide corruption in international business. The Committee on Fiscal Affairs promotes the suppression of tax deductibility of bribes paid to foreign officials. The Public Management Committee (PUMA) and the associated Support for Improvement in Governance and Management in central and eastern European countries (SIGMA) aim at providing support to national integrity strategies. The Centre for Co-operation with Non-Members (CCNM) assists in this work by being the focal point for the development and pursuit of policy dialogue between the OECD and non-member economies.

Central and Eastern Europe and the NIS

Corruption in some of the state institutions of Central and Eastern Europe and the NIS countries detracts from efforts to promote economic growth and engender popular support for democracy. Public servants and politicians in these countries are particularly susceptible to improper conduct due to poorly defined professional requirements and roles, inadequate accountability, weak control mechanisms and low wages. Practices inherited from the days of one-party rule inhibit the development of, and adherence to, high ethical standards.

OECD countries also struggle with problems of unethical behaviour and corruption. They can, however, more readily manage these problems because there exist solid legal and institutional infrastructures that have evolved over time. More recently, the emphasis is shifting to strengthening public ethics through "aspirational" efforts, such as codes of conduct, information campaigns and ethics training.

In most transition countries, such efforts do not suffice since the underlying basic legal and institutional infrastructure is weak or non-existent. The ongoing decentralisation of public administration in these countries creates new opportunities for graft if adequate control mechanisms are not put in place. Moreover, efforts to check corruption will not succeed without sustained, high-level political support.

Since its creation in 1992, *SIGMA* – a joint initiative of the OECD and the European Union, provides continuous assistance in 13 central and eastern European countries (Albania, Bosnia-Herzegovina, Bulgaria, the Czech Republic, Estonia, the former Yugoslav Republic of Macedonia, Hungary, Latvia, Lithuania, Poland, Romania, Slovakia and Slovenia) to strengthen public institutions in order to reduce incentives for corruption and unethical behaviour. Ultimately, the countries seek to achieve the standards of reliable and efficient administration found in EU Member States, something they must do in order to fulfil the "Copenhagen criteria" for EU membership and apply European Community legislation (the *acquis communautaire*).

The SIGMA programme focuses on developing a professional civil service and improving policy-making, co-ordination and regulation. It assists governments in areas relating to administrative reform, review of proposed laws and strategies, assessment of administrative frameworks, training and information-exchange. SIGMA also disseminates comparative information on public administration through published reports, checklists, an internet site, and a bimonthly newsletter. The newsletter, *Public Management Forum*, frequently publishes articles on ethics and integrity in public administration. It further counsels on financial control, budgeting, public procurement and audit. Finally, SIGMA has contributed to the creation of networks of public-administration practitioners where, for example, state auditors, public-procurement officials and managers of the civil service can support colleagues through the exchange of experience, information, laws, and contacts. Internet pages *http://www.oecd.org/puma/sigmaweb* serve these networks.

The *Anti-corruption Network for Transition Economies* assists Eastern European and Former Soviet Union countries to put in place the framework conditions for effectively combating corruption by identifying appropriate political, institutional, and economic reforms. Linking international donors, key government officials and civil society representatives in an informal forum to exchange information about policies and best practices in this field, the Network supports continued anti-corruption strategies by reviewing anti-corruption actions taken in Network countries. It uses as benchmarks existing international instruments, best practices and regional initiatives.

In the aftermath of the Balkan upheavals in 1999, the international community was faced with the urgent and pressing problem of helping to reconstruct the political and economic foundations of those countries in the region. Many organisations heeded the call by Western political leaders to join forces to address the economic, security, and democratisation and human rights problems, legacies of crumbling institutions.

At a meeting in Sarajevo on 15-16 February 2000, the Stability Pact members adopted an *Anti-corruption Initiative* designed to combat corruption on all levels in the region. The OECD, the Council of Europe, the European Commission, the Special Co-ordinator of the Stability Pact, the World Bank and the United States are part of this Initiative which calls for states to take measures to effectively combat corruption on the basis of existing relevant international instruments. Countries commit also to promote good governance, to strengthen the rule of law, to increase transparency and integrity in business operations, and to encourage an active civil society. The OECD has a leading role in the implementation of the action plan as well as in the overall management of the Initiative, together with the Council of Europe.

Asia and the Pacific Region

In Asia as elsewhere, the consequences of corruption on economic development are particularly pernicious. In a bid to counter the malign influence of corruption in the region, the Asian Development Bank (ADB) and the OECD launched the *ADB/OECD Forum On Combating Corruption In The Asia-Pacific Region.*

© OECD 2000

The idea of the Forum emerged from a meeting in Manila in September 1999 on *Combating Corruption in Asian and Pacific Economies* which was sponsored by the OECD and the ADB. The meeting revealed a strong consensus to fight corruption on several fronts.

The experiences described clearly showed that corruption in the Asia-Pacific region cannot recede unless all sectors of the society undertake efforts to stamp it out.

* *Public sector.* Lasting measures taken by governments to counter corruption must be accompanied by law enforcement mechanisms, with a special role for the judiciary. Witness protection programmes are also required to encourage reports of wrong-doing. Transparency can be enhanced through the establishment of competitive public procurement procedures and encouragement of adoption of relevant international rules. Simplification of government procedures can help improve the conditions for international investment.

* *Private sector and Trade Unions.* Effective measures by business and trade associations can take many forms. These can be aimed at making company employees aware of corruption and educating them against it through, for example, the development of codes of conduct, and advocating more dialogue with public officials to propose and implement reforms, including public sector reform, such as more transparent procurement rules.

* *Civil Society.* The involvement of civil society and the media is a critical component in all anti-corruption strategies and can be particularly influential in implementing civic education programmes aimed at fostering an anti-corruption culture. These bodies help to relay policies by assuming greater responsibility for monitoring good governance and integrity in business and government operations. Regional and national networks for civil society as well as increased co-operation with international organisations can also help prevent the misuse of domestic resources.

The Forum serves several purposes for countries in the region. It:

* helps develop well-targeted anti-corruption programmes by providing examples of "success stories" and "best practices" gathered from regional and international initiatives;

* encourages adherence to international anti-bribery standards or norms as found in international agreements, arrangements, or guidelines, such as those of the OECD;

* improves implementation of anti-corruption programmes by assessing progress achieved;

- maximises the use of resources and avoid duplication of work by bringing together regional countries, donors, and international organisations active in promoting anti-corruption efforts in the Asia-Pacific.

The Forum also aims at facilitating the exchange of information and experience via the electronic regional web-site for Asian and Pacific Economies which is part of the OECD Anti-corruption Ring Online, AnCorR Web (see below).

Latin America and the Caribbean

Sharing the concern that bribery and corruption will only be curtailed if co-operation among the various stakeholders is strengthened, the OECD and the Organisation of American States (OAS) organised a conference with the Government of Argentina in summer 1998. The goal was to draw public attention to the anti-corruption actions developed by both organisations to establish and maintain a framework for fighting corruption. Making sure that acts of bribery, both those who give and those who receive, are punished by criminal sanctions is central to these actions but other measures, including, transparent corporate operations and open public procurement practices, can contribute.

The anti-bribery and corruption agreements of both the OECD and the OAS are only as effective as the collective will of the member governments to enforce them. All signatories must respect their international obligations to ratify the agreements and take the necessary steps to implement them at the national level. Where possible, pressure should be brought to bear on countries that show any reluctance to comply with the standards of behaviour set out in the agreements. Each country should be concerned with the performance of its partners and closer co-operation between members of the OAS and the OECD in monitoring the effective implementation of these instruments would be a significant step in increasing international co-operation.

As in other regional initiatives, the need for interaction between governments and civil society to prevent and eliminate corrupt practices was especially highlighted. Corporations and their accountants and auditors can also play a role in improving transparency and accountability. A regional network for Latin America could provide the same services as those developed for the Asia-Pacific region.

A Major Step Forward: The 1997 Bribery Convention

Despite the flurry of international anti-corruption initiatives, none would deny the significance of the step taken in 1997 by OECD and other governments to outlaw the practice of paying bribes in return for international business contracts. As this Convention, including the Recommendations that accompany it, is often a central element in the regional gatherings to consider effective means of fighting corruption, it is natural that it attracts an increasing amount of attention from countries that are serious about fighting corruption. They ask: can other countries join the OECD instruments? What are the conditions for joining? What are the legal consequences of participation? Is joining the Convention the right step for us?

Ultimately, some countries may consider adhering to the OECD anti-bribery instruments. And indeed, the Convention on Combating Bribery in International Business Transactions (Annex I) and the 1997 Revised Recommendation (Annex II) are open to non-members. Argentina, Brazil, Bulgaria, Chile and the Slovak Republic already are signatories to the Convention and are members in the OECD Working Group on Bribery in International Business Transactions.

The 1997 Bribery Convention (Article 13) and the related Commentaries (paragraph 37) explicitly set the conditions and indicate procedures for non-members to accede to the Convention. The Convention is open to non-members that become full participants in the OECD Working Group on Bribery in International Business Transactions, in accordance with procedures for becoming a full participant in any of the OECD subsidiary bodies.

A country wishing to associate itself with the OECD effort to combat bribery in international business transactions must, as a first step, apply formally to the Organisation. In deciding whether to invite an applicant to join, other members of the Convention may well want to assess how the country interested in joining measures up against an objective set of criteria. These criteria include whether the applicant is a "major player" and whether the association will bring "mutual benefit". In applying these criteria, certain essential economic, institutional and legal factors need to be taken into account:

- Assessment of the "major player" criterion requires a look at the country's economic situation. This evaluation will build on the role of a country's companies in international investment and trade. They may be meaningful competitors in the global economy, or relevant actors on a regional scale, or in particularly important or sensitive sectors, such as defence, aviation, construction or telecommunications.

- The appraisal of "mutual benefit" examines an applicant's institutional and legal framework. The existing legal framework for combating bribery on a domestic level, including legislation on the criminalisation of passive bribery will be considered. Another element involves whether the applicant disallows or is willing to discontinue tax deductibility of bribes, and, in general, the extent to which it already can adhere to the standards laid down in the Revised Recommendation. The assessment will also focus on the country's enforcement capacity, particularly to investigate and prosecute bribery cases.

Other factors, of course, might be relevant and would certainly also be given due consideration.

If the assessment process results in a positive evaluation of a country's request, the Organisation could issue an invitation to the country that it observe the workings of the Group for an initial period to be determined. At the end of that period, and depending, in large part, on the country's progress in implementing anti-corruption provisions, the OECD might decide on further action, including an invitation to become a full participant in the Group and to accede to the Convention.

Not all countries serious about fighting corruption will join the Convention and the Working Group. They may decide that other regional initiatives are also compatible with their aims. They may well wish to improve links and co-operation without formal participation. This opens wide opportunities for additional regional events and the other sorts of dialogue and communication that the OECD organises. The Organisation envisages expanding the scope of the information-sharing process through new or extended anti-corruption networks and intensifying its collaboration with different bodies active in the field.

Information Sharing on Anti-corruption Measures

A key element in an effective anti-corruption campaign is the sharing of information and experience on national, regional and international developments and initiatives taken by countries, international organisations, and civil society. The OECD Anti-corruption Unit created one of the world's largest information centres on corruption and bribery, the OECD *Anti-Corruption Ring Online* or *AnCorR* (*http://www.oecd.org/daf/nocorruption/*). Its aim is to facilitate the flow of information, to broaden participation in the core anti-corruption values of the OECD, and to foster continuous dialogue. The web site contains more than 3,000 references to books, journals, papers, and other articles, as well as downloadable or on-line anti-corruption documentation, such as laws, international conventions, anti-corruption strategies and other information.

The AnCorR provides anti-corruption practitioners and individuals with the concrete information necessary to design and implement anti-corruption activities. The site functions as a forum for policy dialogue on corruption, bribery, public governance, money laundering, offshore banking and other topics for both experts and the public at large. It provides the qualitative and quantitative knowledge required to assess all aspects of corruption. It also helps donors to identify current corruption situations in most regions of the world, and provides them with a real-time working tool to co-ordinate their assistance programmes. Different initiatives and their achievements, as well as assistance programmes, can be viewed on the site. Information, research results and ideas can be exchanged.

AnCorR has three main subject areas. The area on *Corruption* provides useful information to follow, understand and anticipate developments in the fight against corruption, and to take effective preventive measures. The *Bribery* area addresses corruption of both the recipients and the suppliers of illicit payments with concrete and action-oriented information on public governance, private sector initiatives, money laundering and offshore banking. Finally, the area on *Law* features anti-corruption legislation, enforcement measures and international instruments that can be downloaded or read online.

AnCorR also acts as a portal to regional and local initiatives. It provides direct access to local initiatives in OECD countries, Latin America and the Middle East and Africa. It links to the three regional networks developed under the auspices of the OECD: the Anti-corruption Network for Transition Economies, the Stability Pact Anti-corruption Initiative for South Eastern Europe and the ADB/OECD Forum on Combating Corruption in the Asia-Pacific Region. These three regional webs enable different constituencies active in the fight against corruption to exchange information and experiences, monitor the implementation of anti-corruption strategies, and pursue policy reforms and harmonisation with international standards. They also help donors to track current situations in the three regions and provide them an additional way to co-ordinate their assistance programmes.

To create synergies and ensure access to a large audience, AnCorR has established partnerships with international organisations, business associations, non-governmental organisations and academic institutions. These players share the same fundamental values as the OECD – democratic political systems, open market economies, and respect for human rights and the rule of law – but differ in their fields of specialisation, prime responsibilities and main constituencies. As such, they permit the web's database to be continuously expanded.

Chapter 12

Dealing with Corruption in Developing Countries

by

Irène Hors*

The need to better understand the phenomena

In many developing countries, corruption exists at all levels in dealings between officials and business people as well as ordinary citizens. It stifles the development dynamic, slows integration into the world economy and jeopardises prospects for sustainable development. It affects economies and societies in many different ways, distorting the mechanisms for awarding contracts, diverting human and capital resources from productive activities and undermining the state and its institutions. Its evils thus imperil political stability and the necessary independence of economic policy.

To better understand the phenomenon of corruption as it manifests itself in developing countries – and to make a contribution to its eradication – the OECD Development Centre in 1996 launched a three-year research activity focused on three broad questions.[1] First, how do corrupt practices affect the economic development process?[2] Second, what are the determinants of corruption in developing countries? Third, how can these countries mount an effective, sustained fight against it? The answers to these questions are emerging in a number of substantial studies that defy summarisation in the brief space available here, but one can provide at least a flavour of some of the key ideas.

Economic Theory's Contribution

The microeconomic approach[3] analyses corruption as the rational behaviour of public and private economic agents reacting to incentives stemming from their milieu. It reveals what features of the direct environment encourage corruption. The

---

* Irène Hors is Administrator in the OECD Development Centre.

environment includes the organisation of government and how public and private persons operate within it, plus the national context itself – the general structure of the machinery of government, whether a genuine exercise of countervailing powers occurs, whether those with power are accountable, and so on.

From this analysis, one can point to a number of measures that can reduce corruption. Economic policy actions include the deregulation of economic activity, lower taxes and adequate, performance-related civil service salaries, aimed at eliminating or reducing the advantage to be gained by resorting to corruption. Bureaucratic reforms can constrain public servants' discretion, and increase procedural transparency and internal checks. The multiplication of systems of checks and balances between the different state and non-state centres of power allows democracy to flourish effectively.

A study on customs fraud and corruption in Senegal and Mali[4] tested these ideas. Confining the study to corruption within the customs administration – a choice justified by the importance of trade policy for the workings of the economy as a whole – made it possible to develop quantified estimates of the degree of corruption,[5] which fell during the 1990s. Econometric tests showed meaningful correlation between the level of corruption and several explanatory variables that reflected, *inter alia,* lower customs duties and the simplification of their structure, reforms aimed at reducing customs officials' discretionary powers and the computerisation of procedures.

An Example of a Successful National Strategy: Hong Kong

To extend this analysis dealing with a single administration, the Development Centre undertook a study of Hong Kong's experience in fighting corruption. Over twenty years, Hong Kong substantially reduced corruption, by means of a strategy in which four characteristics stand out. First, it took co-ordinated action simultaneously to investigate and prosecute corruption in the recent past, to prevent it though organisational reform of government agencies and firms (on request), and to educate the public about its evils. Second, a special commission co-ordinated it, acting independently of the civil service and police, under the direct responsibility of the Governor. Third, it attacked all forms of corruption, without distinction – that involving officials as well as that between private agents, and "low-level" as well as "high-level" corruption. Fourth, and most important, the strategy involved both the public authorities and the business community, and required the constant participation of the population.

One may wonder, however, whether this experience can be replicated elsewhere. Hong Kong enjoyed very special conditions at the time, including a strong political commitment to fight corruption, its status as a British protectorate and abundant human and financial resources. Political and economic constraints and the institutional weaknesses that exist in most developing countries will create obstacles to the implementation of anti-corruption measures and prevent importation of such a strategy without alteration.

Although the economic models go far to analyse the behaviour and incentives driving two parties to an illicit exchange, they do not help to clarify the overall logic behind these phenomena. The corrupt act needs placement within the political and social networks of the two protagonists, and the political dimension of corruption must be taken into account by looking at it from a historical standpoint. Broadening the scope of the analysis in this way affords a better understanding of the difficulties that developing countries face in fighting corruption.

The Potential Role of the Private Sector

Mindful of the foregoing points, the Centre, in collaboration with the UNDP's PACT programme, launched a study[6] on corruption and efforts to fight it in five developing countries: Benin, Bolivia, Morocco, Pakistan and the Philippines. The object is twofold: to gain a better understanding of the determinants of corruption, and to learn from these countries' experience in fighting it. Such knowledge makes possible anti-corruption strategy proposals really adapted to the developing-country context.

Analysis of the situations in these five countries illustrates the close link between corruption and rent seeking. At all levels, the awarding of political and administrative posts or positions that can exploit economic rents (by controlling grants of natural-resource concessions or import licences, for example) can be influenced by the potential resources that they represent. The resulting exchanges of economic privileges in return for political support or allegiance cement the political balance.

Corruption cannot recede unless the authorities demonstrate real determination to act. Such political commitment is not easy to secure, particularly in the economic and social contexts of developing countries. Their leaders may have had to "play the game" in order to get where they are, or they may fear that fighting corruption could undermine the political balance. Mobilising civil society (NGOs and associations) and the media to condemn corruption and oversee government action is generally seen as the best way to generate support for the required political commitment.

The private sector also can act as an important ally. A conference organised by the Development Centre in 1999[7] provided an opportunity to use the experience of multinationals and local firms to explore the sector's potential role in fighting corruption in the developing countries. It is in the interest of private business to operate in a structured environment in which the state, acting via strong institutions, regulates and decides on the rules of competition. The international standards for corporate governance now being developed establish transparency and the firm's social responsibility as priorities. That development, plus firms' increased dependence on the capital markets, prompts firms in developed and developing countries alike to support reforms aimed at increasing integrity.

The experiences described at the conference showed that the private sector can contribute to the fight against corruption in a number of ways:

- Any lasting measures to counter corruption must be accompanied by the nscreation of a political coalition that will defend the values of integrity. The private sector can be one of the major pillars of such a coalition, as in Morocco, for example, where the General Confederation of Moroccan Enterprises backs the new government's anti-corruption reforms.

- Private institutions (employers' and trade associations, networks of entrepreneurs) can help to relay policies aimed at making people aware of corruption and educating them against it. This, for example, is one of the objectives of the Ethics Centres organised in Colombia and the United Arab Emirates by the multinational company Merck.

- Private participation can also take the form of a dialogue with public officials to propose and implement reforms. The National Association of Ecuadorian Entrepreneurs has formulated reforms in six different areas and submitted them to the government.

- The private sector can make up for the lack of resources available to NGOs and the media, and strengthen the role that they play in monitoring and overseeing government action. This is one of the activities of the West African Enterprise Network (WAEN).

- Private compliance with public standards also allows the resources allocated to fight corruption to be reduced as much as possible.[8]

The private sector's commitment to fight corruption does involve a number of difficulties, however. In developing countries, the balance of power between entrepreneurs and government often tips very much in the latter's favour. Entrepreneurs also encounter the so-called "prisoner's dilemma" and "stowaway" problems of co-ordination: it is difficult to reject corruption when competitors continue to resort to it for market access or to gain a favour. Marshalling opposition to corruption also has costs, such as time spent by managers or the cost of reorganising a firm's internal policy, quite apart from real risks of repression. All these factors tempt entrepreneurs to remain passive, taking advantage of reforms, if they occur, undertaken by others who will bear the costs in their stead.

The conference also highlighted the importance of business associations, which can both strengthen the position of entrepreneurs *vis-à-vis* government and solve problems of co-ordination. Aid agencies and non-profit organisations must work with business to strengthen these associations, in ways that make it easier to mobilise the private sector in the anti-corruption fight.

Five Proposals

Base anti-corruption strategies on specifics, not generalities. Corruption is commonplace in the five countries studied, part of the daily lives of entrepreneurs and the population, who endure it and even see it, fatalistically, as an integral part of their culture. The mechanisms that spread it become unofficial norms alongside or replacing official ones. Officials who refuse to play the game get removed from posts of any importance. Businessmen who do the same can find themselves disadvantaged competitively. As public service has become perceived primarily as the least risky way of getting rich quickly, and far from working in the service of the people, minds have become accustomed to the "normality" of corruption. The real obstacles to fighting it lie as much in the interests of the political and administrative pyramid as in the fatalism and ignorance of the victims. Popular fatalism is often sustained by a culture of fear nurtured by precisely the people who benefit from corruption. This makes it essential to discover corruption's specific impact, how it is organised, who benefits and who suffers. Such information is crucial for strategy and action to mobilise the population. Identifying and condemning corruption eloquently but in general terms does not suffice, and can even be counterproductive in the long term. Excessively vague denunciations that do not result in concrete measures may well debase popular indignation.

Build islands of integrity. Measures to combat corruption locally, in particular administrations (customs, tax, local authorities or hospitals), result in small islands of integrity. They not only directly reduce corruption, but also symbolise importantly the possibilities that lie in the absence of corruption. They help to restore healthy public norms, to reverse the perception of what constitutes normality.

Pursue development. The observed correlation between levels of corruption and development, often cited to justify fighting corruption, also reveal a reverse causality: under-development encourages corruption. What are the main mechanisms? Low civil-service wages foster corruption. Strains between supply and demand for public services give rise to opportunities for it. Because the private sector is insufficiently developed to attract the ambitious, people continue to prefer investing in a "state career". Low education levels keep the population ignorant of its rights and unable to take part in political life. While under-development does not in itself make corruption inevitable, the financial, human and institutional resources available to these countries do not match those found in the developed countries. Political conditions are not always conducive to the kind of massive frontal attack on corruption that was possible in Hong Kong. That strategy depended on the protectorate's extensive investigative and penal powers.

Levy penalties. There must be penalties, and they must symbolise the authorities' genuine commitment. Most countries have systems of detection and punishment. What is really important is not so much to augment them as to strengthen the linkages between them and non-government actors. All too often, reports by inspectors or auditors and the recognition of illicit gains lead to no action. The link between detection and punishment must become systematic if corrupt practices are to become really risky. Investigative information must get circulated, with those having penal responsibilities obliged to act.

Integrate with broader policies. Finally, policies to combat corruption should be incorporated in other government programmes to reduce inequalities, stimulate the private sector, increase tax revenues and improve expenditures, etc. This would allow tackling the corruption problem progressively, building up islands of integrity and simultaneously dismantling the vicious circles that link corruption with under-development. It would also justify the choice of priorities, have the effect of "socialising conflicts" and integrate the debate on corruption into a broader one more likely to mobilise the different groups concerned.

IV
SOCIETY'S GADFLIES

Governments cannot fight corruption alone. The preceding chapters have identified essential partners in the anti-corruption struggle: business and labour organisations, civil society, and the media.

Judging by what those who speak for them have to say, these groups do not shun their role in the fight; in fact, they eagerly seek it. Yet they also have pronounced views, some of which are critical of what governments have accomplished so far. In general, these observations do not concern what has been done. They remind us all that in the fight against corruption we have won a few battles, but we have still not won the war.

Chapter 13

How International Business Combats Extortion and Bribery:
Anti-corruption Efforts by the International Chamber of Commerce

by

Fritz Heimann[*] *and* **Mathias Hirsch**[**]

The International Chamber of Commerce (ICC) is the world business organisation. It represents more than 7 000 member companies in over 130 countries. It promotes an open and international trade and investment system and the market economy. It produces rules that govern the conduct of business across borders, including the ICC Rules of Conduct to Combat Extortion and Bribery in International Business Transactions.

Two Decades of Fighting Bribery

ICC's track record in fighting extortion and bribery dates back more than twenty years. Its member companies have long known that bribery, both foreign and domestic, has a corrosive effect not only on governments but also on the integrity and finances of firms.

Bribery has an insidious influence on a company's moral climate. It requires secrecy and subterfuge to avoid exposure. Off-the-book "slush funds" are often established and masking book entries becomes the norm. The moral deceptions involved lead to awkward questions. Who in corporate management participates in decisions? How much is told to top officers, to corporate accountants and to the company's lawyers? Can the company terminate relations with a sales representa-

---
[*] Fritz Heimann is Counsellor to the General Counsel of General Electric Company; he is also Vice-Chairman of the ICC Standing Committee on Extortion and Bribery.
[**] Mathias Hirsch is Policy Manager of the ICC Standing Committee on Extortion and Bribery.

tive who paid bribes? All of this has a destructive impact on the company's culture. As moral values become compromised and corporate controls undermined, the ill effects will extend far beyond the original bribery transaction.

Financial consequences come in train. While at first glance it may seem advantageous to win a large contract by bribery, side effects, like blackmail, can quickly negate any financial gains. Large, unexplained payments to shadowy "agents" or intermediaries can throw the company's finances into turmoil and call into question the performance of its duty to shareholders. A further financial danger lies in the threat of adverse publicity following exposure. If corrupt practices become publicly known, the impact on a company's reputation is incalculable. The risk of exposure is real. Corrupt regimes often fail, and their successors often delight in detailing their crimes. Disgruntled employees have an interest in exposing the flaws of their superiors. In short, quite apart from being morally indefensible, corrupt practices are too risky and the potential damage to the company's morale too important to make bribery a viable option.

Early Activities

ICC's efforts in combating extortion and bribery in international business transactions began in 1975 when it established a committee chaired by Lord Shawcross, a former Attorney General of Great Britain and Nuremberg prosecutor. The Shawcross committee issued a groundbreaking report in 1977, which called for complementary and mutually supportive action on three fronts: an international treaty to be drawn up by the UN, proposals for actions by national governments and rules of conduct to serve as a basis for corporate self-regulation. The report established an ambitious agenda for action by governments and international organisations. It identified self-regulation by international business as a particularly critical step. To provide a basis for such corporate action, the committee drafted "Rules of Conduct to Combat Extortion and Bribery" that have become widely known as the "ICC Rules".

The Shawcross Report was ahead of its time. Although the UN drafted a convention, it failed to gain sufficient support. Much of the industrialised world claimed that corruption was primarily a problem for developing countries. Leaders of developing countries argued that multinational corporations were the real culprits. International financial institutions were unwilling to confront corruption. The United States made bribery of foreign officials a crime in 1977, but no other country took similar action. During the 1980s corruption largely disappeared from view as an international issue.

Recent Activities

In 1996, following a wave of new scandals, an ICC special committee chaired by Francois Vincke, Secretary General of Petrofina in Belgium, issued a revised version of the ICC Report. Building on the 1977 version, it once again called for a combination of government and private action, this time centred on the OECD rather than the UN, because the OECD had become the most effective institution for developing Recommendations and a Convention against international bribery. In 1999, ICC published a revised version of the ICC Rules, adding a preface on the 1997 Bribery Convention (Annex I). ICC remained in close contact with the OECD Working Group on Bribery in International Business Transactions when the Convention was under development and has participated in the consultation process.

The new ICC Rules go farther than the 1997 Bribery Convention. Whereas the Convention prohibits foreign bribery in connection with "obtaining or retaining business or other improper advantage", the ICC Rules prohibit extortion and bribery for any purpose. Indeed, they not only address the bribery of foreign officials, but also commercial, "private-to-private" bribery. They urge governments to regulate political contributions by enterprises and to ensure that they are publicly recorded. They place new emphasis on mechanisms within companies to enforce corporate codes of conduct.

The ICC Rules deal with the extortion/solicitation of bribes. Extortion and bribery are opposite ends of the same problem; both must be addressed. The first of the ICC Rules reads: "No one may, directly or indirectly, *demand* or accept a bribe". Companies seeking contracts abroad do not willingly open their pockets to corrupt foreign officials. The reality is more complicated. In most cases, they are told or strongly led to believe that without payoffs they will not win business. Blatant and discrete extortion is a fact of international commerce and a stain on it. ICC argued for its inclusion in the text of the 1997 Bribery Convention, but, apart from a brief mention in the preamble decrying "solicitation of bribes", the Convention makes no reference to extortion.

Major Provisions of the ICC Recommendations

The ICC recommendations to governments and international organisations:

- Urge all governments to implement promptly both the 1997 Bribery Convention and the OECD recommendations calling for termination of tax deductibility of bribes.

- Recommend that the OECD establish close liaison with the WTO, to encourage acceptance of the OECD recommendations by the WTO's much larger membership.

- Call on the World Bank and other international financial institutions to play an active role in reducing extortion and bribery. Since the 1996 Report was published, ICC has been pleased by the strong positions against corruption taken by James Wolfensohn and Michel Camdessus, the top officers of the World Bank and the IMF.

- Call for more transparent government-procurement procedures, including disclosure of payments to agents. The World Bank has since changed its procurement rules to require disclosure of agents' commissions.

- Recommend that bidders on government contracts be required to provide undertakings to refrain from bribery, and comply with corporate codes barring extortion and bribery.

- Urge governments to regulate the conditions under which political contributions are made and, where they are permitted, to enact legislation requiring them to be publicly recorded by the payers and accounted for by the recipients.

- Recommend that governments enact legislation providing for auditing by independent professional auditors of the accounts of economically significant enterprises.

- Urge governments to co-operate in criminal investigation and prosecution of extortion and bribery.

The 1996 Rules of Conduct for Companies

The principal provisions of the ICC Rules:

- Prohibit extortion and bribery for any purpose, not just for "obtaining and retaining business".

- Broaden the bribery prohibition to bar not only kickbacks but also its other forms, such as subcontracts and consulting agreements that channel payments to government officials, their relatives, or their business associates.

- Sharpen the provision dealing with the use of agents, to provide that payments to them be limited to "appropriate remuneration for legitimate services", and to require companies to take steps to ensure that agents do not pay bribes.

- Make more explicit the financial provisions of the Rules to prohibit the use of "off-the-books" or secret accounts, and call for the establishment of independent systems of auditing to bring to light any transactions that contravene the Rules.

- Urge Boards of Directors to establish and maintain proper systems of control, to conduct periodic compliance reviews, and to take appropriate action against any director or employee contravening the Rules.

- Provide that political contributions may be made only in accordance with applicable law, that all requirements for public disclosure shall be fully complied with, and that all such contributions must be reported to senior corporate management.

The Rules also call on companies to draw up their own codes, consistent with the Rules and tailored to the particular circumstances of their business. They also ask them to go beyond codes of conduct, which mark only the first step in an anti-bribery programme. To render their codes effective, they should develop clear compliance policies, guidelines and training programmes for implementing and enforcing their codes. A code without an effective follow-up programme becomes simply a public-relations exercise, toothless and serving essentially to reassure shareholders and provide cover for corporate managers if violations occur. For that reason, ICC published *Fighting Bribery: A Corporate Practices Manual* in 1999. It deals with the most important aspects of corporate compliance:

- The definition of bribery.
- The responsibilities of top management.
- The relationship with sales representatives and agents.
- Accounting, auditing and financial controls.
- Money-laundering regulations.
- A survey of laws dealing with political contributions.
- Bribery within the private sector.

Large numbers of business leaders around the world would like to see an end to corruption in business transactions. Yet many companies remain reluctant to act unilaterally by adopting effective codes of conduct, as long as they believe that their competitors will continue to pay bribes. For that reason, ICC views its follow-on programme, including the Manual, as crucial. It must help develop the broad international consensus on the need to fight extortion and bribery that is necessary to overcome this reluctance of individual companies.

Future Work

Looking ahead, ICC has developed a programme of action that will maintain the momentum. ICC's Standing Committee on Extortion and Bribery has under way a project on commercial bribery, a high-priority topic often ignored in discussions, which tend to focus on bribes paid to government officials. Yet private bribery, a serious problem, grows progressively more important with the wave of privatisations in central and eastern Europe, Asia and Latin America. The issues resemble those surrounding bribery of public officials, but differ in some important respects. Because public officials are expected to act in the public interest, private enrichment at the expense of the public interest is considered a breach of public trust. Corporate executives, managers and employees have no direct responsibility for the public good, but must act for the good of their corporations. Corporations have a right to expect that executives, managers and employees will act in firms' best interests, and not accept bribes to line their own pockets or to favour the interests of bribe payers.

What should ICC do about commercial bribery? Because little is known about the subject, ICC is approaching it by stages. A special working group will first identify the areas of major concern, to determine how effectively corporate self-regulation can deal with them. Second, the group will sponsor a legal review to ascertain whether adequate legal remedies exist to deal with private bribery, and whether civil litigation or criminal prosecution can provide the more effective remedy. ICC also aims to discover whether commercial bribery is primarily a domestic problem or has a significant international dimension. The overall objective will be to find the right balance between corporate self-regulation, civil suits and criminal prosecution, as well as between national and international initiatives. Based on this work, ICC will become able to develop proposals for consideration by the OECD' Working Group on Bribery in International Business Transactions. They may consist of recommendations for action by national governments and, if the need is demonstrated, for amendments to the 1997 Bribery Convention.

ICC recognises that several years of work will be required to assure that the objectives of the 1997 Bribery Convention are achieved. It continues actively to promote ratification of the Convention by those signatories that have not yet done so. It also participates in the OECD's monitoring programme to assure effective implementation and enforcement of the Convention by national governments. Effective and consistent enforcement by all signatories will assure that the basic objective of the Convention, to raise the level of integrity for international transactions, will be transformed from an ideal to a reality.

Chapter 14

Beyond the 1997 Bribery Convention:
The Business and Industry Advisory Committee's
Work on Corruption

by
Thomas Pletscher* *and* **April Tash****

Business strongly opposes any kind of corruption, which causes competitive disadvantage for honest business, unpredictability for investments (especially in new markets), and added costs. As long ago as 1976, the OECD addressed this concern by developing its *Guidelines for Multinational Enterprises*, clearly rejecting the paying and asking of bribes in all transactions. Business associations and numerous multinational companies all over the world have endorsed these *Guidelines.*

The 1997 Bribery Convention and Beyond

Because corruption distorts competition and efficiency in markets, and undermines the trust necessary for long-term investment and business operations, business assumes that governments should actively combat the problem. The Business and Industry Advisory Committee (BIAC), the voice of business at the OECD, welcomed the Convention on Combating Bribery of Foreign Public Officials in International Business Transactions (Annex I). BIAC views it as a tool to put all business competitors on an equal footing – in bidding situations, for example. If it functions properly, it should discourage some corruption by adding intolerable risks

---

*   Thomas Pletscher is Executive Secretary and Legal Advisor of the Swiss Federation of Commerce and Industry. He is also Chairman of the Business and Industry Advisory Committee (BIAC) Task Force on Corruption and Bribery, Chairman of the UNICE Working Group on International Business Practices, and Vice-Chairman of the ICC Standing Committee on Extortion and Bribery.

** April Tash was Manager for International Trade and Investment, of the Business and Industry Advisory Committee to the OECD (BIAC).

of criminal liability to the list of bribery's disadvantages. It can make a major contribution to the fight against corruption in the forms of extortion and bribery.

The 1997 Bribery Convention must enter into force, practically as well as formally, for the most important trading partners simultaneously, to ensure that foreign and domestic business competitors will have a "level playing field". Otherwise, competitive distortions will remain, and businesses that wish to eliminate corruption will get disadvantaged. Regrettably, some industrial countries still have not yet ratified the Convention. These holes should be closed rapidly. The monitoring process will disclose whether the envisaged "level playing field" has been achieved, or if some countries lag behind or are advancing too fast; either case distorts competition and causes inefficient economic outcomes.

Extortion and bribery are complex phenomena. One cannot expect solutions to emerge quickly, so a step-by-step approach is the best one. The Convention is just such a step, and not the last one. It had to be limited to those items on which an agreement could be reached in a reasonable time. Other important issues will be dealt with in later phases. Aspects of corruption such as political influence peddling or private corruption apparently need more in-depth research to prepare adequate solutions. Time is an ally in the fight against corruption, but it needs careful handling. Right now, signatory states need time to implement the new measures fully. Changing or amending the new rules too quickly would only divert attention and hinder the full integration of principles into the business policies of individual companies.

The fight against corruption requires practically simultaneous action in many areas, by many institutions. The 1997 Bribery Convention takes the important step of strengthening penal law. Essential complementary measures now must come from both firms and governments. Companies need to change business attitudes and review internal procedures to develop compliance mechanisms. For governments, streamlining legislation and authorisation procedures, improving control mechanisms and reviewing remuneration schemes for officials provide just some examples of areas where a number of countries need improvement.

Extortion of Bribes: a Key Issue

Most current governmental actions focus incompletely on the demand for bribes. Yet business associations report that companies frequently confront explicit direct or indirect solicitation of bribes, despite the anti-bribery measures. In implementing the Recommendation and action programme, OECD governments must assist companies in such extortion situations as efficiently as they attempt to fight against the bribe payers. They have not yet sufficiently recognised this. They cannot attack corruption by addressing only the supply side (bribery). They must deal with the demand side (extortion) as well. Extortion has the same effect as bribery on business trust, and tends to distort competition and raise costs in similar ways. Regrettably, the 1997 Bribery Convention only covers bribery transactions. This is to ignore that companies may be confronted, in particular in non-signatory countries, with difficult extortion and passive bribery situations and be placed at competitive disadvantages.

Requests for bribes often come indirectly, at the early stages of business transactions. In such situations, companies want and require safeguards for their business interests. Therefore, any governmental intervention must take account of the need to guard business secrets. Further, there are often insufficient proofs to enter formal judicial proceedings. Governmental actions must still be possible, and co-operation with honest businesses can help in developing evidence. Moreover, competing companies from different countries often face similar bribe requests. Good international co-ordination among governments could help immensely to encourage more businesses to identify corruption, and to resolve such situations without discrimination against any single competitor. Again, however, businesses will have concerns about maintaining their business-related secrets and relationships, so adequate safeguards should help them without spreading confidential information to competing companies or to other countries.

Because corruption occurs in various forms and practices differ widely among countries, it may not always be obvious that a specific payment or behaviour of a company violates anti-corruption laws. Such uncertainty affects international commerce seriously and may distort competition. Companies would like to have speedy access to reliable information on the legitimacy of certain business transactions, so that they can react appropriately. It must be fast, so that they can react to legitimate business opportunities as quickly as their competitors. Such clearance should be provided by responsible official sources not involved with penal prosecution, in order to protect the substantive rights of companies or individuals in the event of later attempts at prosecution.

Reporting on the situation of corruption also should not be limited to the enforcement of penal sanctions and other measures against paying bribes. Both sides of the coin have to be addressed by a follow-up mechanism. This may lead to the naming of specific countries or situations at an early stage (in a setting with protections for confidentiality), although formal and judicial proofs may be obtained later through investigation.

BIAC appreciates the open attitude of the OECD to work on the solicitation/ extortion problem, which BIAC considers so important that it has developed a full programme detailing its views and recommendations (see below). An informal joint working group has started discussions on the issue of "solicitation". Concrete results from the joint efforts are expected soon.

The BIAC Programme for Combating Solicitation of Bribes

Public Recognition of the Problem

Governments have been reluctant to recognise the problem of solicitation. They feared that companies accused of bribing could defend themselves in penal prosecution if fault by others was acknowledged. Yet this creates the false impression that companies are the source of corruption. Testimony and available evidence indicate that explicit or implicit requests for bribes are more often the "initiating act".

> Governments must publicly recognise the solicitation of bribes and engage themselves to act against it, to assist companies in specific situations, and to co-operate internationally. Declarations by the OECD Ministers as well as National Governments (*e.g.* in parliamentary debates on implementing legislation) could be adequate instruments in this respect.

Integration in Follow-up Programmes

As the current international instruments do not properly address the demand side of bribery, follow-up programmes do not include "receiving" countries in all parts of the world. This gives an unbalanced picture. Necessary data to support active measures against the distorting effects of requests for bribes have not been collected.

> The 1997 Bribery Convention's Annex follow-up mechanisms – especially within the OECD – must include the investigation of explicit or implicit requests for bribes and the sufficiency and functioning of measures to combat them. Such enquiries can be made only in close co-operation with business.

Collecting such data may be difficult. Formal proof will seldom be available and business secrets must be safeguarded. Therefore, it will be necessary to establish reporting bodies as "filters" that can provide the necessary information in anonymous and aggregated form. They must be separated from institutions having judicial or penal-prosecution competence, to avoid compromising both the independence of the judicial process and permitted defendant protections.

Clearance for Transactions

As it may not always be obvious whether a specific transaction violates anti-bribery laws, companies must be able to obtain quick clearance on the legitimacy of specific transactions. The United States provides such a facility in its FCPA. To safeguard basic rights of a defendant in a penal prosecution, such reliable and binding advice, when feasible, should come from offices not related to penal proceedings. The information provided should have restrictions on its use, so as not to prejudice later judicial proceedings. Some exceptions could be established to avoid abuse (although they are not currently offered under US FCPA rules).

> Governments ratifying the 1997 Bribery Convention should establish neutral information points to provide companies with clarity on the legitimacy of specific transactions.

Assistance in Cases of Solicitation

Companies often confront requests for bribes – in the context of large public-procurement contracts, for example. Such cases need specific action. BIAC recommends an international co-operation mechanism. National contact points could alert counterparts in other countries to enquire whether other companies have been confronted with similar requests, as part of a thorough investigation.

> Governments should exchange information about reported attempts to solicit bribes. They should co-operate in joint investigations on substantiated cases. They should respect and safeguard the business secrets involved. The commercial position of reporting persons in the market concerned should not be jeopardised by their co-operation in government investigations.

Co-ordinated Measures

Requesting bribes not only distorts trade but violates good-governance obligations. Whereas large trading countries may limit development assistance programmes or impose binding obligations on recipient countries, this is not the case for most OECD Member countries. International co-operation is needed.

> Governments should engage themselves to co-ordinate their enforcement of good governance and the fight against solicitation of bribes. Development aid and other assistance should be taken into account.

Concluding Remarks

The OECD work should also include private or commercial corruption issues. This implies eliminating differences in the treatment of state and private enterprises – a timely proposal given the progress in privatising formerly public functions. Both state and private companies themselves have a strong interest in keeping their own houses clean, based on market forces. Nevertheless, whereas public officials have more or less clearly defined duties and obligations, not all employees do. Moreover, commissions or similar fees may legitimately compensate justified efforts and services rendered. Prohibited acts should therefore be clearly defined. Some argue that private corruption should not be the object of an international convention or based on criminal-law sanctions. A number of countries address this issue in their unfair competition laws.

The OECD must maintain a close dialogue with business in all areas to ensure realistic implementation and to test the practicability of measures taken. BIAC is well experienced and equipped to play this role for the OECD. Such a dialogue, however, can be conducted fruitfully only among informed partners. In this context, the BIAC network has proved its reliability, even in cases where secrecy is a priority. Its membership includes the major representative business organisations in each of the twenty-nine OECD Member states. BIAC ensures a full representation of the business world's views. BIAC expects that its role as the OECD business voice will continue in the ongoing dialogue at the OECD. It sees a co-operative approach as the key to developing creative and effective tools to combat corruption.

Chapter 15

Why Trade Unions have Mobilised Against Corruption:
Views of the Trade Union Advisory Committee

by
Roy Jones[*]

Trade Union Concerns

In October 1997, three international trade-union organisations, the TUAC, ICFTU and ETUC, issued a joint statement with their employer counterparts, the BIAC, ICC and UNICE, welcoming the agreement on the Convention on Combating Bribery of Foreign Public Officials in International Business Transactions (Annex I), and urging governments to ratify it. In February 1999, when the Convention came into force, the international trade-union movement therefore felt that progress had got under way in the world-wide fight against corruption.

Two central questions concerning trade-union views on fighting corruption are addressed. Why do unions have a direct interest in fighting corruption over and above the interest of our members as concerned citizens? What now needs to happen, from our perspective, in the OECD and beyond to step up the fight against corruption and what can we, as trade unionists, do to help?

The Unions' Interest in Fighting Corruption

The first and main reason for unions' interest is the link between corruption and abuses of freedom of association and other core labour standards. A brief look at the Transparency International list of the most corrupt countries in which to do business shows that, with very few exceptions, these countries have not ratified the core conventions of the ILO, and many of them have received repeated censures from the ILO's Freedom of Association Committee. In contrast, the least corrupt countries have, by and large, good records on Freedom of Association and trade union rights. This relationship exists for many reasons. Corruption is often linked to unaccount-

---

[*] Roy Jones is Senior Policy Advisor to the Trade Union Advisory Committee (TUAC) to the OECD.

able political elites, who suppress trade-union and other human rights to protect their own positions and privileges. Action to implement the ILO's 1998 Declaration on Fundamental Rights at Work and to ensure the observation of Freedom of Association in more countries throughout the world would therefore also be action in the long term to fight corruption.

In our experience, similar relationships also exist at the workplace level. Unionised workplaces are more likely to be associated with cultures of transparency and accountability of management decisions. Therefore they are less likely to be ones in which bribes are surreptitiously sought or paid.

The bribery of public officials also clearly becomes an endemic problem when levels of public-sector pay are so low that in some cases they do not allow public workers to support their families. Again, this problem appears in many of those countries that restrict unions from organising in the public sector and negotiating for public-sector workers. Therefore, giving public servants the right to organise and bargain also becomes part of the fight against corruption.

A second reason for trade-union interest is that the employees who expose corruption in organisations – the whistle-blowers – are likely to suffer victimisation. As representatives of employee interests, we must defend whistle-blowers. In the UK the government recently has introduced legislation protecting them, and the UK Public-Sector UNISON has established a telephone hot line for employees to call if they wish to expose corruption or need protection. South Africa too is developing legislation in this area, but clearly more needs to be done. In some parts of the world the risk to whistle-blowers does not involve just their jobs. Over the last year we received information of trade unionists and employees murdered in countries as far apart as Russia and Guatemala, for exposing corruption in the handling of privatisation contracts.

A third reason for trade union concern is that in a more global economy common rules of the game must prevail. If bribery is not to distort trade and investment, all countries must take common action.

What Must Now Happen

First, encourage more ratifications of the 1997 Bribery Convention. TUAC and the ICFTU work with affiliates in the OECD countries to this end. Second, step up actions to protect whistle-blowers. The 1997 Bribery Convention does not cover them because of variations in national systems for employee protection, but the OECD absolutely must now launch work on this subject, possibly in conjunction with the ILO. Trade unions already have experience in the area through work on health and safety issues and the need to protect representatives who blow the whistle on unsafe or unhealthy working practices. Other governments and social partners should emulate the example of government and union action in Britain and elsewhere on whistle-blower protection. One positive move would be for the OECD Working Group on Bribery in International Business Transactions to set up an ad hoc Group to examine issues related to a whistle-blower clause. Moreover, whistle blowing is a specific manifestation of broader issues of free speech. Naturally, the trade union movement also organises journalists, who have first-hand experience of problems of protection for exposing corruption. Campaigns against corruption must link with those for freedom of expression.

Third, look at the role of corporate codes of conduct and voluntary initiatives to combat corruption. Some see codes as a panacea for dealing with any issue. The labour movement has accumulating experience with them, on a range of issues relating to social responsibility of companies and their environmental impact. Unions can therefore bring a source of transparency to the whole debate on corporate social responsibility. Codes do include genuine attempts by companies to establish ethical or environmental standards for themselves and sometimes their subcontractors or suppliers – sometimes for economic reasons, to protect themselves against consumer or NGO boycotts. Often, however, codes simply become public-relations exercises, which have little practical impact. The key factors, which determine their value, are the monitoring, independent verification and certification procedures that accompany them. Moreover, codes cannot be seen as an alternative to effective government regulation.

Fourth, unions must ensure that they show "zero tolerance" in their own ranks to corruption. Unions, like other organisations, often reflect the societies in which they organise and function, but they also must have a more fundamental vocation of responsibility to their membership.

Fifth, unions can work effectively to negotiate decent wages for public officials. This depends on their having the right to represent and bargain for workers in the public sector.

Sixth, give attention to private corruption, especially in connection with privatisation. Unions disagree very strongly with the argument sometimes heard that privatisation reduces the opportunity for corruption. Corruption affects both the public and the private sectors. Moreover, the privatisation process itself introduces new ethical questions on the role of public officials and private investors. Against this background, the international organisation for public-sector trade unions, "Public Services International", has drawn up a code of ethics for public officials handling these issues.

Seventh, build capacity among the different organisations committed to the anti-corruption fight. The trade unions base their approach here on "partnerships", where the main committed actors, including governments, donor organisations, trade unions, business and civil-society groups come together to share information and experiences, and then to develop joint local, national, regional or multilateral activities. TUAC has welcomed the establishment of the Anti-Corruption Network, housed under the auspices of the OECD, which has the potential to develop along these lines. To be truly effective, such an approach requires governments and donor organisations to commit further financial resources, and to develop broad-based national and locally based anti-corruption projects.

In conclusion, it is clear that unions have a part to play in combating corruption around the world. If this campaign remains one directed from above, it will not reach the roots of the problem. We must mobilise all our populations on this issue, creating coalitions and linking the campaign to a wider agenda. The unions are ready to do their part.

Chapter 16

Instilling an Anti-bribery Corporate Culture

by

Kathryn Gordon[*] *and* **Maiko Miyake**[**]

Bribery and Codes of Corporate Conduct

Although the international business community cannot fight bribery on its own, it nevertheless has a crucial role to play. Many firms have responded to this challenge by adapting management techniques commonly used in many other areas (*e.g.* environment and product quality) to ensure compliance with law and with firms' own standards of conduct and performance. These efforts often begin with a written expression of commitment in various areas – sometimes called a "code of corporate conduct". Such codes are voluntary expressions of commitment, made to influence or control business behaviour for the benefit of the firm itself (*e.g.* to enhance company reputation or to minimise risk of criminal or civil sanctions) and for the communities in which it operates. As concerns bribery, the codes inform the public about the nature of the firm's anti-bribery commitments and about implementation measures that accompany these commitments. They also heighten employees' awareness of corporate policy and enlist their support in the fight against bribery. Issuance of codes is often accompanied by the adoption of special management systems designed to help firms honour their commitments in their day-to-day operations.

Two factors have complicated firms' efforts to clarify and communicate their anti-bribery commitments. First, in some cases, it is not easy to define exactly what constitutes bribery and other corrupt practices. Clear-cut cases do exist (and it is relatively easy to proscribe such behaviour), but greyer areas arise in connec-

---

[*] Kathryn Gordon is Principal Administrator in the Capital Movements, International Investment and Services Division of the OECD Directorate for Financial, Fiscal and Enterprise Affairs.

[**] Maiko Miyake is a Consultant in the Capital Movements, International Investment and Services Division of the OECD Directorate for Financial, Fiscal and Enterprise Affairs.

tion with facilitation payments, gifts and hospitality, conflicts of interest and use of intermediaries. The assessment of what constitutes acceptable practice may also be coloured by local circumstances; but cultural diversity and varying local conditions can also be used as excuses for inappropriate business conduct. Furthermore, some members of the international business community may be justified in claiming they often are more victims of extortion than perpetrators of a crime. Trying to formulate reasonable guidelines for business behaviour in these contexts can present problems.

The second factor is the relative scarcity of widely accepted international principles and pools of expertise upon which firms might draw. The international policy framework for bribery is less developed than in other areas such as labour, human rights and environment. Corporate commitments in human rights and labour relations can take inspiration from an extensive body of international declarations (*e.g.* the UN Universal Declaration of Human Rights and various ILO declarations) and institutional expertise (like that in the ILO). More recently, the Rio Declaration and Agenda 21 have contributed to clarifying corporate environmental responsibilities. Even if companies do not explicitly acknowledge such sources, the concepts and definitions used in the codes reflect their influence. Although several prominent NGOs, business groups, the OECD and other inter-governmental organisations work to strengthen the international framework for bribery, no equivalent, formal expressions of international consensus on business rights and responsibilities exist for bribery and corruption. This is reflected in the heterogeneity of the language and concepts the codes use to describe their anti-bribery commitments.

This chapter looks at business approaches to commitment and implementation in the fight against bribery by examining the texts of 246 codes of corporate conduct issued by individual firms, business associations, non-governmental organisations and international organisations. The codes emanate mainly from businesses and business associations[1] from 24 OECD countries and cover the entire range of economic activity (primary production, manufacturing and industry, services).[2] The Annex to this chapter describes how this inventory was accumulated and the limitations of the analysis.

The first section looks at how the 246 codes treat bribery and corruption, particularly the scope of commitments and the definitions used. It shows that bribery and corruption are among the most commonly cited issues, and that the definitions used and scope of commitments vary among the codes. The second section, on implementation, shows that bribery codes are much more likely to deal with implementation than non-bribery codes. This section is based on the 118 codes in the 246-code inventory that are issued by individual firms.

The results of this research can be summarised as follows. The texts of the bribery codes give little evidence of agreement or convergence in the scope of or definitions used in firms' anti-bribery commitments. Diversity of definitions and concepts dominates the code inventory. This suggests that the international business community still struggles to come to grips with the complex ethical questions that arise in defining appropriate business conduct in this area. Yet evidence that firms agree on implementation procedures is reasonably strong. The codes that mention bribery are more likely to deal with implementation issues than those that do not. The bribery codes also contain more elaborate language on implementation procedures than the non-bribery codes. The procedures noted in the bribery codes cluster heavily around record-keeping/reporting and a number of internal mechanisms, such as signing by executive officers, creation of compliance committees, internal auditing and whistle-blowing facilities.

Anti-bribery Commitments

Twenty-three per cent of the codes in the inventory – 56 of them – deal with bribery and corruption (Table 1). This makes bribery the fourth most commonly cited issue area in the code inventory (the others are labour relations, environment and consumer protection). The 56 codes vary widely in their definitions and commitments. Because of fundamental differences in firms' circumstances, complete homogeneity of the codes' coverage and commitments is neither expected nor desirable. Taken as a whole, however, the bribery codes attest to a lack of consensus on the scope of bribery commitments and on basic vocabulary and concepts used in making these commitments.

The company codes in the inventory encompass a broad range of approaches to bribery, corruption, political contributions and gift giving. Thirty-six per cent of the bribery codes contain only general prohibitory statements (*e.g.* "to reject bribery in all its forms"). Others offer detailed texts on bribery, corruption and influence.[3] Codes address corrupt practices *vis-à-vis* both private and public persons, sometimes dealing with one or the other and sometimes with both. In relation to private bribery, the texts deal variously with customers, suppliers, employees and competitors. Many of the codes contain language prohibiting employees (and sometimes their friends and families as well) from accepting gifts or bribes.

Thus, the codes show a variety of approaches to prohibition: many do not attempt to define "bribery" and "corruption" while others give detailed guidance on the activities that could constitute them. None of the codes examined here use the formula adopted in the 1997 Bribery Convention (Annex I), namely attempting

Table 1. **The Bribery Content of the Studied Codes**

	Percentage of bribery codes*
56 codes mention bribery	
Attributes	
Parties to bribery:	
– Bribery of public officials	62.5
– Bribery of private actors	64.3
– Both	37.5
Proscribed activities:	
Vis-à-vis *public officials:*	
– Giving bribes only	17.9
– Employees offering bribes	41.1
– Political contributions	32.1
Vis-à-vis *private actors:*	
– Giving bribes only	23.2
– Employees offering bribes	58.9
– Receiving bribes by firm's employees	23.2
– Solicitation of bribes by employees	53.6
Conditions under which entertainment and gift giving is prohibited:	
– Excessive entertainment and gift giving	39.3
– Seen as inducement to business	39.3
– Exceeds business practices	30.4
– Violation of laws	19.6
– Damaging corporate image	17.9
– Requirements for internal reporting of gifts	33.9

* These are calculated as: 100 × [the number of codes mentioning attribute] ÷ [the number of codes citing bribery].
Source: OECD.

to obtain "undue/improper advantage". Three of the main themes that emerge are:

- *Parties to bribery.* The codes focus on private bribery and corruption (64% of the bribery codes) about as often as corruption of public officials (63%). Thirty eight per cent mention both.

- *Active versus passive.* The codes deal with both active bribery (giving bribes) and the passive version (receiving them). For private bribery, 59% of the codes prohibit offering active bribes, while 54% prohibit attempts at solicitation.

- *Offering bribes versus actual bribery.* Bribery codes are more likely to go beyond prohibition of actual bribery to banning even the offer of a bribe (regardless of whether a briber is actually paid). For bribery involving public officials, 41% of the codes proscribe offering bribes while only 19% limit the definition to completed ones, and 23% prohibit employees from receiving bribes, while 54% prohibit solicitation.

Nearly half of the bribery codes include "gifts and entertainment" in the definition of bribery. Most codes dealing with bribery do not completely prohibit reception of gifts or entertainment from business partners. Here, the border between acceptable business practice and bribery is, perhaps unavoidably, fuzzy. The codes use a variety of language to provide guidance on what is allowed and what is not. Concepts mentioned include: gifts or entertainment "not excessive in value" (appearing in 39% of the bribery codes); "within the business norm" (30%); "not seen as an inducement of business" (39%); "does not violate the law" (20%), and "does not damage corporate image" (18%). Five per cent define monetary limits. Five per cent distinguish between cash and other items, making gifts and entertainment acceptable under certain conditions but prohibiting any transaction involving cash.

Thirty-two per cent of the bribery codes state that the firms do not make political contributions to persons holding office, candidates or political parties. A number of other issues also appear in some of the codes. Fourteen per cent treat employees and immediate relatives of employees in the same manner. Nine per cent acknowledge cultural differences among countries as a factor in determining appropriate gift giving. Among these codes, only one insists on strict guidelines; the others allow judgements of what is acceptable to be influenced by cultural considerations.

Implementing the Bribery Codes

This section seeks to shed light on how firms go about implementing their codes of conduct, especially in relation to bribery. The codes studied here are "voluntary". Their implementation depends on the willingness of companies and their employees to take action. The codes themselves often contain implementation language; 45% of the 118 corporate codes in the inventory discuss compliance.[4] Businesses face the challenge of implementing their commitments in often large, complex, geographically dispersed operations. Ultimately, whether and how they do so determine whether the commitments have meaning – and these factors, plus the effectiveness of implementation, become central to public perceptions of the significance of the codes.

Code implementation and compliance have two facets. First, by putting in place extensive compliance programmes and letting the public know about them, firms hope to increase the credibility of their codes, in the eyes of both the general public and their employees. Second, when binding laws also cover the areas covered in the codes – as is increasingly the case for bribery – the codes and their implementation procedures often are an important facet of firms' attempts to comply with the law.

The analysis below examines the texts of the 118 company codes for their implementation content. It notes the treatment of record keeping and reporting, which are relevant not only to anti-bribery compliance but also to related issues such as protection of shareholders, asset security and protection against fraud. It also keeps track of 13 other attributes, selected using advice from experts and by looking at the full inventory of codes. They include internal monitoring, monitoring suppliers, reports to Boards of Directors, use of compliance manuals, whistle-blowing facilities, signatures of directors, training, periodic compliance reviews by managers, employee signatures, internal auditing, disciplinary action and active communication. These attributes are defined and sample texts are given in the Box below.

A few caveats are in order concerning the methodology for this analysis of the enforcement content of the codes (see also the Annex to this section). Its drawbacks arise mainly because it often looks at only the "tip of the iceberg", in terms of the range of ways in which firms use try to control business conduct. In addition to codes and closely associated material, which the analysis does capture, firms often produce other written materials and rely on unwritten procedures and practices that affect the codes' implementation. Training, production manuals, record-keeping procedures, disciplinary practices and so on may all touch on code compliance. Individual companies decide what appears in their codes and what appears elsewhere. They do not all draw these lines in the same place. Some of the codes are long, detailed documents while others are brief expressions of commitment that may have ancillary support by materials and practices not included in this code analysis.

This introduces a certain non-comparability in the treatment of the enterprises included in the inventory. Nevertheless, the significance of this problem is likely to be moderated because firms have an incentive to publish the key components of their implementation strategy to reinforce the credibility of their codes. If an important implementation measure has been adopted, a firm is likely to mention it in its code.

The bribery codes are much more likely to deal with implementation issues than the non-bribery codes.[5] The first pair of bars in Figure 1 makes it clear that bribery codes are much more likely than non-bribery codes to make commitments relating to the quality of record keeping and reporting. This shows that firms, in their public pronouncements on implementation of their anti-bribery efforts, recognise the key role played by accurate record keeping and transparency in reducing the opportunity and the incentive for employees to engage in bribery and corrupt practices.

Definition of Attributes Used in Analysis of Bribery Texts

Record keeping and financial reporting: Codes mention attempts to set forth quality standards for record keeping and reporting. Example:

> "... employees shall ... comply with all accepted accounting standards, practices rules, regulation and controls ... Ensure that all entries are promptly and accurately recorded and properly documented – no entry will intentionally distort or disguise the true nature of any transaction."

Compliance discussed: Codes mention implementation of, or compliance with, codes of conduct, other than record keeping and financial reporting. Examples:

> "[Company's name] 'Ethical Business Conduct' and related procedures constitute company wide standards of conduct. This procedure provides an overview of the [Company's name] ethics and business conduct program and employees' responsibilities."

> "As a condition of doing business with [Company's name], each and every factory must comply with this Code of Vendor Conduct."

> A code of conduct has a section titled "Maintaining Compliance".

Codes signed by Executive Officers: A code is signed by the board of directors, the chairman of the board, the president or other top officers. This often takes the form of a signed message to employees as a foreword to the code text, or it can be a signature on the code document itself. Codes are not scored for this attribute when the code text merely says that the chairman or board of directors adopted the code.

Internal monitoring mentioned: Codes mention that the company monitors or has a compliance/implementation system for its own company codes of conduct. Codes addressed to suppliers or other business partners are not scored for this attribute. Example:

> "The structure includes the Corporate Responsibility Committee of the Board of Directors and the Leadership Committee, which have oversight responsibility; the Compliance Council, whose duties include education, monitoring and response; and all employees of the Company."

Existence of whistle-blowing facility: Codes mention the company ombudsman, with clear indication of where to contact this person, *e.g.* address, telephone number and EM address. Example:

> "Call the [company's] Human Resources toll-free hotlines (ex. 1-800...) to report any possible violations of law or other violations of the Code of Business Conduct."

Definition of Attributes Used in Analysis of Bribery Texts *(cont.)*

Appointed compliance officer or committee: Codes mention company appointment of compliance officers or committees to execute compliance programmes. Example:

> "… we have established a 'Corporate Compliance Committee' to oversee our compliance efforts and ensure that the Company has necessary policies and systems in place to train employees in their legal responsibilities, monitor compliance and correct any deficiencies in compliance programs."

Use of compliance manuals: Codes mention the existence of compliance manuals, or themselves look like manuals (give thorough guidance on what to do under certain circumstances, or have Questions and Answers). Examples:

> "Many of the statements made here are backed up by detailed policies and procedures. These are available on the internal policy and procedure web-site at: [internet address given]."

> "'Handle a Concern' explains the many ways you can get a policy question answered, or report a concern or possible violation".

> 'What to Watch Out For' lists some of the things that may indicate a policy problem."

Reference to disciplinary actions: Codes mention that the companies will take disciplinary actions in the case of non-compliance with the codes. Example:

> "Failure to act in compliance with the Code is likely to result in disciplinary action against both the employee committing the breach and others who condone it."

Report to the Boards of Directors: Codes mention that the Boards of Directors receive reports on compliance activities. Example:

> "The Committee will report annually through the Managing Director to the Board of Directors."

Training for compliance mentioned: Codes state explicitly that employees will be trained in code implementation or monitoring. Example:

> "Each operating group and division will establish a training program. The program will be designed to ensure that all employees have an awareness of the [Company's name] Integrity Statement and the standards of conduct and legal requirements that are relevant to their work at a level of detail appropriate to their job functions."

Active communication: Codes mention specific activities to disseminate information about them. For example, codes are displayed on bulletin boards in factories, or

---

Definition of Attributes Used in Analysis of Bribery Texts *(cont.)*

shown to newly hired employees, or new or existing employees are required to acknowledge regularly (*e.g.* annually) that they have read them. Example:

> "Ethics and business conduct booklets will be approved by the Committee and distributed within the company as the Committee directs."

Endorsement by employees: Codes have a section in which employees are requested to sign that they have read the codes and will comply with them. Example:

> "This booklet contains an acknowledgement to sign as a statement of your personal commitment to integrity. It's a way for each of us to pledge to uphold the principles of high ethical standards and to comply with all company policies."

Monitoring suppliers: Codes mention that the companies monitor activities of their suppliers and business partners, as opposed to monitoring their own activities (internal monitoring). Example:

> "[Company's name] intends to monitor compliance with our Partnership Guidelines and to undertake on-site inspection of partners' facilities."

Periodic review by managers: Codes mention that it is the task of managers to monitor compliance and conduct periodic reviews. Example:

> "Management is responsible for instituting regular reviews of compliance..."

Other types of compliance measures are also more prevalent in bribery codes. The second pair of bars in Figure 1, labelled "compliance discussed", includes any code that mentions any of the more specific compliance measures shown subsequently in the figure. The bribery codes are almost twice as likely (61% of them) to discuss implementation as those that do not (35% of them). In considering these statistics, note that the codes labelled as bribery codes generally extend beyond bribery in coverage; for example, 78% of them also mention environmental management.

There is no "one size fits all" approach to implementation and compliance. The bribery codes show a distinctive approach to implementation.[6] "Record keeping and reporting" is the single most important implementation measure in the bribery codes, while the non-bribery codes hardly mention it. The bribery codes are also much more likely to mention a range of more specific internal measures – signing of codes by executive officers (57% of them), internal monitoring (57%), whistle-blowing (41%), compliance officers or committees (34%), use of compliance manuals

Figure 1.a. **Implementation and Company Codes:
a Comparison of Bribery Codes with Non-bribery Codes**

Per cent

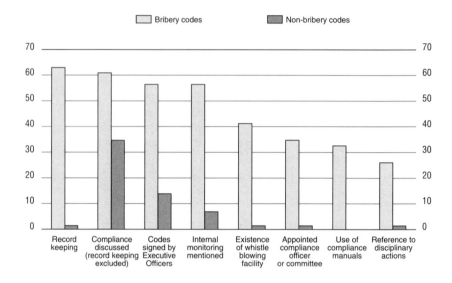

Figure 1.b. **Implementation and Company Codes:
a Comparison of Bribery Codes with Non-bribery Codes**

Per cent

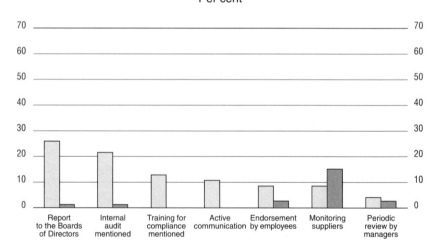

Source: OECD.

(32%) and reference to punitive action (27%). Despite the intense interest shown in third-party auditing by NGOs and trade unions, only two of the 118 company codes mention this implementation method (financial auditing is not included in this count).

The codes on gift-giving also exhibit different approaches to implementation. Almost 34% of them require employees to report giving and receiving gifts or entertainment. Often, however, the report is required "only when the gifts/entertainment exceed business norms". Some 12.5% of the codes require prior approval for accepting gifts and entertainment, but 86% of these ask employees to seek approval only when the gifts and entertainment exceed business norms.

On the whole, firms show considerable agreement as to the "choice of weapons" in the fight against bribery. This emerging consensus may facilitate the growth of standardised management systems for dealing with bribery and corruption issues.[7] If so, developments in this area will parallel trends in environmental management, where standardised management systems (especially ISO 14001) have gained widespread acceptance.

Implications for Anti-bribery Practitioners

The fight against bribery needs to be conducted on a broad front, marshalling support from a wide variety of actors on a wide variety of issues. The management and control techniques used in this fight remain under development in both the private and the public sectors. The analysis here suggests that, despite considerable progress on developing a consensus on management control, a need persists for international dialogue and consensus building on exactly what kinds of behaviour – especially corporate behaviour – should be proscribed. A number of private and inter-governmental organisations have made contributions. Particularly noteworthy are the activities of Transparency International, the ICC and the OECD's Working Group on Bribery in International Business Transactions. The revised OECD Guidelines for Multinational Enterprises also contain a wide definition of bribery and corruption, covering public officials, private-to-private bribery, gift giving and political contributions.[8]

It would be helpful for all if the international community could work on an international declaration defining basic recommendations in relation to bribery and corruption. Multinational enterprises, which now operate in a complex patchwork of legal and political frameworks, could draw on it as they formulate and revise their own anti-bribery commitments.

Notes

1. Businesses and business groups issued the majority of codes in the inventory. A few were issued by NGOs, alliances of labour and business, and inter-governmental organisations.

2. see Gordon, Kathryn and Maiko Miyake (1999), *Deciphering Codes of Corporate Conduct: A Review of Their Contents*, OECD Directorate for Financial, Fiscal and Enterprise Affairs Working Papers on International Investment, Number 99/2, October, for a more detailed description of the inventory.

3. For example, one US code states that federal regulators may be offered complimentary donuts and coffee, but that they must pay for their own sandwiches.

4. Unlike the previous section (which was based on the full inventory of 246 codes), this one looks only at the 118 codes in the inventory that are issued by individual firms. The other main issuers – non-governmental organisations and business associations – may not have the same perspective on implementation as individual firms.

5. The bribery and non-bribery codes differ in more than just their treatment of bribery itself. The firms issuing bribery codes tend to be very large, extractive-industry firms or capital-intensive manufacturers (often of branded durables or products with an important public-sector clientele). Some financial services and telecommunications firms and very large conglomerates are also represented. The issuers of the non-bribery codes tend to be much smaller. Their activities are more likely to be in branded apparel, toy or sporting goods manufacturing or mass retailing. For many of these firms, the codes tend to concentrate on other sets of commitments, especially those relating to core labour standards in the supply chain.

6. As noted in the text, the non-bribery codes' coverage of implementation issues is relatively cursory. Their distinctive implementation feature (*i.e.* the feature stronger in them than in the bribery codes) seems to be a comparatively strong orientation to supply-chain issues (see second to last pair of bars in the graph).

7. A number of standardised management systems already have been proposed in this area (*e.g. ECS 2000 in Japan*).

8. For further detail on the guidelines consult *http://www.oecd.org/daf/investment/guidelines/index.htm*.

Annex

Methodology and Limitations

Definition of Codes of Corporate Conduct

The definition of code of corporate conduct used in this study is: The codes of corporate conduct are broadly defined as commitments voluntarily made by companies, associations or other entities, which put forth standards and principles for the conduct of business activities in the marketplace. This definition includes self-obligations and negotiated instruments. It excludes codes of corporate governance.

Collection of Codes

The OECD Secretariat (Trade Directorate) contacted OECD Member countries, BIAC and TUAC for the identification of codes to be included in the inventory. A number of OECD Member countries provided contact names and in some cases also code titles and texts. Following the initial communication, the Secretariat sent letters to 77 prospective respondents across the OECD between April and October 1998. The letters asked recipients to identify up to 20 codes that they thought were significant in their country or elsewhere in the OECD area.

The process resulted in an initial collection of over 200 codes of corporate conduct. Some were excluded from the inventory because they were codes of corporate governance, company credos or incomplete documents. 246 codes were eventually collected. The items in the inventory are coded as individual codes. Hence if a firm has several codes of conduct – *e.g.* a code on outsourcing and another on the general behaviour of employees – the codes were counted separately.

Limitations

This study has several methodological limitations:

- Because of the way the codes were collected, the set of codes is neither a random nor a representative sample of the codes issued by the business communities in various countries.

- There was little consensus on the definition of codes of corporate conduct when the request was communicated. As a result, the nature of codes included in the inventory varies widely, from codes designed to influence employees' conduct to sourcing principles. For some firms, several codes are in the inventory. In other cases, the inventory contains only one code, though the firm may have other codes as well. Some of the texts in the inventory also contain training material. Scoring was based on this entire information set and therefore may not be fully comparable across code issuers.

The overall code analysis aggregates over a number of important sectoral and geographical factors. This makes it hard to use the overall aggregates to make inferences about key concerns that the economics literature on self-regulation has raised. For example, the overall inventory cannot be used to determine the extent to which the social and economic processes driving the corporate-codes movement have led to uniformity in firms' commitments.

Chapter 17

Citizens Against Corruption:
Calling Governments to Account

by

Michael H. Wiehen[*]

Governments, business and Civil Society (CS) play the most influential governance roles in today's era of globalisation. CS has itself revived in a recent megatrend – in Europe and North America in the 1970s, in Latin America and Eastern Europe in the 1980s, and in Africa and parts of Asia in the 1990s. A global proliferation of CS organisations works at the grass-roots and policy levels in the developing and developed worlds, promoting democracy, human rights, civil rights, development and other objectives. What is CS, and how does it function? What does it do in the global effort to fight and prevent corruption?

Definition of Civil Society

There is no single accepted definition. CS includes organisations, structures and networks separate from the legislative, administrative and judicial power of the state and, many would argue, from business, but interacting with both in a variety of ways. Alexis de Toqueville credited the strength of democracy in the United States to the proliferation and vigour of "a thousand different types" of associations of citizens pursuing a common purpose. Thus, "Civil Society" is a new term for a social force with a historical pedigree. The role of CS in demanding accountability from government involves the most basic questions about power, participation, transparency and democracy.

In the working definition used in this chapter, CS consists of groups of individuals, sometimes groups of groups, who have agreed to act collectively for the common good, to influence and stimulate democratic action, and to analyse and educate

---

[*]   Michael H. Wiehen is Chairman of Transparency International – Germany.

public debate. CS organisations define themselves by selective membership (trade unions, university teachers), by religious choice (churches or social-activity groups), by professional interests (groups like "Professors for Freedom of Information" and chambers of commerce), and by broad or narrow issues (being for or against something). Their wide range includes:

- Broad environmental groups (Greenpeace, IUCN, the World Wide Fund for Nature) and special-interest environmental groups (like the "Society for the Protection of the Snail Darter").
- Groups for gender-related issues.
- Groups for solar and renewable power or against nuclear power.
- Groups pursuing broad developmental issues or regional economic development, as in Sub-Saharan Africa.
- Groups to help protect rivers or mountains, or people or animals near rivers or mountains, or humans and nature in specific areas ("The Mountain Institute").
- Groups for Human Rights.
- Groups for Civil Rights.
- Groups against Corruption.

The term "Civil Society" combines many advantages: it is abstract, therefore applicable to a wide range of concrete situations; it is class-unspecific; it is political; and it is neutral ideologically. It reflects the realisation that people are not simply socio-economic variables, but active and participating citizens. CS reflects the acceptance of pluralism (the liberal argument), the expansion of participation (the democratic argument) and the mobilisation of cultural energies (the efficiency argument).

CS encompasses the expertise and networks needed to address almost any issue of common concern. It has a vocation for attacking corruption, most of which involves two principal actors, the government and the private sector. As power devolves from the centre to local authorities, opportunities for corruption shift downward, to people in more direct contact with CS. The ability of CS to monitor, detect and reverse the activities of public officials in its midst is enhanced by proximity and familiarity with local issues.

Authoritarian regimes normally repress CS, although they may establish "captive" groups to give the appearance of having it. Only the development of political democracy allows it to flourish. Without democratisation (or at least political liberalisation) there will be no true CS and thus no potential partner in government. A "predatory" state normally is not democratic, doesn't know the difference between private and public and is exploitative, amoral and corrupt. Just as a state can be predatory or oriented toward the common good, CS does not necessarily pursue the common good, and not all CS organisations necessarily follow lofty ideals. Some, for example, were founded solely as vehicles for receiving much-coveted donor development assistance for the personal benefit of their founders. Such organisations obviously cannot be part of the solution in the fight against corruption, but they are instead a thorny part of the problem.

The CS dealt with in this chapter does pursue the common good and does have lofty ideals. It consists of civic communities, with norms of trust and co-operation, which facilitate common projects with collective action. In some countries a "progressive state" has co-opted CS into public responsibility.

How Does Civil Society Obtain its Legitimacy?

Democratically elected government has the legitimacy to deal with all over-arching issues of the common good, but it often lacks the global reach, despite its efforts to network, associate with others and form groupings (such as the EU, the OECD, NATO, the IMF or the World Bank). Business has the means to operate globally, but it is driven by the profit motive, not humanitarian concerns. Only CS has the public mandate and the global potential to declare the improvement of peoples' lives a paramount priority, put the enhancement of the human condition above all other priorities – and do something meaningful about it.

But does CS actually have a mandate? After all, the public at large does not elect its leaders and people. Organisations with wide membership and much individual financial support (like Greenpeace or Amnesty International) can legitimately claim to have mandates from these broad bases of support. Others, funded by governments or exclusive business groups, may well represent particular interests and thus would have no public mandate.

Does Transparency International (TI), the global anti-corruption organisation, have a public mandate? TI has managed to mobilise significant government and official support but it also enjoys much broad-based public support, especially for its approximately 70 National Chapters world-wide. Its individual membership is comparatively small, but TI practices full transparency regarding its funding support and its objectives. Mandate or no mandate, it is the only organisation that focuses exclusively and globally on the fight against corruption. TI certainly has demonstrated that CS organisations can provide the impetus, the force and the leadership to wage this global fight, and, more generally, place new subjects effectively on the public agenda. Its efforts have helped set the framework for actions by government and business.

New international conventions and national laws and regulations make bribery and kickbacks less pervasive and intrusive. As in other areas, CS organisations can provide the leadership in monitoring the progress of government and business in implementing such measures. The public will trust only such empowered CS organisations to report progress objectively. Government, business and often CS itself usually underestimate their potential power.

How Can Civil Society Act Against Corruption?

CS organisations can fight or prevent corruption in many different ways:

- By expressly addressing bribery and extortion in public or private sector life.

- By demanding more transparency in government activities such as procurement, licensing, permits, service monopolies etc., to minimise the opportunities for corruption.

- By demanding Freedom of Information laws, to give CS and the public access to administration information, which will also reduce the opportunities.

- By monitoring the implementation of environmental laws and commitments, and concentrating on corruption suspicions.

- By monitoring implementation of the 1997 Bribery Convention (Annex I) in domestic law and practice.

- By more general monitoring and auditing of government activities.

- By serving on oversight bodies.

- By monitoring campaign expenditures.

Even beyond the groups focussing specifically on corruption, like TI, many CS organisations work against it – rarely as a major objective but often as a minor one. Some have demonstrated great effectiveness. Many CS people and organisations have a fundamental interest in achieving effective integrity systems for their own countries. The Hong Kong Independent Commission against Corruption (ICAC) has an entire department devoted to community relations and advisory committees that incorporate significant involvement by the private sector and other elements of CS. "Neighbourhood watch" schemes, now established in many countries, organise citizens to support policing efforts. In some countries, consumer groups help to identify hazardous products on sale.

Transparency International

As the only single-purpose CS anti-corruption group working globally, TI addresses corruption in all its aspects and manifestations. Only TI deals systematically with:

- The social and environmental causes and effects of corruption, and damage from it.
- The economic and political impacts of corruption.
- The institutional aspects of fighting and preventing corruption.
- The content and quality of the relevant national and international laws, regulations and administrative practices.
- Enforcement.
- Business positions and efforts regarding corruption, institutional programmes including codes of conduct, compliance programs, etc., and offers of guidance to business.
- The entire Integrity Systems of countries, including the democratic process, judicial systems, Ombudsmen, Auditors General, Independent Anti-Corruption Agencies, Commissions and Offices and public-procurement systems. TI's "Source Book", which exists in about 12 languages and can be accessed on the Internet (*http://www.transparency.org*), describes this work in detail.

Founded in 1993, TI has its international secretariat (TI-S) in Berlin, but it works primarily through its National Chapters (NCs) in roughly 70 countries. The NCs are largely independent, both financially and in their choices of priorities. All the NCs in OECD Member countries have among their highest priorities support for the implementation of the 1997 Bribery Convention. NCs in developing or transition countries primarily address domestic corruption issues.

Many CS organisations co-operate with TI and its National Chapters, in general or on specific issues and campaigns. TI always welcomes the opportunity to join forces with others to build an even stronger case and to rely on such combined support. It has a fundamental aim to build broad coalitions against corruption by bringing together groups that are expressly non-partisan and non-confrontational.

Thanks to the Internet and e-mail, CS groups can, at minimal cost, stay in close touch around the globe and mount effective mass campaigns on short notice. They have become so effective, in fact, that the Financial Times has called CS the "Internet-Guerrilla" – a term most organisations would be proud of. TI's global and national work could not be nearly as effective without electronic communications.

Specific Civil-society Anti-corruption Activities

Support for the 1997 Bribery Convention

TI has supported OECD's work against corruption from the very beginning. It participated as an observer in many working meetings of the OECD Working Group on Bribery in International Business Transactions, often submitting detailed suggestions and recommendations, and frequently using its own access to the media to highlight the importance of early government agreement on joint OECD action. This "instant impact" was possible because TI was founded by and continues to attract many senior professionals with long experience in international development administration. In 1997, three major OECD Member countries withheld their agreement to the common approach and tried to hide behind their domestic business communities, arguing that they could not agree to something that might adversely affect export opportunities. TI mobilised a number of top business leaders, who wrote letters to their government ministers urging full support for the OECD approach. This strategy worked successfully.

TI and all its NCs in the OECD area then publicly supported the convention approach to criminalise bribery of foreign officials, as well as all the flanking recommendations. The Convention is narrower and more specific, but more binding than the originally intended "soft law" recommendations, which now accompany it, namely the abolishment of tax deductibility, the strengthening of accounting and auditing requirements and the reform of export-credit schemes. In many OECD Member countries the NCs publicly demanded quick ratification and passage of the necessary laws, participated in public hearings before national parliaments and in some cases even participated in drafting the legislation. TI also submitted first a more general set of recommendations, and later a very detailed list of technical suggestions, to the EU Commission and the OECD, on how national export-credit schemes should be modified to minimise the use of official credits or credit guarantees for business deals obtained or retained by corruption. Parallel submissions went to several of the OECD Member governments. TI shares all such actions with the media and usually attracts considerable attention.

When the OECD started reviewing the national legislation and administrative action by which member states converted the Convention into national law, it invited TI to prepare and submit its own independent evaluations. Its NCs wrote them for a good number of countries, and the OECD Working Group on Bribery in International Business Transactions (although not necessarily the national government representatives in it) much appreciated them. TI and its NCs are now gearing up to perform a similar "independent evaluation" function for reviewing actual compliance and the application of these national laws and regulations, to assure as high a degree of equal treatment across the OECD as is feasible. TI also has been consulted on and actively participates in the various outreach activities of the OECD, in order to convince at least the remaining major trading nations to join the Convention.

Many of the NCs work very actively to bring to the attention of their business communities the new legal situation created by the recent criminalisation of bribery of foreign officials in international business transactions. As US businessmen have learned since the promulgation of the FCPA in 1977, good, straightforward codes of conduct and solid compliance programmes will help exonerate them if one of their employees is caught bribing. Business houses in all OECD Member countries should develop such codes of conduct. TI assists companies that want to learn about successful models and the associated compliance programmes. Although many management consultant firms now offer "integrity services" commercially, TI can help steer companies in the right direction. It sees this as a very important contribution to addressing the supply side of bribery.

Support for Other Anti-corruption Activities, International and National

As late as 1996, the European Commission tended to leave all anti-corruption activities to the OECD and the member states. A TI memorandum in late 1995, demanding that the Commission use its legal and political instruments to address corruption, helped bring about a change of direction. In May 1997 the Commission issued a formal report to the Council of Ministers and the European Parliament entitled "A Union Policy toward Fighting Corruption". TI and in particular TI-Belgium remain in constant contact with the Commission and have contributed to many debates and documents prepared at the Commission.

The 23 members of the Organisation of American States (OAS) agreed in December 1996 on the "Inter-American Convention" against corruption. TI-USA as well as all the NCs in OAS member states were deeply involved in the drafting and the passage of the Convention, and continue their efforts to get all signatories to ratify it.

The Government of Bénin recently approved a new "Code d'Éthique et de Moralisation des Marchés Publics", a comprehensive integrity pact in the form of a decree that will be integrated in existing legislation on public procurement. The new code aims at obtaining from both bidders and government officials a formal commitment to abstain from corrupt practices during the bidding process and the implementation of contracts. This active renunciation of corrupt practices in public procurement will be compulsory for all competitive tendering, and the code makes provision for appropriate sanctions in case of violation. The code provides for civil society's monitoring role in the process, with the possibility of recruiting qualified experts to evaluate independently the bidding process and contract implementation. This involvement of CS in the control mechanisms will be critical to the success of the initiative at the implementation stage. TI-Bénin as well as TI-S were actively involved and played an important role in supporting the development of the new code.

In Mauritius, it had been felt for some time that the country had procurement legislation inadequate to prevent manipulation and corruption. In 1998 the Government invited TI-Mauritius to help draft a better law, in collaboration with other CS representatives. The Parliament finally adopted the Procurement Transparency and Equity Bill in April 1999.

In Nigeria, the recently elected President (and former Chairman of TI's Advisory Board), Olusegun Obasanjo, has asked his friends in TI for advice and help in installing anti-corruption measures throughout the administration. At this writing, TI and other CS representatives are helping to rewrite Nigeria's procurement code.

In Ukraine, the Parliament in June 1999 adopted a Law, drafted by TI-Ukraine, setting up the Ad Hoc Investigative Parliamentary Commission. The Commission, which includes national Deputies and representatives from all parties and groups, can investigate all cases involving corruption at high official levels.

The TI Integrity Pact (IP)

TI felt early on that governments embarking on major anti-corruption reforms should demonstrate their determination to bring about real change by establishing so-called "islands of integrity" (today called "Integrity Pacts" (IP)), for the implementation of one or more major investment projects. The concept has had very successful application in several cases and is under serious consideration for a number of others. TI developed the IP concept in the mid-1990s. Its main criteria are:

- A formal pact or contract between a government office (the "principal") inviting tenders for a public project and the companies tendering for the project (the "bidders").

- An undertaking by the principal that its officials will not demand or accept any bribes.

- A statement by each bidder that it has not paid any bribes in order to obtain the contract, and an undertaking that it will not do so in the future.

- An undertaking by each bidder to disclose all payments made in connection with the contract to anybody, including agents and other middlemen.

- Undertakings on behalf of a bidding company will be made "in the name and on behalf of the company's Chief Executive Officer".

- Bidders are advised to have company codes of conduct clearly rejecting the use of bribes and other unethical behaviour, and compliance programmes to implement the codes throughout their companies.

- A pre-announced set of sanctions for any violation by a bidder of its statements or undertakings, including some or all of the following:

  - Denial or loss of the contract.

  - Forfeiture of the bid security.

  - Liability for damages to the principal and the competing bidders.

  - Blacklisting by the principal for an appropriate period.

The IP is intended to accomplish two objectives:

- To enable companies to abstain from bribing by providing assurances to them that their competitors will do the same, and that government procurement agencies will undertake to prevent corruption, including extortion, by their officials and follow transparent procedures.

- To enable governments to reduce the high cost and the distortionary impact of corruption on public procurement.

From the outset it has been expected that CS groups in a country would play a key role in overseeing and monitoring the correct and full implementation of its IPs. The IP idea has now been used in several cases involving major investment and supply contracts as well as privatisation and licensing. Significant refinements include resort to international arbitration under the auspices of the Arbitration Court of the ICC, and use of the concept for the selection of consultants.

Broader application should considerably reduce opportunities for corruption in major international investment projects and privatisations. In one such case, the construction of the "Linea H Subway" in Buenos Aires, TI-Argentina not only arranged for the application of the IP concept to the major contracts, but also persuaded the city's government to hold several open hearings. The hearings opened to public debate all relevant issues, such as the location of the line and the stations, the process for selecting contractors, the costs and the economic and social impact of the project. They were extremely popular and led to significant modifications of the plans. This high degree of transparency will make it much more difficult if not impossible to manipulate the process of choosing contractors and building the subway according to specifications.

In another case, the privatisation of Panama's telephone company, the government invited TI-Panama to observe and monitor the entire process of selecting the "best" bidder for the company. TI-Panama insisted on and was granted unrestricted access to all the relevant documents and access to all the decision meetings. This enabled TI-Panama eventually to announce that it had monitored the process and found everything in order. In the end, the government obtained a sale price 30% above the estimated proceeds. All parties were satisfied.

The TI-NC in Colombia (TICOL) has been singularly effective in persuading the Vice-President, senior officials and many other public figures of the benefits and advantages of a high degree of transparency in public procurement, of using an Integrity Pact and of a strong CS monitoring role. These procedures govern the selection of operators for "community telecommunication points" (value US$ 80 million), and TICOL may well repeat this success for other projects.

Civil Society Influencing National Anti-corruption Activities

TI has just launched the Local Government Integrity Programme. Recognising that corruption at the local level has significantly increased over the last few years, TI will apply its usual evolutionary and coalition-building approach. It seeks to bring influential elements of CS into international alliances and national coalitions with their own governments to analyse and address local problems. TI has joined hands in this effort with the Global Coalition for Africa.

In 1997 TI-Bangladesh did a systematic survey of how corruption affected people throughout the country. The survey returns revealed that a very large number of people had to pay bribes for hospital admissions, to obtain drugs, indeed to get any medical attention at all. They had to bribe schoolmasters to get their children enrolled and again to get them passing report cards. They had to bribe the police if they needed any assistance. TI-B took this dramatic and shocking survey report to the President of Bangladesh and obtained her commitment to introduce reforms and address all the major issues one-by-one. TI-B is now monitoring the implementation of this reform program, keeping the public at large informed along the way through media reports. The TI-NCs in Argentina and Malaysia are conducting similar surveys.

In Argentina, Poder Ciudadano (an NC with several thousand members) has experimented with CS action in a number of different ways. For example, in 1998 it collected information throughout Buenos Aires on the prices paid by the hospitals for major consumption items (bed sheets, aspirin, other drugs, toilet paper, etc.), and found major discrepancies, suggesting that in several cases corruption and sweetheart deals were at work. They published this information in full detail in the local press – and when they repeated the survey a few months later, they learned that all hospitals now were buying at the lowest prices.

TCC-Brazil keeps and regularly publishes a "Corruption Scoreboard": it monitors six daily newspapers and three weekly magazines for corruption cases involving members of the executive, the legislature and the judiciary at federal, state and municipality levels. For the first quarter of 1999 it identified 76 cases, of which a third (26) appeared in federal executive offices. TCC-Brazil has recently listed several other CS organisations with which it co-operates including notably: *Associação Juízes para a Democracia* (Association of Judges for Democracy), *Instituto Ethos, Associação Brasileira de Empresários pela Cidadania* (Brazilian Association of CEOs for Business and Social Responsibility), *Controladoria Geral do Municipio de Rio de Janeiro* (General Control of the Rio de Janeiro Municipality) and UNACON (National Union of Analysts and Technicians in Finance and Control).

In Germany, TI-Deutschland collaborates with several other NGOs in an effort to obtain a freedom of information law, on the assumption that more transparency in general, and better access to procurement documentation of the states and municipalities in particular, should reduce the unacceptably high corruption, especially in German municipalities.

In Bulgaria, a coalition of CS groups in which TI-Bulgaria collaborates has prepared a systematic analysis of corruption vulnerability in the country and is now designing, together with government departments, a programme for addressing the most vulnerable entry points for corruption.

In Slovakia, Premier Mikulas Dzurinda and TI-Slovakia agreed to work out a National Anti-Corruption Programme. TI-Slovakia will also co-supervise transparency in procedures of public tendering and state-debt settlement. On the legislative front, government will seek TI-Slovakia's help in drafting legislation on public procurement and rights to information.

The Government of Senegal, at the initiative of the President, called a "national consultation" on the quality of public services. This meeting gathered representatives from the employers associations and the trade unions, as well as grassroots and civil-society organisations. It looked closely at good-governance issues. The organisers accepted as a basis for discussion a set of proposed reforms, which had come from a workshop organised by the TI-NC in formation in Senegal, the Forum Civil, on "Transparency in the Management of Public Affairs". The Forum Civil will play an important role in the process, with its president co-chairing a commission debating "Civil Society and Public Administration."

The TI Corruption Perceptions Index and TI Bribe Payers Index

Since 1995, TI has published each year in the autumn its *Corruption Perceptions Index* (CPI), which ranks countries on how people perceive them in terms of the likelihood of being asked to pay bribes when doing business there. The CPI has become one of TI's most effective public-information products, carefully read by both business people and governments. Occasionally a head of state or government gets upset about what he calls "slanderous" information. More often, governments take this information to heart and acknowledge that they had better address the problem. In the autumn of 1999, TI published for the first time a companion measure – the *Bribe Payers Index* (BPI). It ranks the 19 leading exporting countries in terms of the degree to which they are perceived as the homes of bribe-paying companies. Although their methodologies differ, the two indices now cover both the supply and demand sides of corruption.

The CPI, a composite index, draws on 17 different polls and surveys from ten independent institutions, carried out among business people, the general public and country analysts. It focuses on corruption in the public sector and defines corruption as the abuse of public office for private gain. Among the ten sources are Gallup International, the *Wall Street Journal*, the World Economic Forum (Davos), the Political and Economic Risk Consultancy, the *World Competitiveness Yearbook* issued by the Institute for Management Development and the Economist Intelligence Unit. A Steering Committee of leading international experts in econometrics, statistics and corruption regularly reviews TI's methodology for using the results of these polls and surveys. Because TI will include in the annual CPI only countries for which recent surveys from at least three different institutions exist, the composition of the list varies from year to year; countries occasionally drop in or out of the index. Therefore both a country's specific rank in a given year and the comparability of annual scores from year to year for a given country (the "country trend") have limited significance. If a country drops out of the CPI for a year, it would be quite wrong and misleading for it to rejoice that "we no longer have a problem with corruption", as has happened. Despite these limitations, the CPI's clear general message has indeed been heard loudly and clearly year after year, judging by its press coverage around the globe.

The 1999 CPI ranks 99 countries (the 1998 CPI included 85). The five best-ranked countries in 1999 were Denmark, Finland, New Zealand, Sweden and

Canada. The five lowest-ranked were (in ascending order) Cameroon, Nigeria, Indonesia, Azerbaijan and Uzbekistan.

The BPI comes from a special international survey carried out for TI by the Gallup International polling organisation, with 770 respondents in 14 major emerging-market countries (Argentina, Brazil, Colombia, Hungary, India, Indonesia, Morocco, Nigeria, the Philippines, Poland, the Russian Federation, South Africa, South Korea and Thailand). This list of respondents' countries excludes those that traditionally deal primarily with one supplier country, as well as China, in which it was not possible to run the survey. The respondents included chief executives of major companies, chartered accountants, bi-national chambers of commerce, major commercial banks and commercial law offices. They answered a comprehensive questionnaire about trends over past years, reasons for the use of bribery, the response to the 1997 Bribery Convention and other aspects of transnational corruption. The BPI ranks the 19 leading exporting countries. The five best-ranked were Sweden, Australia, Canada, Austria and Switzerland. The five lowest-ranked were China, South Korea, Chinese Taipei, Italy and Malaysia.

Based on the comprehensive survey data collected for the BPI, TI has also recently produced an Industrial Sector Ranking, listing major business sectors on a cross-country basis. They include agriculture, arms and defence, banking and finance, civil aircraft, health care and social work, power, petroleum and energy, industry and mining, public works and construction, and telecommunications.

Neither the CPI nor the BPI is based on hard empirical data measuring actual corruption (those data are not now available); they reflect the perceptions of the respondents. TI accepts that some gap may exist between perception and reality. Yet the perceptions represent the best information available, and they will influence investors and other business people. Countries interested in attracting more business, or expanding their exports, would be well advised to pay close attention to them. (Further information is available at the TI website *www.transparency.org*).

The International Anti-corruption Conference (IACC)

Every two years, in meetings organised by TI since 1997, experts from around the globe interested in fighting and reducing corruption gather for a week of intensive discussions and sharing of experience. Delegates come from governments, international organisations, business, civil society and academia. At the meeting in Lima, Peru in 1997, the 8th IACC adopted the "Lima Declaration", which contains a wealth of suggestions and demands regarding the global fight against corruption. The 9th IACC, in Durban, South Africa in October 1999, heard uplifting fundamental commitments to corruption fighting by leaders of countries, institutions, private companies and civil-society organisations. The 1600 participants from more than a hundred countries agreed on the "Durban Commitment". Both the Lima Declaration and the Durban Commitment are accessible on the TI website.

Media Contacts and Support for Investigative Journalism

Print and electronic media can be powerful allies in the fight against corruption. In many countries they have made major contributions to a better understanding of the dangers and costs of corruption, put pressure on ruling elites to mend their ways, and often supported anti-corruption activities, whether CS or legislative initiatives. In some countries the tradition of investigative journalism has helped uncover many scandals (including the Lockheed scandal in the 1970s, which led to the US FCPA). In many other countries such journalism does not yet exist. TI has on several occasions collaborated with others in offering relevant training and technical expertise to journalists. TI-Deutschland in June 1999 ran an intensive two-day workshop for journalists; it was made possible thanks to funding by another CS organisation.

Achievements so Far

At a conference in early 1999 in Washington, chaired by US Vice President Al Gore, the US Secretary of the Treasury, Mr. Robert Rubin, called TI a "terrific organization" which has been "largely responsible for putting corruption on the international agenda and making it possible for (global or G-8) summit meetings to address this issue". That is perhaps the major achievement of CS over the last decade: putting corruption and the need to do something meaningful about it on the international agenda.

Thinking back to the three pillars of society – government, business and CS – only CS could possibly have undertaken this task and succeeded. Governments, or members of governments, have always been among the culprits and they are vulnerable. Businessmen on occasion may have felt that they had little choice but to bribe, but they do clearly represent the supply side of corruption, even recognising a significant degree of solicitation from the government side. Thus CS has taken up the challenge to call governments and business to task. Yet corrective action must come from them. CS can only keep the spotlight focused on the cancerous wound and monitor the healing process – or the further deterioration.

Although awareness of serious damage from corruption has grown rapidly and widely, and more and more societies have begun to take some action to brake and reverse it, recent revelations make one wonder whether the cancerous growth has even slowed, let alone halted. One can observe veritable orgies of corruption in too many countries, and despair. Yet despair means inaction, and inaction by the decent will mean free play for the corrupt – at the expense of all. CS reflects the engagement and support of a phenomenal group of individuals, around the globe. Networks have been built and they function. Effective tools have been developed and applied. People understand increasingly better the causes and processes of corruption. Surely, this is not the moment to give up.

Chapter 18

Recovering the Rage:
Media and Public Opinion

by
Sheila S. Coronel[*]

Introduction

In 1972, two rookie reporters of the *Washington Post* exposed the burglary and attempted wiretapping, apparently on orders from the White House, of the Democratic Party headquarters at the Watergate building in the US capital. Since then, the series of articles written by Bob Woodward and Carl Bernstein alleging the complicity of President Richard Nixon's aides in political espionage has become the stuff of journalistic legend. Watergate became the symbol of the might of investigative reporting. Although the truth was somewhat more complex, the popular mythology soon came to accept that the president of the most powerful nation on earth was forced to resign because two enterprising reporters showed how he had abused the prerogatives of his position.

The myth remains compelling a quarter of a century later. In truth, Nixon resigned, not because of what the Woodward-Bernstein exposés contained, but because thorough probes undertaken by several government bodies later yielded evidence of illegal acts committed by the president's aides. The Washington Post deserves the credit not for toppling the president, but for breaking the story of his aides' indiscretions, putting it on the news agenda, and framing it as one of wrong-doing at the highest levels of government.

Watergate's most lasting impact is perhaps on journalism itself. It inspired an entire generation of US journalists. Even outside the United States, it set the standard for what the press can do. Hollywood helped by glamorising the reporters' role.

---

[*] Sheila S. Coronel is Executive Director of the Philippine Centre for Investigative Journalism, Philippines.

Yet beneath the glamour lay the essential truth: two dogged journalists following the trail of wrongdoing to no matter where it led them, no matter the consequences. It is a somewhat romantic notion. Still, a generation after Watergate, when citizens and governments in many countries are overwhelmed by widespread malfeasance and when it has become obvious that there are too few checks on the excesses of power, renewed interest has bloomed in the role of a free press and of enterprising journalists in ensuring that officials and institutions are held responsible for their actions.

Today, the idea of the press as watchdog and catalyst of change is widely accepted in most democracies, even if only in theory. In countries with fragile and corrupt democratic institutions, and where the rule of law is at best erratic, journalists soon realise that their role is not just to record events passively. Because other institutions are weak or compromised, the press has ended up doing what the police, the courts, parties and parliaments should do: exposing malfeasance, calling for reforms and mobilising public action against corruption.

In recent years, the importance of a free and independent press has been demonstrated most dramatically in new or "transitional" democracies. In these countries, the fear of media exposure often acts as the only deterrent to official abuse. In some notable instances, media exposés have compelled corrupt officials to resign. If they don't, public pressure forces governments to bring to justice those guilty of malfeasance. Because of investigative reporting, wrong policies get reversed, extravagant projects get shelved and politicians whose misbehaviour has been exposed lose elections.

It is little wonder that the dramatic impact of investigative reporting has caught the attention of donors and multilateral institutions in search of mechanisms to improve governance. What journalists have known all along – the importance of the press in ensuring the accountability of powerful institutions – experts now preach as if it were an original notion. It is not. The idea of the press as Fourth Estate, as a check on the excesses of government, is deeply embedded in liberal democratic theory. The importance of the freedom of information, and citizens' access to it, has been enshrined in some countries' laws and constitutions since the 18th century.

Today, as the 21st century begins, the world becomes ever more complex and the power of big public and private institutions over citizens' lives becomes even more pervasive, the old precepts of a free press and the free flow of information need no reinvention. The problem is that in many countries, whether they are old autocracies or new democracies, these principles are observed more in the breach. Stringent laws, monopolistic media ownership, and sometimes brute force seriously hinder the ability of the press to be an effective watchdog. In 1998, 24 journalists were killed because of their work. In 1999, 77 journalists were in prison, some of them for more than 10 years, because authorities were displeased with their reporting.

State controls are not the only constraints. Serious reporting is difficult to sustain in media markets that put a premium on the shallow and the sensational. In many newsrooms, even in affluent countries, tight budgets do not allow for the investment in time and resources that investigative journalism requires. In many countries, journalists do not have the experience and the training to do in-depth reporting. Even if they did, the pecuniary and political interests of media owners limit the freedom of journalists to conduct exposés. The obstacles to investigative journalism, in terms of both state control and anarchic media markets, remain formidable. In fact, the astonishing thing is that this kind of reporting thrives at all, sometimes in the least hospitable of environments.

The Press as Democracy's Watchdog

The most instructive case is that of Latin America, where it is widely acknowledged that sustained investigative reporting on corruption, human rights violations and other forms of wrongdoing has helped build a culture of accountability in government. There, media exposure, particularly of corruption in high places, has brought down governments. The downfall of two presidents – Fernando Collor de Mello of Brazil and Carlos Andres Perez of Venezuela – was due largely to investigative reporting on their complicity in corrupt deals.

In 1992, Brazilian magazines printed exposés on Collor de Mello's involvement, through his campaign treasurer, in the extortion of bribes from companies in exchange for favourable government treatment. The Brazilian Congress formed a body to investigate the charges and eventually the president was forced to resign. Not long afterward, a Venezuelan newspaper ran articles alleging that President Perez was unable to account for $17 million in discretionary funds and that he made money by speculating on the local currency. In reaction, the Venezuelan Congress began impeachment proceedings, prompting Perez to step down from office.

Elsewhere in Latin America, the media have raked up similarly damaging charges against high officials. The Argentinean press has found evidence of President Carlos Menem's involvement in financial scandals. In Panama, a team of investigative reporters showed how a local bank with close ties to the government was used by a Colombian drug cartel to launder profits from the narcotics trade. Such reporting has made the press a credible – and prestigious – institution that enjoys the public's support and trust. In the fledgling democracies of the region, the press has stood out as the one institution that has functioned effectively and independently.

This success has come at a great cost. The New York-based Committee to Protect Journalists (CPJ) tallied 117 journalists killed in Latin America from 1988 to 1998. Most of the murders took place in countries where the judiciary is weak and corrupt, therefore unable and unwilling to defend press rights. Because the courts are dishonest and inept, the killers seldom get punished. Those who wish the press ill – whether they are officials, drug cartels, or insurgent movements involved in illicit trades or the protection of crime – can operate with impunity.

It is obvious that at the most basic level, a free press – and investigative reporting – are possible only where journalists enjoy some protection. Constitutional and legal provisions are necessary, but even where they exist, they do not always ensure that the media can report without fear or favour. The rights of journalists must be upheld by an independent judiciary and protected by the rule of law. In Latin America and the Philippines (where 33 journalists have been killed since 1986), many of those murdered were the victims of small-town bosses able to terrorise communities because weak states cannot enforce the law and provide protection to their citizens, journalists included.

That is why the press often seems caught in a chicken-and-egg situation. Its freedoms are not guaranteed unless other democratic institutions perform their functions well; but these institutions are unable to do so because there is no independent check on their performance, in part because the press is threatened and bullied. It is often up to crusading journalists to break this impasse despite the risks.

Legal Constraints on Reporting

Certainly, the job of journalists can be made much easier. In many countries, stringent libel and defamation laws keep the media in thrall. Because these laws penalise erring reporters with prison terms, journalists become wary about doing exposés that could land them in jail. In addition, the prospect of long, expensive litigation and hefty penalties daunts media proprietors who are more concerned with profit margins than public service.

In many countries, truth is not considered a defence in libel, and journalists can be compelled to reveal their sources on pain of contempt of court or a prison term. Contempt charges have also been used to clamp down on critical reporting on the courts. In September 1999, Canadian journalist Murray Hiebert, then Malaysia bureau chief of the *Far Eastern Economic Review*, was jailed for four weeks for an Article that a local judge deemed derogatory to the judiciary in that country. Journalists writing articles questioning an official's actions or motives have also been tried for treason and sedition. In Nigeria, four journalists were convicted in 1995 as "accessories after the fact to treason" for reporting on a supposed coup plot. In Croatia, merely reporting facts considered insulting or harmful to a government official's reputation is ground for a libel suit. There were some 500 lawsuits pending against journalists in that country in 1998, including 130 criminal libel suits with fines totalling over $13 million.

In many places, politicians file suits indiscriminately, knowing that the mere threat of a court case often succeeds in squelching further reporting on a controversy. Even when reporters are not actually hauled off to jail, they have to get a lawyer, pay bail, attend court hearings and compile evidence to back their case. This is tedious work that takes them away from what they should be doing – reporting.

If investigative reporting is to take off, libel and defamation must be decriminalised. As press groups in various countries have argued, civil suits are sufficient to provide redress for aggrieved citizens. The experience of many countries has shown that stringent laws do not actually curb sensationalism and irresponsible reporting; instead, these statutes have mainly been used to clamp down on serious journalists who expose official wrongdoing. There is also a need to liberalise other laws, including those that impose strict licensing requirements for newspaper publication or allow the government to seize or close down publications or ban programmes considered a threat to "national security," "public order," or "national unity."

Although less onerous, laws such as the Official Secrets Act remain in force in many Commonwealth countries and are a real damper to investigations because they make government records inaccessible. In contrast, few countries have freedom of information statutes. Even where there are disclosure laws, record keeping in many new democracies is primitive, and a culture of secrecy still rules in bureaucracies.

Investigative reporting becomes unnecessarily excruciating, and sometimes impossible, if journalists do not get routine access to essential public records like corporate registrations, property records, audit reports and disclosure statements of officials. Procedures that simplify access to such records, instead of making them subject to the discretion of officials, make it easier for reporters to do their jobs.

In truth, the requisites for investigative journalism are not difficult to put in place even in the most fragile of democratic regimes: legal guarantees and protection for the press, accessibility of public records, and a community of committed journalists. Joel Simon, the CPJ's Latin America co-ordinator, writes: "While enormous financial investments and strong political will are needed to create an independent judiciary or truly competitive political parties, a free press requires no financial investment or direct government support. All that is needed is for the government to allow journalists to work without fear of reprisal."

Investing in Investigative Journalism

The institutionalisation of a free press is of course the first step. To sustain investigative reporting, however, a *laissez-faire* approach will not suffice. Investigative journalism requires an investment in time, resources for research, and the development of reportorial talent. Unfortunately, such investment is lacking. In many newsrooms in the world, media proprietors compete with their rivals by offering sex, sleaze and sensation instead of in-depth reports. The media market is so crowded and so anarchic that the tendency is to appeal to the lowest common denominator of public taste. In this environment, investigative reports are crowded out of the newscasts and the news pages by the routine reportage of events and the other distractions that are passed off as news.

Investigative reporting is a risky business. It threatens to upset the cosy relationships between media owners and their friends among the upper crust of business and politics. Press proprietors are wary that investigating such issues as corporate irresponsibility might turn off advertisers. Given these obstacles, the only way that investigative reports can make any headway in the media free market is to show that they can sell newspapers and news programs and that there is an audience for serious reporting.

The truth is that in many countries, investigative reports do sell. They generate a great deal of public reaction and bring recognition to news organisations. The key is to get newsrooms to initiate and invest in investigations despite the costs and the risks. One way is to convince them of the rewards, in terms of increased audience share, name-brand recognition or professional prestige. Awards for investigative reporting offer one way to encourage this trend.

Other, less tangible benefits are perhaps even more important. Carefully researched, high-impact investigative reports help build the media's credibility and support among the public. The press as an institution is strengthened if journalists have demonstrated that they serve the public interest by uncovering malfeasance and abuse. A credible press is assured of popular backing if it is muzzled or otherwise constrained. Such support may not be forthcoming if journalists squander their freedoms on the superficial and the sensational.

Restraining Media Excesses

The development of investigative reporting can in fact be seen as one way to curb some of the excesses of a free press. This is especially true in new democracies. A media explosion often follows the fall of dictatorships. After Ferdinand Marcos was toppled in 1986, for example, scores of new newspapers and radio stations sprang up in the Philippines, as citizens basked in the novelty of a free press. In Indonesia, hundreds of new newspapers opened after the 32-year reign of President Suharto ended in May 1998. Indonesians called it the "euphoria press". Euphoria is a wonderful thing, but it does not always give birth to good journalism. There is a lack of skilled journalists to staff the news organisations created by the media boom. The boom also results in intense competition, which often means racing for the headlines and sacrificing substance and depth.

Investigative reporting offers a way out of these problems. It addresses the problem of skills by forcing journalists to sharpen research and reporting techniques. It helps resolve the problem of sensationalism because investigative reports require sobriety and depth. They also help sell newspapers and give publications a competitive edge. If constantly exposed to excellent reporting, audiences develop a more discerning palate and will learn to tell the difference between fast-food journalism and substantial reading fare. In time, they may even get weaned from the merely distracting and entertaining, and will demand more in-depth reporting. Unless exposed to new ideas and better kinds of journalism, audiences will stagnate and news organisations will be stuck pandering to their undeveloped tastes.

Apart from improving the quality of the media and the audience, investigative reporting helps widen the scope of journalistic freedom. By constantly digging for information, by forcing government and the private sector to release documents and by subjecting officials and other powerful individuals to rigorous questioning, investigative journalists expand the boundaries of what is possible to print or air.

At the same time, they accustom officials to an inquisitive press. Officials eventually realise that releasing information benefits the government. Absent a flow of official information, journalists will tend instead to report lies, rumours, and speculations, with no one the better for it. It may take time, but officials must be convinced that informed citizens make better citizens, even if in the process government takes a beating in the press. Any government, no matter how corrupt or autocratic, has reform-minded officials and bureaucrats who appreciate the journalists' role and are willing to co-operate with reporters in the release of information. In the long term, the constant give and take between journalists and officials helps develop a culture – and a tradition – of disclosure.

This, in turn, buttresses the media's capacity to play their watchdog role. Investigative journalism gives the media not only more bark, but also more bite, making them better watchdogs. The better the media, the more able they are to find proof of wrongdoing, the more they can hold powerful individuals and institutions accountable.

Dictators like Marcos and Suharto could rob their countries blind not only because they controlled the levers of power, but also because they muzzled the media. Such plunder by similar regimes in Africa and Latin America was possible partly because of an acquiescent press. Would these leaders have been able to get away with their crimes if inquisitive journalists had dogged their trail and exposed their abuses? Probably not. This is why democracies need skilled journalists with the ability and the courage to ask tough questions and to keep an eye on those who wield power and create wealth. Otherwise, they risk being trapped in a cycle of plunder and abuse.

Increasingly, in many parts of the world, the realisation dawns that democracy does not bring an end to corruption, cronyism or environmental devastation. Abuses merely take new forms. Corruption, for example, becomes more decentralised, no longer concentrated in the head of state and his family; many more snouts crowd around the public trough and it becomes ever more important to guard it. The criminal waste of public resources continues in scandalous proportions and very often, unless the media expose these crimes and unmask the criminals, reforms do not take place.

Investigating Corruption

Not all reporters have the inclination or the skills to be investigative journalists. Exposing malfeasance requires not only the nose, but also the doggedness, to sniff out wrongdoing and follow its trail. Patience and perseverance count, especially with tedious detail. Other requisites are a basic knowledge of laws, the capacity to understand bureaucratic procedures, and the ability to chase documents that will provide evidence of malfeasance. Good investigative journalists know where to find sources that will provide reliable information and help them piece together how wrongdoing was committed. Increasingly, a familiarity with computer-assisted research tools (e.g. the use of computer databases and the internet) is indispensable for investigative reporters.

All of these traits can be learned. In many cases, special training, such as in reading financial statements, constructing databases and internet searching, has proved useful in honing investigative skills. Manuals for investigative reporters, including those that provide tips on where appropriate documents can be found and the procedures for accessing them, arm journalists with the tools they need for conducting research. In time, and with practice, journalists master these tools and sharpen the instinct for reporting on corruption. They are also able to develop a network of sources that will provide information on official wrongdoing.

In many countries, corruption actually is rarely hidden from public view. Petty corruption – policemen taking bribes from erring motorists or fixers who demand a fee in exchange for facilitating a permit or a license – is fairly easy to document. Reporters can interview victims or simply go through the processes themselves to see whether they are asked to make payoffs.

Corruption on a grander scale is harder but not impossible to investigate. Many times, insiders in an organisation will, for whatever reason, play the role of whistle-blower. Often, they are only waiting to be asked the right questions by an inquisitive journalist. All reporters, after all, are constantly on the lookout for their "Deep Throat". In other circumstances, business or political rivals can be tapped for information. Businessmen who lose bids for government contracts may be willing to speak about how bribes have been extorted from them. Sometimes, police or other investigators are only too eager to share with journalists what they have found.

Evidence of actual payoffs may be difficult to find, so investigative journalists instead seek out lapses in established procedures or conflicts of interest. Sometimes, they can discern patterns of irregular decision-making or awarding of contracts to favoured firms, even if proof of actual bribery is not available. Another area ripe for investigation is the lifestyle and public behaviour of government officials. For example, it may be difficult to show that judges are paid off, but reporting on judges meeting with litigants or lawyers with cases pending in their courts may be sufficient to demonstrate breaches of ethical conduct. Reporters who find tax examiners driving Volvos and sporting Rolex watches should start following the money trail.

The more sophisticated types of corruption are the most difficult to report on, especially when they involve dummy firms and shareholders, corporate layering, overseas bank accounts and offshore companies. In an era of digital convergence, transnational money flows and international crime, investigating corruption becomes more challenging than ever. Even the most talented investigative journalists can reach a dead end when investigating complex transactions that cross national borders and legal jurisdictions. Yet even in these instances, it may be possible to get the co-operation of lawyers, accountants, official regulators and investigators, as well as business rivals or company insiders who may have reason to blow the whistle.

Journalists should of course develop a certain scepticism about their sources. It is easy for corruption investigations to be manipulated. Reporters are often fed information by sources with something to gain from an exposé. The challenge is to steer clear of partisan politics and remain independent of vested interests. No matter how careful, journalists will be accused of the basest motives. This is par for the course; reporters eventually learn to be patient and to realise that only after several exposés will they be able to prove their independence and develop a reputation for credibility and trustworthiness.

The public's trust is earned if journalists are careful about their methods. Investigative reporting has come under fire in the United States, where reporters have been accused of being too trigger happy with the use of undercover and surveillance methods. The ABC network, for example, was penalised in court for allowing its journalists to seek employment in a grocery store and to use hidden cameras to show how the Food Lion grocery chain was selling stale meat. In 1998, a reporter of the *Cincinnati Enquirer* resorted to accessing the internal voice mail of employees of Chiquita Brands in the course of researching a story on the company's business practices. He was widely criticised for using illegal methods to get a story and later for revealing his source in the course of court proceedings.

The easy availability of surveillance equipment, such as video cameras or tape recorders that fit neatly into a small pocket, makes it tempting for journalists to take shortcuts. If they are to have the public's confidence, journalists should be more self-critical about their methods and ethics. They must also be willing to disclose the methods they use in their investigations.

The ideal for the press is still self-regulation. Codes of Ethics that clearly define appropriate conduct and lay down the principles that journalists should uphold must be drawn up and strictly enforced, at the level either of the news organisation or of the media community as a whole. Journalists should also engage each other and their readers or viewers in discussions on the conduct of the press and its methods of work. These discussions can take place in various forums, including conferences, online newsgroups, industry publications, or newspaper columns. There should also be mechanisms, such as press ombudsmen or press councils, through which aggrieved readers or viewers can seek redress or at least air their views. This way, the media themselves become accountable.

The media represent a powerful institution that deserves to be subjected to the same examination as others. There is no reason why the power of investigative reporting should not be used to probe the excesses of the media as well. For example, media corruption – as in bribes or favours given to reporters in exchange for favourable coverage – is an issue that most journalists refuse to discuss publicly. Like corruption elsewhere, corrupt practices in the media will persist if they are not brought into the open and subjected to scrutiny and reform.

There are other issues too. One is wages and benefits. In many countries, journalists are poorly paid in comparison to those in other professions. This is one reason why petty corruption – such as envelopes of cash given out during press conferences – persists in many developing countries. Better salaries help keep reporters honest, and they ensure that the best of them stay in the profession instead of seeking better remuneration elsewhere. Competitive pay for journalists also ensures that the media attract the best and the brightest. High levels of skill, probity, and behaviour are demanded of investigative journalists, yet the media industry is niggardly and often unwilling to provide adequate compensation for reportorial integrity and talent.

The Journalism of Outrage and Hope

The danger, of course, is that sustained reporting on corruption would lead to widespread cynicism about government. Investigative reports must make an impact in terms of policy reversals or personnel changes, or at least the initiation of official investigations of the wrongdoing that they have exposed. Otherwise, citizens will think that nothing can be done, and they will view exposés as yet another distraction proffered by the media.

Often, news organisations that have invested in an exposé will try to make sure that something does happen, by eliciting reactions to their investigation or writing follow-up stories that examine what has been done. Sometimes, all the media get involved in an issue, with reporters from various news organisations investing resources to follow up on a particularly explosive revelation. This was the case with Watergate, when both television and print reporters followed the trail of the story for many months after the initial *Washington Post* investigation.

Investigative journalists are lone-ranger types: many of them work best alone or in small teams. In many countries, they are now realising that if reforms are to be sustained, there must be a conscious effort to develop a community of journalists who can trade techniques and sources as well as provide each other support when they are being hounded by the powerful. The role of press organisations is important in this regard. These groups can act as lobbyists for journalists' rights and for greater access to information. They can monitor infringements on press freedom and develop mechanisms to assist and protect journalists. Press groups can also help improve skills through training and internships.

In the 1990s, groups defending press freedom have been set up by journalists in several Latin American countries to document and protest abuses against the press. These groups have organised seminars on press rights and mobilised fact-finding missions and international delegations to look into infringements of media freedom. In 1998, journalists from Indonesia, Thailand and the Philippines got together to form the Southeast Asian Press Alliance, a watchdog group to promote press freedom in the region. The alliance facilitates exchanges of information among press groups, keeps track of press-freedom violations, and conducts training seminars.

Journalists alone cannot solve social ills. Civil society plays a role and eventually, the wheels of government have to be set in motion to fight malfeasance. At best, journalism plays a catalytic role. Investigative reports enrich public debate and put on the news agenda issues that should be of concern to citizens. By probing, for example, the consequences of corruption in terms of the quality of government services or the magnitude of the waste of public resources, journalists help readers to understand the problems of governance and to make decisions about who they should vote for and what changes they should demand. At their best, exposés should make people angry rather than cynical, and move citizens to action. Outrage makes change possible.

Ideally, investigative reporting should help raise the level of public discourse by bringing issues of corruption away from personal attacks or partisan politics to the level of policy and institutional reform. Apart from the psychic rewards of exposing crooks, "naming and shaming" are important because they make corruption visible and intelligible to the public. Investigative journalists should look not only at who is responsible for the wrongdoing they have uncovered and how it was done, but also at why it was possible and how it can be corrected. For this reason, it may sometimes be good to feature the work of reformers, whistle-blowers and organisations combating corruption. Citizens need to be informed about innovations that have worked or reforms that have been implemented – and what still needs to be done – so they can temper their outrage with a measure of hope.

Abbreviations and Acronyms

ADB	Asian Development Bank
AnCorR	OECD Anti-Corruption Ring Online
BIAC	Business and Industry Advisory Committee to the OECD
BIS	Bank of International Settlement
CIS	Commonwealth of Independent States
CoE	Council of Europe
EBRD	European Bank for Reconstruction and Development
EC	European Commission
ECOJ	Official Journal of the European Commission
ETUC	European Trade Union Confederation
EU	European Union
FATF	Financial Action Task Force
FCPA	US Foreign Corrupt Practices Act
G7	Group of Seven most industrialised nations
GNP	Gross National Product
IASC	International Accounting Standards Committee
IBRD	International Bank for Reconstruction and Development
ICC	International Chamber of Commerce
ICFTU	International Confederation of Free Trade Unions
IDA	International Development Association
IAPC	International Auditing Practices Committee
IFAC	International Federation of Accountants
ILO	International Labour Organization
IMF	International Monetary Fund
IOSCO	International Organisation of Securities and Exchange Commissions
MNEs	Multinational Enterprises
NGO	Non Government Organisations
NIS	Newly Independent States (of the former Soviet Union)
OAS	Organisation of American States
OECD	Organisation for Economic Co-operation and Development

OECD Directorates
CCNM	Centre for Co-operation with Non-Members
CFA	Committee on Fiscal Affairs
DAC	Development Assistance Committee
DAFFE	Directorate for Financial, Fiscal and Enterprise Affairs
PUMA	Public Management Service
SIGMA	Support for Improvement in Governance and Management in Central and Eastern European Countries – OECD unit administrating the EU programme PHARE

OSCE	Organisation for Security and Co-operation in Europe
TI	Transparency International
BPI	Bribe Payers Index
CPI	Corruption Perceptions Index
IP	Integrity Pact
NC	National Chapter
TI-S	International Secretariat
TUAC	Trade Union Advisory Committee to the OECD
UNICE	Union of Industrial and Employer's Confederations
UNCITRAL	United Nations Commission on International Trade Law
UNDP	United Nations Development Program
USAID	United States Agency for International Development
WTO	World Trade Organisation

Suggested Further Reading

ACEMOGLU D., VERDIER T., "Property Rights, Corruption and the Allocation of Talent: A General Equilibrium Approach", Paper No. 1494, Centre for Economic Policy Research Discussion, October 1996.

> In this article, the authors show that property rights are essential to ensure sufficient rewards to ex-ante investments. Because enforcement of property rights influences the ex-post distribution of rents, there is room for corruption.

ADES A., DI TELLA R., "The New Economics of Corruption: A Survey and Some New Results", *Political Studies*, Vol. 45, No. 3, 1997, pp. 496-515.

> This economic article presents indices of corruption and offers an econometric analysis of the causes of corruption and the relative effectiveness of the various instruments for controlling the phenomenon. The key variables are a country's wealth, the level of education, the extent of political competition, economic outreach and the independence of the judicial system.

ALATAS S.H., *Corruption: Its Nature, Causes and Functions,* Avebury, Gower Publishing Company, 1990.

> This multidisciplinary book gives a detailed explanation of the causes and consequences of corruption in contemporary Asian societies and features chapters on the history of corruption in the Roman Empire and ancient China. The author presents and offers a critique of functionalist theories.

ANECHIARICO F., JAMES J.B., *The Pursuit of Absolute Integrity; How Corruption Control Makes Government Ineffective,* University of Chicago Press, 1998.

> Proliferating regulations and oversight mechanisms designed to prevent or root out corruption have turned out to be seriously undermining the ability to govern. By constraining decision makers' discretion, shaping priorities and causing delays, corruption control has contributed to the contemporary crisis in public administration just as corruption itself has.

BARDHAN P., "The Economics of Corruption in Less Developed Countries: A Review of Issues" in *The Role of Governance in Economic Development*, Development Centre Studies, OECD, 1997, pp. 15-44 (also available in French).

> This review of economic literature offers a detailed digest of work dealing with problems of efficiency, growth, differential corruption levels from one country to another, and incentive policies that could hopefully reduce those levels. (Another version of this can be found in the Journal of Economic Literature, Vol. 35, 1997, pp. 1320-1346.)

BECK P., MAHER M., ESCHOEGL A., "The Impact of the Foreign Corrupt Practices Act on US Exports", *Managerial and Decision Economics*, No. 12, 1991, pp. 295-303.

For the authors, there is no compelling empirical evidence that American firms are being penalised by the FCPA. The (methodologically complex) debate and attempts at quantification have been given new impetus by Hines and by Elliott (see below).

BERG W., *Bananenrepublik Deutschland. Korruption der ganz alltägliche Skandal*, Mod. Verlagsgesellschaft, 1997.

This book describes how corruption works in every day life and where the line with gifts is to be drawn. It also reviews mechanisms used in multinational and other big enterprises to make a "carrier".

BORGHI M., MEYER-BISCH P. (Eds.), *La Corruption, l'Envers des Droits de l'Homme*, Ed. Universitaires de Fribourg (Switzerland), Collection interdisciplinaire, série "Droits de l'homme", 1995.

The book is a collection of some twenty articles that are a mixture of sociological, legal, and economic policy approaches, along with works by theorists and practitioners of the fight against corruption.

BRUNETTI A., *Politics and Economic Growth*, Development Centre Studies, OECD, 1997 (also available in French).

The author uses surveys of the private sector and econometric methods to try to quantify the effects on investment and growth, in some one hundred countries, of institutional factors such as democracy, governmental stability, the credibility of economic policies, political violence and corruption. This review of literature, on a subject that sparked the interest in good governance, shows the relationships between political instability and corruption.

BUITENEN P. van, *"Unbestechlich für Europa. Ein EU-Beamter kämpft gegen Misswirtschaft und Korruption"*, Brunnen Verlag, 1999.

The author used to be an official in the EU Commission. He describes how corruption influences political decisions in Brussels.

CARTIER-BRESSON J. (Ed.), *Analyses et Contrôle de la Corruption*, Montchrétien, Collection Finance et Société, Association d'Économie Financière, 1997.

This book features a range of analysis of corruption in developed and developing countries and summarises the controversies surrounding the definition and impact of the phenomenon, before explaining the nature of French laws seeking to prevent corruption. The last part of the book contains contributions from organisations such as France's Central Corruption Prevention Department, the Group of Experts of the Council of Europe and OECD's DAFFE.

CHAGNOLLAND J-P., RAVENEL B. (Eds.), *Confluences Méditerranée: Corruption et Politique en Europe du Sud*, No. 15, 1995.

This issue features political sociology articles on corruption in southern Europe, providing material for comparative analysis concerning France, Spain, Greece and Italy, focusing on the roles of the main players: elected officials, businesses, civil servants, judges and journalists. Contributions from practitioners of the anti-bribery struggle in France and Italy illustrate the anti-corruption strategies that have been adopted.

CLARK W.A., *Crime and Punishment in Soviet Officialdom: Combating Corruption in the Political Elite 1965-1990*, M.E. Sharpe, 1993.

> This book gives an analysis of political corruption and and attempts to battle it in the Soviet elite. It examines how corruption fits into the structure of the bureaucracy and the society, the various attitudes to it, gives data on its prevalence and the future of legal reform in the successor states.

CLARKE M. (Ed.), *Corruption: Causes, Consequences, and Control*, St. Martin's Press, 1983.

> The book is a collection of writings on corruption and the fight against it in developed countries (United Kingdom, Netherlands, Italy), developing countries (in Latin America, Africa and Asia) and Soviet-style regimes.

CLINARD M.B., *Corporate Corruption: The Abuse of Power,* Praeger Publishers, 1990.

> In this book the author describes unethical and illegal behavior of America's giant corporations and their executives. He shows how corporate bribery is commonly used and leads to a breakdown of ethics in contemporary society.

Crime Law and Social Change, Vol. 23, No. 4, 1995.

> This journal's special issue on corruption is devoted to recent corruption cases in the British and Norwegian oil industry and the Banco Ambrosiano scandal.

CROTTY J., *Measures to Address Corruption Problems in Tax and Customs Administration*, Paper prepared for Presentation at the 8th International Anti-corruption Conference, Lima-Peru September 7-11, 1997.

> An approach to promote integrity and reduce corruption in customs administrations is outlined in this paper. It accepts, as a given, that incentives and opportunities exist in all revenue-collecting agencies to engage in corrupt practices and, based on this premise, attempts to provide the framework for the legal and administrative procedures that are necessary to detect, punish, and reduce such undesirable behaviour.

DE SPELLVILLE B., *Hong Kong: Policy Initiatives Against Corruption*, OECD Development Centre, 1997 (also available in French).

> This books takes a close look at the history, organisation and credibility of Hong Kong's Independent Commission Against Corruption (ICAC). The body's exemplary success stems from on a broad-based approach to the battle that incorporates prevention, enforcement and education, as well as to a substantial budget.

DELLA PORTA D., MENY Y. (Eds.), *Democracy and Corruption in Europe*, Pinter, 1996 (also available in French (La Découverte, 1995), Italian (Liguori Editore) and Portuguese (Editorial Inquérito)).

> This book contains socio-political analyses of corruption as a flaw of democratic societies in France, Italy, the United Kingdom, Germany, Spain, Russia and Japan, as well as in Franco-African relations. The overview is supplemented by a presentation of the various economic

approaches to corruption. The book offers the beginnings of a comparative analysis of corruption in democratic societies. It is an initial European exploration of the subject.

DELLA PORTA D., VANUCCI A., *Corrupt Exchanges: Actors, Resources and Mechanisms of Political Corruption (Social Problems and Social Issues)*, Aldine De Gruyter, 1999.

This sociological study explores the workings of corruption in Italy, focusing on influence-peddling, through votes for favours and government jobs in exchange for political allegiance. It shows how tainted politicians protected by the system soon become arrogant and greedy. The book draws on court trials to dissect three corruption cases and offers a socio-political and organisational theory about connivance-based forms of Italian corruption involving clans, businesses and political factions.

Déviances et Société: La Justice Face à la Corruption, Vol. 20, No. 3, 1996.

This issue of the journal features in-depth analyses by political scientists and legal experts of the causes of corruption and reactions that have been building up over the past decade, focusing on cases in France, the United Kingdom, Spain, Italy, Germany and Switzerland.

ELLIOTT K. A. (Ed.), *Corruption and the Global Economy*, Washington DC, Institute for International Economics, 1997.

This book examines corruption through incisive contributions by specialists in the subject: Glynn et al. on the end of the Cold War and America's desire for an international law similar to the FCPA; Rose-Akerman and Mauro on economics; Johnston on political science; Pieth on international efforts and the various treaties; Heimann on initiatives and the role of the private sector. In his lengthy conclusion, Elliott offers a wealth of information on the various controversies about the causes of corruption (too much government?), the consequences (diverse?), the cost of international corruption, disputed evaluations of the effects of the FCPA and the relative effectiveness of the various corruption-fighting weapons in existence.

Finance & Development: Fighting Corruption Worldwide, March 1998 (also available in French).

This issue features contributions by three experts working for international organisations (World Bank and IMF) on problems of international or regional co-operation in fighting corruption, and on problems with quantifying corruption's harmful effects.

GUPTA S., DAVOODI H., ALONSO-THERME R., *Does Corruption Affect Inequality and Poverty,* Working Paper WP/98/76, Washington, International Monetary Fund, 1998.

High and rising corruption increases income inequality and poverty by inter alia reducing economic growth, the progressivity of the tax system, the level and effectiveness of social spending and the formation of human capital. Policies that reduce corruption will also lower income inequality and poverty.

HARRISS-WHITE B., WHITE G., "Corruption, Liberalisation and Democracy", *IDS Bulletin (Liberalisation and the New Corruption)*, Vol. 27, No. 2, 1996.

The authors find that, in most of the major developing economies, economic liberalisation and democratisation have not had the effects on corruption that most economists and political experts were expecting. It seems that in China and India, corruption has in fact increased in the wake of liberalisation, and that South Korea saw an explosion of corruption following democratisation. The authors therefore speak in terms of old corruption, stemming from economic rents and authoritarian regimes, and new corruption, which is taking root along with liberalisation and democratisation. Articles on India, China, South Korea, the Philippines, Thailand and Argentina illustrate the theory and expose the obstacles facing the anti-corruption strategies of the international organisations as they take on deep-rooted corruption.

HEIDENHEIMER A., JOHNSTON M., LEVINE V.T., *Political Corruption: A Handbook*, New Brunswick, Transactions Publishers, 1989.

This book is a must for any researcher beginning to look into the subject. It combines some sixty articles dealing with a wide range of disciplines, methods and points of view. Readers can grasp the nature of the major controversies that existed before the subject came into fashion in the 1990s. The book is divided into sections on, inter alia: definitions, historical analyses of the creation of modern and contemporary States, work on corruption and influence-peddling, studies on corruption in the major developing economies, developed countries and Soviet-style regimes, thoughts on the processes that give rise to scandals, and how perceptions of the phenomenon are changing, depending on the manner in which economic and political power is legitimated. Reading a variety of articles (*e.g.* those by Huntington, Leff, Nye and Scott) provides an introduction to the debate between functionalists, who saw corruption as speeding transitions to modernity, and reformers.

HINES J., *Forbidden Payment: Foreign Bribery and American Business after 1977*, Working Paper, No. 5266, National Bureau of Economic Research, 1995.

The author points to an econometric study to claim that US exports declined after FCPA took effect, putting American firms at a disadvantage without diminishing the global phenomenon of corruption.

"Host Country Tax Treatmant of Foreign Bribes and Commissions: Belgium, Canada, Denmark, France, Germany, Ireland, Italy, Japan, the Netherlands, Spain, Swizerland, United Kingdom, United States", *Tax Management International Forum*, Vol. 18, No. 3, September 1997, BNA International Inc.

A quarterly comparative discussion of international tax law problems by distinguished practitioners in major industrial countries

INTERNATIONAL CHAMBER OF COMMERCE, *Fighting Bribery, a Corporate Practices Manual,* ICC Publishing SA, 1999.

The book describes, based on case studies and corporate codes of conduct, how companies can develop strategies against bribery. It also advises managers and employees to the need to be alert to the dangers of bribery and suggests means they can use to combat it.

International Social Science Journal: Corruption in Western Democracies, No. 149, 1996 (also available in French).

This issue features social science contributions about corruption in Western democracies. It explores the multiplicity of definitions and corruption in France and Italy. It offers comparative analyses of the phenomenon in Europe and a study of corruption at international level.

JAIN A.K. (Ed.), *Economics of Corruption,* Kluwer Academic Publishers, 1998.

Essential elements of different economic and legal approaches that have been used to understand corruption are brought together in this book. It proposes to shift away from the bribery-type activities to corruption that distorts economic policies and attempts to define and model corruption.

JAMIESON A., "Political Corruption in Western Europe: Judiciary and Executive in Conflict", *Conflict Studies*, Vol. 288, RISCT, March 1996.

The author notes the increasing frequency of conflict between the executive branch, economic interests and the judiciary during investigations. Independent judges are indispensable.

JOHNSON S., KAUFMANN D., ZOIDO-LOMBATON P., *Corruption, Public Finances, and the Unofficial Economy,* WPS No. 2169, World Bank, August 1999, No. 2169.

On the basis of a sample of 49 Latin American, OECD the authors demonstrate that countries with a large unofficial economy tend to grow more slowly. The size of the unofficial economy is increased by the ineffective and discretionary administration of tax and regulatory regimes as well as corruption.

JOHNSTON M., *What Can Be Done about Entrenched Corruption,* Paper presented at the Annual World Bank Conference on Development Economics 1997, 1998.

This political science article makes a distinction between political and administrative corruption to show how to achieve a low level of corruption in the major developing economies thanks to a succession of reforms ensuring the credibility of economic commitments, human rights, civil liberties and political competition. Such reforms should make it possible to boost growth and enhance the responsibility of civil servants, thereby yielding more credibility and civil liberties. The journal's same issue features an article by Rose-Akerman reporting on the current state of economic analysis.

Journal Of Law And Society: Corruption of Politics and Politics of Corruption, Vol. 23, No. 1, 1996.

A special issue on corruption, scandals, the potential for deterioration and the crisis of legitimisation of the State in Western democracies (USA, France, Italy, United Kingdom, Israel).

KLITGAARD R., *Controlling Corruption*, University of California Press, 1988 (French translation available from Nouveaux Horizons, 1995).

The first book devoted to the fight against corruption in the major developing economies. Drawing on several case studies and a great deal of economic and management analysis, the author proposes an anti-corruption programme based on a gradual enhancing of transparency. The strategy is a mixture of prevention, enforcement, government performance evaluation, the appointment of auditors and the creation of specialised agencies.

KLITGAARD R., *Adjusting to Reality,* Institute for Contemporary Studies, California, 1991.

How can governments shift from controlling economic development to facilitating it? How can the market place be made to serve the poor as well as the advantaged?

KRUG S., *Korruption in verschiedenen Wirtschaftssystemen,* Universitätsverlag, 1997.

Corruption is to be found in all economic systems. It only differs in size and shape. Processes in economies in transition can be slowed down or speeded up by corruption.

LAMBSDORFF J., *An Empirical Investigation of Bribery in International Trade*, University of Göttingen, 1997.

The author proposes an initial econometric method for quantifying the proclivity of exporting countries to pay bribes to foreign civil servants. The method, which is still being discussed, has sparked a debate over the developed democratic countries' lack of morality in international trade.

LANGE H., LÖHR A., STEINMANN H., *Working across Cultures, Ethical Perspectives for Intercultural Management*, Kluwer Academic Publishers, 1998.

This book offers a collection of texts on economic and legal aspects of international corruption, values and ethics in the corporate transformation process and reflection on cross-cultural issues of business ethics.

LANGSETH P., STAPENHURST R., *National Integrity System Country Studies*, EDI, World Bank, 1997.

The authors present the World Bank's anti-corruption strategy based on the concept of good governance. It entails public sector reform, the presence of reformers in government, and a mobilisation of civil society, including the private sector, to support them. Details of the strategy are described in the cases of Uganda and Tanzania. The report highlights the many economic and political obstacles along the path to integrity in the major developing economies.

LEON P. de, *Thinking about Political Corruption,* M.E. Sharpe, 1993.

According to the author, the US political system encourages or condones political corruption. Based on this perspective, the author develops a theoretical model of political corruption that enables one to understand the ways in which the costs of corruption might be alleviated.

LITTLE W., POSADA-CARBO E. (Eds.), *Political Corruption in Europe and in Latin America*, Macmillan, 1996.

The book is made up of three parts. Part I presents historical analyses of pre-20th century corruption, Part II offers methods to assess corruption in European countries (Spain, Italy, France, United Kingdom), and Part III features studies of corruption in Latin America (Brazil, Mexico, Paraguay, Venezuela).

MANACORDA S., *La Corruzione Internazionale del Pubblico Agente*, Casa Editrice Dott. Eugenio Jovese, 1999.

Criminological and international penal law aspects are taken into account to describe various aspects of international corruption. This book also describes the influence of various anti-corruption conventions on the Italian domestic legislation.

MANFRODI C. A., *Soborno Transnacional,* Abeledo-Perrot, 1998.

> Transnational corruption in the context of global capitalism. The author describes influence of the FCPA, the OAS convention and the 1997 Bribery Convention on national legislation.

MAURO P., "The Effects of Corruption on Growth, Investment and Government Expenditure" in Elliott, op. cit., pp. 83-108.

> This econometric study has been cited very frequently to show the economic cost of corruption. For the author, corruption sharply reduces investment and growth and creates heavy distortions in government spending in favour of the sectors offering the greatest bribes (construction/public works and arms, to the detriment of education).

MENY Y., *La corruption de la République*, Fayard, 1992.

> One of the first books to deal with corruption in a reputedly upright European democracy (France). The author stresses the problems of financing party politics and the patterns of opportunity arising from the dimness with which conflicts of interest are perceived, and from multiple office-holding, lucrative private sector jobs for civil servants and the blurring of the borders between the public and private sectors.

Mondes en Développement : De l'Ancienne à la Nouvelle Corruption dans les Pays en Développement, No. 102, 1998.

> This issue is composed of two parts. The first presents three economic articles dealing with the causes and consequences of corruption, as well as strategies for combating it. The second features socio-political studies of corruption in sub-Saharan Africa, Latin America, Russia and China.

MOODY-STUART G., *Grand Corruption*, World View Publishing, 1997.

> The scale and means of corruption in business transactions between the North and the South is a source of confusion for many businessperson. The line between legitimate trade and corruption is a fine one and not always recognisable. Apart from that, in many cultures bribery is accepted as an inevitable part of business. More transparency is needed and principles of fair dealing should be applicable throughout the world.

MORRIS S.D., *Corruption and Politics in Contemporary Mexico*, University of Alabama Press, 1991.

> For a better understanding of the politics in Mexico a systematic analysis of corruption is essential. This book is based on reports from the Mexican press, a public opinion poll as well as on personal interviews. Scandals and examples of corruption are discussed. The central question is whether, in fact corruption has enhanced or diminished the stability of the Mexican government. The reasons that many anti-corruption efforts have failed are examined.

NOOHAN J., *Bribes*, Macmillan, 1984.

> One of the first to take a socio-judicial approach to corruption, based on numerous case studies.

OECD DEVELOPMENT CENTRE, UNDP, *Corruption & Integrity Improvement Initiative in Developing Countries*, Paris, 1998.

> Includes articles by the leading specialists on the subject, dealing with relationships between corruption and the economy and political regimes, weapons to combat it and actions taken by international organisations.

OECD, *Public Sector Corruption, an International Survey of Prevention Measures*, Paris, OECD, 1999.

> If governments seek to provide their citizens with a trustworthy and effective framework for economic and social life, integrity is a fundamental precondition. To prevent corruption, specific prevention techniques and effective law and law enforcement are crucial. The book gives an overview of the measures 15 OECD countries are currently using to protect their domestic public institutions against corruption.

OECD, *Ensuring Ethical Conduct in the Public Service: From Analysis to Action*, Paris, OECD, 2000 (forthcoming).

> This book analyses the main challenges public services are facing as well as the different approaches in managing government ethics in OECD countries. It introduces the OECD Principles for Managing Ethics in the Public Service that serve as a practical instrument for managers to review their public service environment.

Parliamentary Affairs: Sleaze: Politics, Private Interests and Public Reaction, Vol. 48, No. 4, 1995.

> The relationship between scandals and corruption in Western democracies is addressed by a large number of contributors using cases from the United Kingdom, the United States, Denmark, France, Germany, Greece, Ireland and Italy. This compilation provides the basis for a comparative analysis of corruption in market democracies.

PENA Y ESTADO, *Corrupción de Funcionarios Públicos*, Editores del Puerto, 1995.

> A collection of papers relating to corruption, good governance and control. What could be the solution for the corruption problem?

PERRY P.J., *Political Corruption and Political Geography*, Dartmouth Pub. Co., 1997.

> This book aims to break down the taboo of political corruption. Corruption is considered as both part of the geographical context in which human activity takes place and as a spatially variable condition explicable at least in part in terms of other geographies.

PIETH M., EIGEN P. (Eds.), *Korruption im internationalen Geschäftsverkehr. Bestandsaufnahme, Bekämpfung, Prävention*, Luchterhand, 1999.

> The damage caused by international corruption world-wide is severe. It is necessary to tackle this phenomenon on a global scale. Cases of national and international corruption are analysed by various authors. Managers, politicians but also law enforcement agencies looking for effective means to prevent and combat corruption find instruments to do so in this book.

POLINSKY A. M., SHAVELL S., *Corruption and Optimal Law Enforcement*, Working Paper No. 6945, National Bureau of Economic Research, 1999.

> An analysis of the corruption of law enforcement agents: payment of bribes to agents so that they will not report violations. Corruption dilutes deterrence because bribes payments are less than sanctions.

"The Political Consequence of Corruption: A Reassessment", *Comparative Politics*, 1986, pp. 459-477.

> This landmark article presents the first major typology explaining how the severity of the harmful effects of corruption depends on the nature of dealings between the people being corrupted and those corrupting them, and the number, frequency and organisation of their transactions.

Political Corruption and Public Policy in America, Cole Publishing Company, 1982.

> The book presents different definitions of corruption and analyses corruption from the standpoint of political systems, focusing on the role of money in politics. This classic work ends with a study of American political machines, Watergate and the difficulties of carrying out reforms.

Political Studies: Political Corruption, Vol. 45, No. 3, 1997.

> This review looks at political corruption, the problems it poses and research prospects, presenting economic and socio-economic studies and case studies on Italy, Russia and the fight against corruption in the United Kingdom and the European Union.

Revue Internationale de Politique Comparée: La corruption, Vol. 4, No. 2, 1997.

> This journal publishes comparative analyses only. The articles in this issue include: studies on corruption in Western Europe, corruption in the French and Spanish Socialist parties, corruption in South-East Asia, corruption in South Korea and Nigeria, corruption in Africa and East Asia and international corruption and sub-Saharan Africa. The bibliographies are very comprehensive.

RIDER B.A.K. (Ed.), *Corruption: The Enemy Within*, Kluwer Law International, 1997.

> A selection of papers presented at the 14th International Symposium on Economic Crime which centred on the prevention and control of corrupt practices. Corruption and associated crimes attack from within the integrity and therefore the efficiency of institutions, both in public and private sectors. The control of corrupt practices requires an integrated strategy involving preventive and response measures. Various aspects of corruption are addressed on a multidisciplinary basis and cover a variety of jurisdictions.

RIJCKEGHEM C. van, WEDER B., *Corruption and the Rate of Temptation: Do low wages in the Civil Service Cause Corruption?*, Working Paper WP/97/73, Washington, International Monetary Fund, 1997.

> Two efficiency wage models of corruption in the civil service are developed and tested. The empirical evidence points to a negative relationship between corruption and wages across developing countries.

ROSE-ACKERMAN S., *Corruption and Government: Causes, Consequences, and Reform*, Cambridge University Press, 1999.

> In this book, the author, who is the international specialist on the subject who has written numerous economic articles in most of the journals that have addressed this topic, summarises her economic analysis of corruption in the major developing economies. She sets out the causes, consequences and ways of fighting corruption – political (democratisation), economic (institutional and legal reforms) and international (the roles of multilateral organisations). A landmark book on corruption in the most developed economies, it draws on numerous case studies and features an extremely complete bibliography.

ROSE-ACKERMAN S., *Corruption: A Study in Political Economy*, Academic Press, New York, 1978.

> The definitive academic microeconomic analysis of corruption as a phenomenon that brings political, bureaucratic and economic markets into contact. The author dissociates legislative and administrative corruption and proposes counter-measures tailored to each situation. The frame of reference is the American model of pluralistic democracy.

ROSENN K.S., *Corruption and Political Reform in Brazil: The Impact of Collor's Impeachment*, University of Miami North-South Center, 1999.

> Examining the fall of Fernando Collor de Mello, the book focuses on linkages between corruption and political reform, such as people seeking to maximise personal returns, processes that impede financial accountability and the impact of power.

SAVONA E.U., MEZZANOTTE, L., *La Corruzione in Europa*, Carocci Editore, 1998.

> An analysis is given of corruption in various countries of the European Union. This analysis is based on studies of various cases throughout various countries. The structure of corruption is examined, paying attention to the people involved, the instruments and methods used. Examples can be found of different forms in which corruption may occur: systemic, sporadic and occasional corruption.

SCOTT J.C., *Comparative Political Corruption*, Englewood Cliffs, Prentice-Hall, 1972.

> The book for political scientists. It sets forth all of the problems, analysing the various forms of corruption (economic exchanges and social exchanges) as methods of exerting politico-economic influence unique to each type of regulatory system. For the author, corruption cannot be analysed without a detailed study of its functions and the forms of legitimisation of economic and political power it makes possible through the exchanges typical of influence-peddling: favours, privileges and government contracts or appointments in exchange for votes, money or loyalty. The typologies of influence-peddling and patrimonialistic systems are illustrated with case studies involving Thailand, American political machines, India and Ghana.

SHLEIFER A., VISHNY R.W., *Corruption*, Working Paper No. 4372, National Bureau of Economic Research, 1993.

> Two propositions about corruption. First the structure of government institutions and the political process form a very important determinant of the level of corruption. Second, the illegality of corruption and the need for secrecy make it distortionary and costly. This might explain why in some developing countries, corruption is so high and so costly to development.

SIGMA, *Promoting Performance and Professionalism in the Public Service,* SIGMA Paper No. 21, Paris, OECD, 1997.

> A report on human resources management practices in the public administrations of Albania, Estonia, Hungary and Poland. It aims to determine to what extent the implementation of a specific law for employment in the administration would lead to significant changes in personnel management or in the preconditions for management, selection and promotion of staff.

STAPENHURST R., KPUNDEH S.J. (Eds.), *Curbing Corruption: Toward a Model for Building National Integrity,* World Bank, 1999.

> On the basis of experiences gathered in various countries like Hong Kong, China, Singapore and Bolivia and case studies from Tanzania, Uganda and Sierra Leone, the authors establish an overview of the costs of corruption and suggest strategies of how to combat it.

TANZI V., "Corruption Around the World: Causes, Consequences, Scope and Cures", *Staff Papers*, Vol. 45, No. 4, Washington, International Monetary Fund, 1998, pp. 559-594.

> The phenomenon is now out in the open and is being studied in all countries, because the end of the Cold War has put an end to the hypocrisy and cleared the way for information making it conceivable to battle corruption.

TANZI V., DAVOODI H., *Corruption, Public Investment and Growth,* Working Paper WP/97/139, Washington, International Monetary Fund, 1997.

> Corruption and especially "grand" corruption distorts the entire decision making process connected with public investment projects. The degree of distortion is higher with weaker auditing institutions.

THEOBALD R., *Corruption, Development and Underdevelopment,* Macmillan, 1990.

> This work takes a multidisciplinary approach, blending history, sociology and political science, with major issues involving corruption, dealing with the problem in respect to the major developing economies and developed countries alike.

THOMPSON D.F., *Ethics in Congress: From the Individual to Institutional Corruption,* Brookings Institute, 1995.

> The demand for accountability in the political environment has rendered traditional codes of conduct inadequate. Less familiar forms of corruption, such as implicit understanding and political advantage are identified.

TRANSPARENCY INTERNATIONAL, *The TI Source Book*, 1996.

> The reference work of the non-governmental organisation for the fight against corruption, setting forth its analytical framework and its analysis of various weapons (democratisation, mobilisation of civil society, administrative reforms, improvements to the legal and judicial system, creation of a corps of auditors, freedom of the press, international aid).

TRANSPARENCY INTERNATIONAL (USA), *Corporate Anti-corruption Programs: A Survey of Best Practices*, Washington, 1996.

> A handbook with sample codes of ethics containing anti-corruption clauses, and hypothetical case studies on use of the codes and compliance with FCPA.

WEBSTER W.H. (Ed.), CSIS GLOBAL ORGANISED CRIME PROJECT, *Russian Organised Crime: Global Organised Crime Project*, 1997.

> The breadth and depth of Russian organised crime and corruption is analysed in order to understand the corrupt state, the corruption in bureaucracy and the systematic roots of corruption and criminality in Russia.

WEI S-J, *Corruption in Economic Development*, WPS No. 2048, World Bank, February 1999.

> Corruption is a major obstacle to economic development. International pressure against corruption is useful, but more critical is reform of domestic institutions and a focus on the incentive problem. Abuse of power by public officials should not pay.

WEI S-J, *How Taxing is Corruption on International Investors?*, Working Paper No. 6030, National Bureau of Economic Research, 1997.

> What are the effects of corruption on foreign direct investment? Bilateral investment from 14 source countries to 45 host countries in the period 1990-91. The paper contains three central findings.

WOODALL B., *Japan under Construction: Corruption, Politics and Public Works*, University of California Press, 1996.

> A profile is given of the institutionalised system of bid-rigging in the public construction market. The powerful positions of unelected bureaucrats is explored, detailing recent scandals and reform movements.

WORLD BANK, *Helping Countries Combat Corruption: The Role of the World Bank*, Washington, 1997.

> The Bank's definitive work on the subject since fighting corruption has become a priority for the organisation. Indispensable for grasping the Bank's motives and the proposed policies.

WORLD BANK, *World Development Report 1997: The State in a Changing World,* Washington, 1997 (also available in French).

> The World Bank's general survey of its new approach to State intervention in the major developing economies based on the concept of good governance: the State is both the problem and the solution. Each chapter enumerates the problems (arbitrary action, a lack of transparency and fragility of institutions) and proposed solutions (liberalisation, administrative reforms and mobilisation of civil society). An advantage of the book is that the conclusion explains how to tailor the available resources to each type of politico-economic regime. Chapter 6 ("Restraining Arbitrary State Action and Corruption") sets forth the essence of the World Bank's strategy.

ZIMMERMAN, Joseph, *Curbing Unethical Behavior in Government*, Greenwood Pub Group, 1994.

Governments need to initiate special efforts to eliminate unethical behaviour by public officers and employees. Special controls should be installed to detect and deter unethical behaviour.

Convention on Combating Bribery of Foreign Public Officials in International Business Transactions

Adopted by the Negotiating Conference on 21 November 1997

Preamble

The Parties,

Considering that bribery is a widespread phenomenon in international business transactions, including trade and investment, which raises serious moral and political concerns, undermines good governance and economic development, and distorts international competitive conditions;

Considering that all countries share a responsibility to combat bribery in international business transactions;

Having regard to the Revised Recommendation on Combating Bribery in International Business Transactions, adopted by the Council of the Organisation for Economic Co-operation and Development (OECD) on 23 May 1997, C(97)123/FINAL, which, *inter alia*, called for effective measures to deter, prevent and combat the bribery of foreign public officials in connection with international business transactions, in particular the prompt criminalisation of such bribery in an effective and co-ordinated manner and in conformity with the agreed common elements set out in that Recommendation and with the jurisdictional and other basic legal principles of each country;

Welcoming other recent developments which further advance international understanding and co-operation in combating bribery of public officials, including actions of the United Nations, the World Bank, the International Monetary Fund, the World Trade Organisation, the Organisation of American States, the Council of Europe and the European Union;

Welcoming the efforts of companies, business organisations and trade unions as well as other non-governmental organisations to combat bribery;

Recognising the role of governments in the prevention of solicitation of bribes from individuals and enterprises in international business transactions;

Recognising that achieving progress in this field requires not only efforts on a national level but also multilateral co-operation, monitoring and follow-up;

Recognising that achieving equivalence among the measures to be taken by the Parties is an essential object and purpose of the Convention, which requires that the Convention be ratified without derogations affecting this equivalence;

Have agreed as follows:

Article 1
The Offence of Bribery of Foreign Public Officials

1.   Each Party shall take such measures as may be necessary to establish that it is a criminal offence under its law for any person intentionally to offer, promise or give any undue pecuniary or other advantage, whether directly or through intermediaries, to a foreign public official, for that official or for a third party, in order that the official act or refrain from acting in relation to the performance of official duties, in order to obtain or retain business or other improper advantage in the conduct of international business.

2.   Each Party shall take any measures necessary to establish that complicity in, including incitement, aiding and abetting, or authorisation of an act of bribery of a foreign public official shall be a criminal offence. Attempt and conspiracy to bribe a foreign public official shall be criminal offences to the same extent as attempt and conspiracy to bribe a public official of that Party.

3.   The offences set out in paragraphs 1 and 2 above are hereinafter referred to as "bribery of a foreign public official".

4.   For the purpose of this Convention:

   a) foreign public official" means any person holding a legislative, administrative or judicial office of a foreign country, whether appointed or elected; any person exercising a public function for a foreign country, including for a public agency or public enterprise; and any official or agent of a public international organisation;

   b) "foreign country" includes all levels and subdivisions of government, from national to local;

   c) "act or refrain from acting in relation to the performance of official duties" includes any use of the public official's position, whether or not within the official's authorised competence.

Article 2
Responsibility of Legal Persons

   Each Party shall take such measures as may be necessary, in accordance with its legal principles, to establish the liability of legal persons for the bribery of a foreign public official.

Article 3
Sanctions

1.   The bribery of a foreign public official shall be punishable by effective, proportionate and dissuasive criminal penalties. The range of penalties shall be comparable to that applicable to the bribery of the Party's own public officials and shall, in the case of natural persons, include deprivation of liberty sufficient to enable effective mutual legal assistance and extradition.

2.   In the event that, under the legal system of a Party, criminal responsibility is not applicable to legal persons, that Party shall ensure that legal persons shall be subject to effective, proportionate and dissuasive non-criminal sanctions, including monetary sanctions, for bribery of foreign public officials.

3.   Each Party shall take such measures as may be necessary to provide that the bribe and the proceeds of the bribery of a foreign public official, or property the value of which corresponds to that of such proceeds, are subject to seizure and confiscation or that monetary sanctions of comparable effect are applicable.

4.   Each Party shall consider the imposition of additional civil or administrative sanctions upon a person subject to sanctions for the bribery of a foreign public official.

Article 4
Jurisdiction

1.   Each Party shall take such measures as may be necessary to establish its jurisdiction over the bribery of a foreign public official when the offence is committed in whole or in part in its territory.

2.   Each Party which has jurisdiction to prosecute its nationals for offences committed abroad shall take such measures as may be necessary to establish its jurisdiction to do so in respect of the bribery of a foreign public official, according to the same principles.

3.   When more than one Party has jurisdiction over an alleged offence described in this Convention, the Parties involved shall, at the request of one of them, consult with a view to determining the most appropriate jurisdiction for prosecution.

4.   Each Party shall review whether its current basis for jurisdiction is effective in the fight against the bribery of foreign public officials and, if it is not, shall take remedial steps.

Article 5
Enforcement

Investigation and prosecution of the bribery of a foreign public official shall be subject to the applicable rules and principles of each Party. They shall not be influenced by considerations of national economic interest, the potential effect upon relations with another State or the identity of the natural or legal persons involved.

Article 6
Statute of Limitations

Any statute of limitations applicable to the offence of bribery of a foreign public official shall allow an adequate period of time for the investigation and prosecution of this offence.

Article 7
Money Laundering

Each Party which has made bribery of its own public official a predicate offence for the purpose of the application of its money laundering legislation shall do so on the same terms for the bribery of a foreign public official, without regard to the place where the bribery occurred.

Article 8
Accounting

1.   In order to combat bribery of foreign public officials effectively, each Party shall take such measures as may be necessary, within the framework of its laws and regulations regarding the maintenance of books and records, financial statement disclosures, and accounting and auditing standards, to prohibit the establishment of off-the-books accounts, the making of off-the-books or inadequately identified transactions, the recording of non-existent expenditures, the entry of liabilities with incorrect identification of their object, as well as the use of false documents, by companies subject to those laws and regulations, for the purpose of bribing foreign public officials or of hiding such bribery.

2.   Each Party shall provide effective, proportionate and dissuasive civil, administrative or criminal penalties for such omissions and falsifications in respect of the books, records, accounts and financial statements of such companies.

Article 9
Mutual Legal Assistance

1.   Each Party shall, to the fullest extent possible under its laws and relevant treaties and arrangements, provide prompt and effective legal assistance to another Party for the purpose of criminal investigations and proceedings brought by a Party concerning offences within the scope of this Convention and for non-criminal proceedings within the scope of this Convention brought by a Party against a legal person. The requested Party shall inform the requesting Party, without delay, of any additional information or documents needed to support the request for assistance and, where requested, of the status and outcome of the request for assistance.

2.   Where a Party makes mutual legal assistance conditional upon the existence of dual criminality, dual criminality shall be deemed to exist if the offence for which the assistance is sought is within the scope of this Convention.

3.   A Party shall not decline to render mutual legal assistance for criminal matters within the scope of this Convention on the ground of bank secrecy.

Article 10
Extradition

1.   Bribery of a foreign public official shall be deemed to be included as an extraditable offence under the laws of the Parties and the extradition treaties between them.

2.   If a Party which makes extradition conditional on the existence of an extradition treaty receives a request for extradition from another Party with which it has no extradition treaty, it may consider this Convention to be the legal basis for extradition in respect of the offence of bribery of a foreign public official.

3.   Each Party shall take any measures necessary to assure either that it can extradite its nationals or that it can prosecute its nationals for the offence of bribery of a foreign public official. A Party which declines a request to extradite a person for bribery of a foreign public official solely on the ground that the person is its national shall submit the case to its competent authorities for the purpose of prosecution.

4.   Extradition for bribery of a foreign public official is subject to the conditions set out in the domestic law and applicable treaties and arrangements of each Party. Where a Party makes extradition conditional upon the existence of dual criminality, that condition shall be deemed to be ful-

filled if the offence for which extradition is sought is within the scope of Article 1 of this Convention.

Article 11
Responsible Authorities

For the purposes of Article 4, paragraph 3, on consultation, Article 9, mutual legal assistance and Article 10, on extradition each Party shall notify to the Secretary-General of the OECD an authority or authorities responsible for making and receiving requests, which shall serve as channel of communication for these matters for that Party, without prejudice to other arrangements between Parties.

Article 12
Monitoring and Follow-up

The Parties shall co-operate in carrying out a programme of systematic follow-up to monitor and promote the full implementation of this Convention. Unless otherwise decided by consensus of the Parties, this shall be done in the framework of the OECD Working Group on Bribery in International Business Transactions and according to its terms of reference, or within the framework and terms of reference of any successor to its functions, and Parties shall bear the costs of the programme in accordance with the rules applicable to that body.

Article 13
Signature and Accession

1.	Until its entry into force, this Convention shall be open for signature by OECD members and by non-members which have been invited to become full participants in its Working Group on Bribery in International Business Transactions.

2.	Subsequent to its entry into force, this Convention shall be open to accession by any non-signatory which is a member of the OECD or has become a full participant in the Working Group on Bribery in International Business Transactions or any successor to its functions. For each such non-signatory, the Convention shall enter into force on the sixtieth day following the date of deposit of its instrument of accession.

Article 14
Ratification and Depositary

1.	This Convention is subject to acceptance, approval or ratification by the Signatories, in accordance with their respective laws.

2.	Instruments of acceptance, approval, ratification or accession shall be deposited with the Secretary-General of the OECD, who shall serve as Depositary of this Convention.

Article 15
Entry into Force

1.	This Convention shall enter into force on the sixtieth day following the date upon which five of the ten countries which have the ten largest export shares set out in DAFFE/IME/BR(97)18/FINAL (annexed), and which represent by themselves at least sixty per cent of the combined total exports of those ten countries, have deposited their instruments of acceptance, approval, or ratification. For each signatory depositing its instrument after such entry into force, the Convention shall enter into force on the sixtieth day after deposit of its instrument.

2.   If, after 31 December 1998, the Convention has not entered into force under paragraph 1 above, any signatory which has deposited its instrument of acceptance, approval or ratification may declare in writing to the Depositary its readiness to accept entry into force of this Convention under this paragraph 2. The Convention shall enter into force for such a signatory on the sixtieth day following the date upon which such declarations have been deposited by at least two signatories. For each signatory depositing its declaration after such entry into force, the Convention shall enter into force on the sixtieth day following the date of deposit.

Article 16
Amendment

Any Party may propose the amendment of this Convention. A proposed amendment shall be submitted to the Depositary which shall communicate it to the other Parties at least sixty days before convening a meeting of the Parties to consider the proposed amendment. An amendment adopted by consensus of the Parties, or by such other means as the Parties may determine by consensus, shall enter into force sixty days after the deposit of an instrument of ratification, acceptance or approval by all of the Parties, or in such other circumstances as may be specified by the Parties at the time of adoption of the amendment.

Article 17
Withdrawal

A Party may withdraw from this Convention by submitting written notification to the Depositary. Such withdrawal shall be effective one year after the date of the receipt of the notification. After withdrawal, co-operation shall continue between the Parties and the Party which has withdrawn on all requests for assistance or extradition made before the effective date of withdrawal which remain pending.

Annex

Statistics on OECD Exports

	OECD Exports		
	1990-1996 US$ million	1990-1996 % of Total OECD	1990-196 % of 10 largest
United States	287 118	15.9	19.7
Germany	254 746	14.1	17.5
Japan	212 665	11.8	14.6
France	138 471	7.7	9.5
United Kingdom	121 258	6.7	8.3
Italy	112 449	6.2	7.7
Canada	91 215	5.1	6.3
Korea (1)	81 364	4.5	5.6
Netherlands	81 264	4.5	5.6
Belgium-Luxembourg	78 598	4.4	5.4
Total 10 Largest	**1 459 148**	**81.0**	**100**
Spain	42 469	2.4	
Switzerland	40 395	2.2	
Sweden	36 710	2.0	
Mexico (1)	34 233	1.9	
Australia	27 194	1.5	
Denmark	24 145	1.3	
Austria*	22 432	1.2	
Norway	21 666	1.2	
Ireland	19 217	1.1	
Finland	17 296	1.0	
Poland (1)*	12 652	0.7	
Portugal	10 801	0.6	
Turkey*	8 027	0.4	
Hungary **	6 795	0.4	
New Zealand	6 663	0.4	
Czech Republic ***	6 263	0.3	
Greece *	4 606	0.3	
Iceland	949	0.1	
Total	**1 801 661**	**100**	

Notes: * 1990-1995; ** 1991-1996; *** 1993-1996.
Source: OECD, (1) IMF.

Concerning Belgium-Luxembourg: Trade statistics for Belgium and Luxembourg are avail-able only on a combined basis for the two countries. For purposes of Article 15, paragraph 1 of the Convention, if either Belgium or Luxembourg deposits its instrument of acceptance, approval or ratification, or if both Belgium and Luxembourg deposit their instruments of acceptance, approval or ratification, it shall be considered that one of the countries which have the ten largest exports shares has deposited its instrument and the joint exports of both countries will be counted towards the 60 per cent of combined total exports of those ten countries, which is required for entry into force under this provision.

Appendix A

Commentaries on the Convention on Combating Bribery of Foreign Public Officials in International Business Transactions

Adopted by the Negotiating Conference on 21 November 1997

General:

1.   This Convention deals with what, in the law of some countries, is called "active corruption" or "active bribery", meaning the offence committed by the person who promises or gives the bribe, as contrasted with "passive bribery", the offence committed by the official who receives the bribe. The Convention does not utilise the term "active bribery" simply to avoid it being misread by the non-technical reader as implying that the briber has taken the initiative and the recipient is a passive victim. In fact, in a number of situations, the recipient will have induced or pressured the briber and will have been, in that sense, the more active.

2.   This Convention seeks to assure a functional equivalence among the measures taken by the Parties to sanction bribery of foreign public officials, without requiring uniformity or changes in fundamental principles of a Party's legal system.

Article 1. The Offence of Bribery of Foreign Public Officials:

Re paragraph 1:

3.   Article 1 establishes a standard to be met by Parties, but does not require them to utilise its precise terms in defining the offence under their domestic laws. A Party may use various approaches to fulfil its obligations, provided that conviction of a person for the offence does not require proof of elements beyond those which would be required to be proved if the offence were defined as in this paragraph. For example, a statute prohibiting the bribery of agents generally which does not specifically address bribery of a foreign public official, and a statute specifically limited to this case, could both comply with this Article. Similarly, a statute which defined the offence in terms of payments "to induce a breach of the official's duty" could meet the standard provided that it was understood that every public official had a duty to exercise judgement or discretion impartially and this was an "autonomous" definition not requiring proof of the law of the particular official's country.

4.   It is an offence within the meaning of paragraph 1 to bribe to obtain or retain business or other improper advantage whether or not the company concerned was the best qualified bidder or was otherwise a company which could properly have been awarded the business.

5.   "Other improper advantage" refers to something to which the company concerned was not clearly entitled, for example, an operating permit for a factory which fails to meet the statutory requirements.

6.   The conduct described in paragraph 1 is an offence whether the offer or promise is made or the pecuniary or other advantage is given on that person's own behalf or on behalf of any other natural person or legal entity.

7.   It is also an offence irrespective of, inter alia, the value of the advantage, its results, perceptions of local custom, the tolerance of such payments by local authorities, or the alleged necessity of the payment in order to obtain or retain business or other improper advantage.

8.   It is not an offence, however, if the advantage was permitted or required by the written law or regulation of the foreign public official's country, including case law.

9.   Small "facilitation" payments do not constitute payments made "to obtain or retain business or other improper advantage" within the meaning of paragraph 1 and, accordingly, are also not an offence. Such payments, which, in some countries, are made to induce public officials to perform their functions, such as issuing licenses or permits, are generally illegal in the foreign country concerned. Other countries can and should address this corrosive phenomenon by such means as support for programmes of good governance. However, criminalisation by other countries does not seem a practical or effective complementary action.

10.   Under the legal system of some countries, an advantage promised or given to any person, in anticipation of his or her becoming a foreign public official, falls within the scope of the offences described in Article 1, paragraph 1 or 2. Under the legal system of many countries, it is considered technically distinct from the offences covered by the present Convention. However, there is a commonly shared concern and intent to address this phenomenon through further work.

Re paragraph 2:

11.   The offences set out in paragraph 2 are understood in terms of their normal content in national legal systems. Accordingly, if authorisation, incitement, or one of the other listed acts, which does not lead to further action, is not itself punishable under a Party's legal system, then the Party would not be required to make it punishable with respect to bribery of a foreign public official.

Re paragraph 4:

12.   "Public function" includes any activity in the public interest, delegated by a foreign country, such as the performance of a task delegated by it in connection with public procurement.

13.   A "public agency" is an entity constituted under public law to carry out specific tasks in the public interest.

14.   A "public enterprise" is any enterprise, regardless of its legal form, over which a government, or governments, may, directly or indirectly, exercise a dominant influence. This is deemed to be the case, inter alia, when the government or governments hold the majority of the enterprise's subscribed capital, control the majority of votes attaching to shares issued by the enterprise or can appoint a majority of the members of the enterprise's administrative or managerial body or supervisory board.

15.   An official of a public enterprise shall be deemed to perform a public function unless the enterprise operates on a normal commercial basis in the relevant market, *i.e*, on a basis which is substantially equivalent to that of a private enterprise, without preferential subsidies or other privileges.

16.   In special circumstances, public authority may in fact be held by persons (*e.g.*, political party officials in single party states) not formally designated as public officials. Such persons, through their *de facto* performance of a public function, may, under the legal principles of some countries, be considered to be foreign public officials.

17.   "Public international organisation" includes any international organisation formed by states, governments, or other public international organisations, whatever the form of organisation and scope of competence, including, for example, a regional economic integration organisation such as the European Communities.

18.   "Foreign country" is not limited to states, but includes any organised foreign area or entity, such as an autonomous territory or a separate customs territory.

© OECD 2000

19.   One case of bribery which has been contemplated under the definition in paragraph 4.c is where an executive of a company gives a bribe to a senior official of a government, in order that this official use his office – though acting outside his competence – to make another official award a contract to that company.

Article 2. Responsibility of Legal Persons:

20.   In the event that, under the legal system of a Party, criminal responsibility is not applicable to legal persons, that Party shall not be required to establish such criminal responsibility.

Article 3. Sanctions:

Re paragraph 3:

21.   The "proceeds" of bribery are the profits or other benefits derived by the briber from the transaction or other improper advantage obtained or retained through bribery.

22.   The term "confiscation" includes forfeiture where applicable and means the permanent deprivation of property by order of a court or other competent authority. This paragraph is without prejudice to rights of victims.

23.   Paragraph 3 does not preclude setting appropriate limits to monetary sanctions.

Re paragraph 4:

24.   Among the civil or administrative sanctions, other than non-criminal fines, which might be imposed upon legal persons for an act of bribery of a foreign public official are: exclusion from entitlement to public benefits or aid; temporary or permanent disqualification from participation in public procurement or from the practice of other commercial activities; placing under judicial supervision; and a judicial winding-up order.

Article 4. Jurisdiction:

Re paragraph 1:

25.   The territorial basis for jurisdiction should be interpreted broadly so that an extensive physical connection to the bribery act is not required.

Re paragraph 2:

26.   Nationality jurisdiction is to be established according to the general principles and conditions in the legal system of each Party. These principles deal with such matters as dual criminality. However, the requirement of dual criminality should be deemed to be met if the act is unlawful where it occurred, even if under a different criminal statute. For countries which apply nationality jurisdiction only to certain types of offences, the reference to "principles" includes the principles upon which such selection is based.

Article 5. Enforcement:

27.   Article 5 recognises the fundamental nature of national regimes of prosecutorial discretion. It recognises as well that, in order to protect the independence of prosecution, such discretion is to be exercised on the basis of professional motives and is not to be subject to improper influence by concerns of a political nature. Article 5 is complemented by paragraph 6 of the Annex to the 1997 OECD Revised Recommendation on Combating Bribery in International Business Transactions,

C(97)123/FINAL (hereinafter, "1997 OECD Recommendation"), which recommends, inter alia, that complaints of bribery of foreign public officials should be seriously investigated by competent authorities and that adequate resources should be provided by national governments to permit effective prosecution of such bribery. Parties will have accepted this Recommendation, including its monitoring and follow-up arrangements.

Article 7. Money Laundering:

28.   In Article 7, "bribery of its own public official" is intended broadly, so that bribery of a foreign public official is to be made a predicate offence for money laundering legislation on the same terms, when a Party has made either active or passive bribery of its own public official such an offence. When a Party has made only passive bribery of its own public officials a predicate offence for money laundering purposes, this article requires that the laundering of the bribe payment be subject to money laundering legislation.

Article 8. Accounting:

29.   Article 8 is related to section V of the 1997 OECD Recommendation, which all Parties will have accepted and which is subject to follow-up in the OECD Working Group on Bribery in International Business Transactions. This paragraph contains a series of recommendations concerning accounting requirements, independent external audit and internal company controls the implementation of which will be important to the overall effectiveness of the fight against bribery in international business. However, one immediate consequence of the implementation of this Convention by the Parties will be that companies which are required to issue financial statements disclosing their material contingent liabilities will need to take into account the full potential liabilities under this Convention, in particular its Articles 3 and 8, as well as other losses which might flow from conviction of the company or its agents for bribery. This also has implications for the execution of professional responsibilities of auditors regarding indications of bribery of foreign public officials. In addition, the accounting offences referred to in Article 8 will generally occur in the company's home country, when the bribery offence itself may have been committed in another country, and this can fill gaps in the effective reach of the Convention.

Article 9. Mutual Legal Assistance:

30.   Parties will have also accepted, through paragraph 8 of the Agreed Common Elements annexed to the 1997 OECD Recommendation, to explore and undertake means to improve the efficiency of mutual legal assistance.

Re paragraph 1:

31.   Within the framework of paragraph 1 of Article 9, Parties should, upon request, facilitate or encourage the presence or availability of persons, including persons in custody, who consent to assist in investigations or participate in proceedings. Parties should take measures to be able, in appropriate cases, to transfer temporarily such a person in custody to a Party requesting it and to credit time in custody in the requesting Party to the transferred person's sentence in the requested Party. The Parties wishing to use this mechanism should also take measures to be able, as a requesting Party, to keep a transferred person in custody and return this person without necessity of extradition proceedings.

Re paragraph 2:

32.   Paragraph 2 addresses the issue of identity of norms in the concept of dual criminality. Parties with statutes as diverse as a statute prohibiting the bribery of agents generally and a statute directed specifically at bribery of foreign public officials should be able to co-operate fully regarding cases whose facts fall within the scope of the offences described in this Convention.

Article 10. Extradition

Re paragraph 2:

33.   A Party may consider this Convention to be a legal basis for extradition if, for one or more categories of cases falling within this Convention, it requires an extradition treaty. For example, a country may consider it a basis for extradition of its nationals if it requires an extradition treaty for that category but does not require one for extradition of non-nationals.

Article 12. Monitoring and Follow-up:

34.   The current terms of reference of the OECD Working Group on Bribery which are relevant to monitoring and follow-up are set out in Section VIII of the 1997 OECD Recommendation. They provide for:

  i) receipt of notifications and other information submitted to it by the [participating] countries;

  ii) regular reviews of steps taken by [participating] countries to implement the Recommendation and to make proposals, as appropriate, to assist [participating] countries in its implementation; these reviews will be based on the following complementary systems:

  – a system of self evaluation, where [participating] countries' responses on the basis of a questionnaire will provide a basis for assessing the implementation of the Recommendation;

  – a system of mutual evaluation, where each [participating] country will be examined in turn by the Working Group on Bribery, on the basis of a report which will provide an objective assessment of the progress of the [participating] country in implementing the Recommendation.

  iii) examination of specific issues relating to bribery in international business transactions;

  ...

  v) provision of regular information to the public on its work and activities and on implementation of the Recommendation.

35.   The costs of monitoring and follow-up will, for OECD Members, be handled through the normal OECD budget process. For non-members of the OECD, the current rules create an equivalent system of cost sharing, which is described in the Resolution of the Council Concerning Fees for Regular Observer Countries and Non-Member Full Participants in OECD Subsidiary Bodies, C(96)223/FINAL.

36.   The follow-up of any aspect of the Convention which is not also follow-up of the 1997 OECD Recommendation or any other instrument accepted by all the participants in the OECD Working Group on Bribery will be carried out by the Parties to the Convention and, as appropriate, the participants party to another, corresponding instrument.

Article 13. Signature and Accession:

37.   The Convention will be open to non-members which become full participants in the OECD Working Group on Bribery in International Business Transactions. Full participation by non-members in this Working Group is encouraged and arranged under simple procedures. Accordingly, the requirement of full participation in the Working Group, which follows from the relationship of the Convention to other aspects of the fight against bribery in international business, should not be seen as an obstacle by countries wishing to participate in that fight. The Council of the OECD has appealed to non-members to adhere to the 1997 OECD Recommendation and to participate in any institutional follow-up or implementation mechanism, *i.e*, in the Working Group. The current procedures regarding full participation by non-members in the Working Group may be found in the Resolution of the Council concerning the Participation of Non-Member Economies in the Work of Subsidiary Bodies of the Organisation, C(96)64/REV1/FINAL. In addition to accepting the Revised Recommendation of the Council on Combating Bribery, a full participant also accepts the Recommendation on the Tax Deductibility of Bribes of Foreign Public Officials, adopted on 11 April 1996, C(96)27/FINAL.

Appendix B

State of Ratification

Countries having deposited their instrument of ratification of the Convention*

Country	Date of Deposit of Instrument of Acceptance, Approval or Ratification	Date of Examination by the Working Group
1. Iceland	17 August 1998	October 1999
2. Japan	13 October 1998	October 1999
3. Germany	10 November 1998	April 1999
4. Hungary	4 December 1998	October 1999
5. United States	8 December 1998	April 1999
6. Finland	10 December 1998	July 1999
7. United Kingdom	14 December 1998	December 1999
8. Canada	17 December 1998	July 1999
9. Norway	18 December 1998	April 1999
10. Bulgaria	22 December 1998	July 1999
11. Korea	4 January 1999	July 1999
12. Greece	5 February 1999	July 1999
13. Austria	20 May 1999	December 1999
14. Mexico	27 May 1999	February 2000
15. Sweden	8 June 1999	October 1999
16. Belgium	27 July 1999	October 1999
17. Slovak Republic	24 September 1999	February 2000
18. Australia	18 October 1999	December 1999
19. Spain	14 January 2000	March 2000
20. Czech Republic	21 January 2000	March 2000
21. Switzerland	31 May 2000	February 2000

---

* In order of ratification received by the Secretary General, by 21 June 2000.

Revised Recommendation of the Council on Combating Bribery in International Business Transactions

Adopted by the Council on 23 May 1997

THE COUNCIL,

Having regard to Articles 3, 5a) and 5 b) of the Convention on the Organisation for Economic Co-operation and Development of 14 December 1960;

Considering that bribery is a widespread phenomenon in international business transactions, including trade and investment, raising serious moral and political concerns and distorting international competitive conditions;

Considering that all countries share a responsibility to combat bribery in international business transactions;

Considering that enterprises should refrain from bribery of public servants and holders of public office, as stated in the OECD Guidelines for Multinational Enterprises;

Considering the progress which has been made in the implementation of the initial Recommendation of the Council on Bribery in International Business Transactions adopted on 27 May 1994, C(94)75/FINAL and the related Recommendation on the tax deductibility of bribes of foreign public officials adopted on 11 April 1996, C(96)27/FINAL; as well as the Recommendation concerning Anti-corruption Proposals for Bilateral Aid Procurement, endorsed by the High Level Meeting of the Development Assistance Committee on 7 May 1996;

Welcoming other recent developments which further advance international understanding and co-operation regarding bribery in business transactions, including actions of the United Nations, the Council of Europe, the European Union and the Organisation of American States;

Having regard to the commitment made at the meeting of the Council at Ministerial level in May 1996, to criminalise the bribery of foreign public officials in an effective and co-ordinated manner;

Noting that an international convention in conformity with the agreed common elements set forth in the Annex, is an appropriate instrument to attain such criminalisation rapidly.

Considering the consensus which has developed on the measures which should be taken to implement the 1994 Recommendation, in particular, with respect to the modalities and international instruments to facilitate criminalisation of bribery of foreign public officials; tax deductibility of bribes to foreign public officials; accounting requirements, external audit and internal company controls; and rules and regulations on public procurement;

Recognising that achieving progress in this field requires not only efforts by individual countries but multilateral co-operation, monitoring and follow-up;

General

I.   **RECOMMENDS** that Member countries take effective measures to deter, prevent and combat the bribery of foreign public officials in connection with international business transactions.

II.   **RECOMMENDS** that each Member country examine the following areas and, in conformity with its jurisdictional and other basic legal principles, take concrete and meaningful steps to meet this goal:

  i) criminal laws and their application, in accordance with section III and the Annex to this Recommendation;

  ii) tax legislation, regulations and practice, to eliminate any indirect support of bribery, in accordance with section IV;

  iii) company and business accounting, external audit and internal control requirements and practices, in accordance with section V;

  iv) banking, financial and other relevant provisions, to ensure that adequate records would be kept and made available for inspection and investigation;

  v) public subsidies, licences, government procurement contracts or other public advantages, so that advantages could be denied as a sanction for bribery in appropriate cases, and in accordance with section VI for procurement contracts and aid procurement;

  vi) civil, commercial, and administrative laws and regulations, so that such bribery would be illegal;

  vii) international co-operation in investigations and other legal proceedings, in accordance with section VII.

Criminalisation of Bribery of Foreign Public Officials

III.   **RECOMMENDS** that Member countries should criminalise the bribery of foreign public officials in an effective and co-ordinated manner by submitting proposals to their legislative bodies by 1 April 1998, in conformity with the agreed common elements set forth in the Annex, and seeking their enactment by the end of 1998.

  DECIDES, to this end, to open negotiations promptly on an international convention to criminalise bribery in conformity with the agreed common elements, the treaty to be open for signature by the end of 1997, with a view to its entry into force twelve months thereafter.

Tax Deductibility

IV.   **URGES** the prompt implementation by Member countries of the 1996 Recommendation which reads as follows: "that those Member countries which do not disallow the deductibility of bribes to foreign public officials re-examine such treatment with the intention of denying this deductibility. Such action may be facilitated by the trend to treat bribes to foreign officials as illegal."

Accounting Requirements, External Audit and Internal Company Controls

V.   **RECOMMENDS** that Member countries take the steps necessary so that laws, rules and practices with respect to accounting requirements, external audit and internal company controls are in line with the following principles and are fully used in order to prevent and detect bribery of foreign public officials in international business.

A. Adequate accounting requirements

i) Member countries should require companies to maintain adequate records of the sums of money received and expended by the company, identifying the matters in respect of which the receipt and expenditure takes place. Companies should be prohibited from making off-the-books transactions or keeping off-the-books accounts.

ii) Member countries should require companies to disclose in their financial statements the full range of material contingent liabilities.

iii) Member countries should adequately sanction accounting omissions, falsifications and fraud.

B. Independent External Audit

i) Member countries should consider whether requirements to submit to external audit are adequate.

ii) Member countries and professional associations should maintain adequate standards to ensure the independence of external auditors which permits them to provide an objective assessment of company accounts, financial statements and internal controls.

iii) Member countries should require the auditor who discovers indications of a possible illegal act of bribery to report this discovery to management and, as appropriate, to corporate monitoring bodies.

iv) Member countries should consider requiring the auditor to report indications of a possible illegal act of bribery to competent authorities.

C. Internal company controls

i) Member countries should encourage the development and adoption of adequate internal company controls, including standards of conduct.

ii) Member countries should encourage company management to make statements in their annual reports about their internal control mechanisms, including those which contribute to preventing bribery.

iii) Member countries should encourage the creation of monitoring bodies, independent of management, such as audit committees of boards of directors or of supervisory boards.

iv) Member countries should encourage companies to provide channels for communication by, and protection for, persons not willing to violate professional standards or ethics under instructions or pressure from hierarchical superiors.

Public procurement

VI. **RECOMMENDS:**

i) Member countries should support the efforts in the World Trade Organisation to pursue an agreement on transparency in government procurement;

ii) Member countries' laws and regulations should permit authorities to suspend from competition for public contracts enterprises determined to have bribed foreign public officials in contravention of that Member's national laws and, to the extent a Member applies procurement sanctions to enterprises that are determined to have bribed domestic public officials, such sanctions should be applied equally in case of bribery of foreign public officials.[*]

iii) In accordance with the Recommendation of the Development Assistance Committee, Member countries should require anti-corruption provisions in bilateral aid-funded procurement, promote the proper implementation of anti-corruption provisions in international development institutions, and work closely with development partners to combat corruption in all development co-operation efforts.[**]

International Co-operation

VII. **RECOMMENDS** that Member countries, in order to combat bribery in international business transactions, in conformity with their jurisdictional and other basic legal principles, take the following actions:

i) consult and otherwise co-operate with appropriate authorities in other countries in investigations and other legal proceedings concerning specific cases of such bribery through such means as sharing of information (spontaneously or upon request), provision of evidence and extradition;

ii) make full use of existing agreements and arrangements for mutual international legal assistance and where necessary, enter into new agreements or arrangements for this purpose;

iii) ensure that their national laws afford an adequate basis for this co-operation and, in particular, in accordance with paragraph 8 of the Annex.

Follow-up and institutional arrangements

VIII. **INSTRUCTS** the Committee on International Investment and Multinational Enterprises, through its Working Group on Bribery in International Business Transactions, to carry out a programme of systematic follow-up to monitor and promote the full implementation of this Recommendation, in co-operation with the Committee for Fiscal Affairs, the Development Assistance Committee and other OECD bodies, as appropriate. This follow-up will include, in particular:

i) receipt of notifications and other information submitted to it by the Member countries;

ii) regular reviews of steps taken by Member countries to implement the Recommendation and to make proposals, as appropriate, to assist Member countries in its implementation; these reviews will be based on the following complementary systems:

– a system of self-evaluation, where Member countries' responses on the basis of a questionnaire will provide a basis for assessing the implementation of the Recommendation;

– a system of mutual evaluation, where each Member country will be examined in turn by the Working Group on Bribery, on the basis of a report which will provide an

---

[*] Member countries' systems for applying sanctions for bribery of domestic officials differ as to whether the determination of bribery is based on a criminal conviction, indictment or administrative procedure, but in all cases it is based on substantial evidence.

[**] This paragraph summarises the DAC recommendation, which is addressed to DAC members only, and addresses it to all OECD Members and eventually non-member countries which adhere to the Recommendation.

© OECD 2000

objective assessment of the progress of the Member country in implementing the Recommendation.

iii) examination of specific issues relating to bribery in international business transactions;

iv) examination of the feasibility of broadening the scope of the work of the OECD to combat international bribery to include private sector bribery and bribery of foreign officials for reasons other than to obtain or retain business;

v) provision of regular information to the public on its work and activities and on implementation of the Recommendation.

IX. **NOTES** the obligation of Member countries to co-operate closely in this follow-up programme, pursuant to Article 3 of the OECD Convention.

X. **INSTRUCTS** the Committee on International Investment and Multinational Enterprises to review the implementation of Sections III and, in co-operation with the Committee on Fiscal Affairs, Section IV of this Recommendation and report to Ministers in Spring 1998, to report to the Council after the first regular review and as appropriate there after, and to review this Revised Recommendation within three years after its adoption.

Co-operation with non-members

XI. **APPEALS** to non-member countries to adhere to the Recommendation and participate in any institutional follow-up or implementation mechanism.

XII. **INSTRUCTS** the Committee on International Investment and Multinational Enterprises through its Working Group on Bribery, to provide a forum for consultations with countries which have not yet adhered, in order to promote wider participation in the Recommendation and its follow-up.

Relations with international governmental and non-governmental organisations

XIII. **INVITES** the Committee on International Investment and Multinational Enterprises through its Working Group on Bribery, to consult and co-operate with the international organisations and international financial institutions active in the combat against bribery in international business transactions and consult regularly with the non-governmental organisations and representatives of the business community active in this field.

Annex

Agreed Common Elements of Criminal Legislation and Related Action

1) *Elements of the offence of active bribery*

   i) *Bribery* is understood as the promise or giving of any undue payment or other advantages, whether directly or through intermediaries to a public official, for himself or for a third party, to influence the official to act or refrain from acting in the performance of his or her official duties in order to obtain or retain business.

   ii) *Foreign public official* means any person holding a legislative, administrative or judicial office of a foreign country or in an international organisation, whether appointed or elected or, any person exercising a public function or task in a foreign country.

   iii) *The offeror* is any person, on his own behalf or on the behalf of any other natural person or legal entity.

2) *Ancillary elements or offences*

   The general criminal law concepts of attempt, complicity and/or conspiracy of the law of the prosecuting state are recognised as applicable to the offence of bribery of a foreign public official.

3) *Excuses and defences*

   Bribery of foreign public officials in order to obtain or retain business is an offence irrespective of the value or the outcome of the bribe, of perceptions of local custom or of the tolerance of bribery by local authorities.

4) *Jurisdiction*

   Jurisdiction over the offence of bribery of foreign public officials should in any case be established when the offence is committed in whole or in part in the prosecuting State's territory. The territorial basis for jurisdiction should be interpreted broadly so that an extensive physical connection to the bribery act is not required.

   States which prosecute their nationals for offences committed abroad should do so in respect of the bribery of foreign public officials according to the same principles.

   States which do not prosecute on the basis of the nationality principle should be prepared to extradite their nationals in respect of the bribery of foreign public officials.

   All countries should review whether their current basis for jurisdiction is effective in the fight against bribery of foreign public officials and, if not, should take appropriate remedial steps.

5) *Sanctions*

   The offence of bribery of foreign public officials should be sanctioned/punishable by effective, proportionate and dissuasive criminal penalties, sufficient to secure effective mutual legal assistance and extradition, comparable to those applicable to the bribers in cases of corruption of domestic public officials.

Monetary or other civil, administrative or criminal penalties on any legal person involved, should be provided, taking into account the amounts of the bribe and of the profits derived from the transaction obtained through the bribe.

Forfeiture or confiscation of instrumentalities and of the bribe benefits and the profits derived from the transactions obtained through the bribe should be provided, or comparable fines or damages imposed.

6) *Enforcement*

In view of the seriousness of the offence of bribery of foreign public officials, public prose-cutors should exercise their discretion independently, based on professional motives. They should not be influenced by considerations of national economic interest, fostering good political relations or the identity of the victim.

Complaints of victims should be seriously investigated by the competent authorities.

The statute of limitations should allow adequate time to address this complex offence.

National governments should provide adequate resources to prosecuting authorities so as to permit effective prosecution of bribery of foreign public officials.

7) *Connected provisions (criminal and non-criminal)*

   – *Accounting, recordkeeping and disclosure requirements*
     In order to combat bribery of foreign public officials effectively, states should also ade-quately sanction accounting omissions, falsifications and fraud.

   – *Money laundering*
     The bribery of foreign public officials should be made a predicate offence for purposes of money laundering legislation where bribery of a domestic public official is a money laun-dering predicate offence, without regard to the place where the bribery occurs.

8) *International co-operation*

Effective mutual legal assistance is critical to be able to investigate and obtain evidence in order to prosecute cases of bribery of foreign public officials.

Adoption of laws criminalising the bribery of foreign public officials would remove obstacles to mutual legal assistance created by dual criminality requirements.

Countries should tailor their laws on mutual legal assistance to permit co-operation with countries investigating cases of bribery of foreign public officials even including third coun-tries (country of the offeror; country where the act occurred) and countries applying different types of criminalisation legislation to reach such cases.

Means should be explored and undertaken to improve the efficiency of mutual legal assistance.

Annex 3

Recommendation of the Council on the Tax deductibility of Bribes to Foreign Public Officials

Adopted by the Council on 11 April 1996

THE COUNCIL,

Having regard to Article 5 b) of the Convention on the Organisation for Economic Co-operation and Development of 14th December 1960;

Having regard to the OECD Council Recommendation on Bribery in International Business Transactions [C(94)75/FINAL];

Considering that bribery is a widespread phenomenon in international business transactions, including trade and investment, raising serious moral and political concerns and distorting international competitive conditions;

Considering that the Council Recommendation on Bribery called on Member countries to take concrete and meaningful steps to combat bribery in international business transactions, including examining tax measures which may indirectly favour bribery;

On the proposal of the Committee on Fiscal Affairs and the Committee on International Investment and Multinational Enterprises:

I. RECOMMENDS that those Member countries which do not disallow the deductibility of bribes to foreign public officials re-examine such treatment with the intention of denying this deductibility. Such action may be facilitated by the trend to treat bribes to foreign public officials as illegal.

II. INSTRUCTS the Committee on Fiscal Affairs, in cooperation with the Committee on International Investment and Multinational Enterprises, to monitor the implementation of this Recommendation, to promote the Recommendation in the context of contacts with non-Member countries and to report to the Council as appropriate.

Annex 4

Recommendation on Anti-corruption Proposals for Aid-Funded Procurement

**Endorsed by the Development Assistance Committee
at its High Level Meeting, 6-7 May 1996**

1.   DAC Members share a concern with corruption:

- It undermines good governance.

- It wastes scarce resources for development, whether from aid or from other public or private sources, with far-reaching effects throughout the economy.

- It undermines the credibility of, and public support for, development co-operation and devalues the reputation and efforts of all who work to support sustainable development.

- It compromises open and transparent competition on the basis of price and quality.

2.   The DAC, therefore, firmly endorses the need to combat corruption through effective prohibition, co-ordinated in a multilateral framework to ensure harmonised implementation. Other meaningful and concrete measures are also required to ensure transparency, accountability and probity in the use of public resources in DAC Members' own systems and those of partner countries, who themselves are increasingly concerned with this problem.

3.   In its efforts to curb corruption, the DAC recognises that opportunities may exist for corrupt practices in aid-funded procurement. Together with other efforts to deal with corruption, the DAC hereby expresses its firm intention to work to eliminate corruption in aid procurement.

4.   The DAC therefore recommends that Members introduce or require anti-corruption provisions governing bilateral aid-funded procurement. This work should be carried out in co-ordination with other work being undertaken in the OECD and elsewhere to eliminate corruption, and in collaboration with recipient countries. The DAC also recommends that its Members work to ensure the proper implementation of their anti-corruption provisions and that they draw to the attention of the international development institutions to which they belong, the importance of proper implementation of the anti-corruption provisions envisaged in their rules of operation.

5.   The DAC will follow up on the effect given to this Recommendation within one year.

6.   DAC Members will work closely with development partners to combat corruption in all development co-operation efforts.

Annex 5

Recommendation of the Council on Improving Ethical Conduct in the Public Service Including Principles for Managing Ethics in the Public Service

Adopted by the Council on 23 April 1998

THE COUNCIL,

Having regard to Article 5 b) of the Convention on the Organisation for Economic Co-operation and Development;

Considering that ethical conduct in the public service contributes to the quality of democratic governance and economic and social progress by enhancing transparency and the performance of public institutions;

Considering that increased public concern with confidence in government has become an important public and political challenge for OECD Member countries;

Recognising that public sector reforms are resulting in fundamental changes to public management that pose new ethical challenges;

Recognising that although governments have different cultural, political and administrative environments, they often confront similar ethical challenges, and the responses in their ethics management show common characteristics;

Recognising that Member countries are concerned to address ethical standards in public life by strengthening the efforts made by governments to improve ethical conduct;

Having regard to the political commitment of governments of Member countries, demonstrated by their actions to review and redefine their public service ethics framework;

Considering that public service integrity is essential for global markets to flourish and for international agreements to be respected;

Having regard to the Convention on Combating Bribery of Foreign Public Officials in International Business Transactions which was signed on 17 December 1997;

Having regard to other recent developments which further advance international understanding and co-operation in promoting ethical culture in the public service, such as the Resolution on Action Against Corruption, including the International Code of Conduct for Public Officials, passed by the United Nations on 12 December 1996, the Inter-American Convention Against Corruption adopted by the Organization of American States in March 1996, the Programme of Action Against Corruption approved by the Council of Europe in November 1996, including the preparation of a model European Code of Conduct for Public Officials, and the adoption by the European Council of the Action Plan to Combat Organized Crime on 28 April 1997 and the Convention on the Fight against Corruption involving Officials of the European Communities or Officials of Member States of the European Union on 26 May 1997;

Recognising the need of Member countries to have a point of reference when combining the elements of an effective ethics management system in line with their own political, administrative and cultural circumstances;

On the proposal of the Public Management Committee;

I.   **RECOMMENDS** that Member countries take action to ensure well-functioning institutions and systems for promoting ethical conduct in the public service. This can be achieved by:

- developing and regularly reviewing policies, procedures, practices and institutions influencing ethical conduct in the public service;

- promoting government action to maintain high standards of conduct and counter corruption in the public sector;

- incorporating the ethical dimension into management frameworks to ensure that management practices are consistent with the values and principles of public service;

- combining judiciously those aspects of ethics management systems based on ideals with those based on the respect of rules;

- assessing the effects of public management reforms on public service ethical conduct;

- using as a reference the Principles for Managing Ethics in the Public Service set out in the Annex to ensure high standards of ethical conduct.

II.   **INSTRUCTS** the Public Management Committee to:

- analyse information provided by Member countries on how they apply these principles in their respective national contexts. The purpose of the analysis is to provide information on a comparative basis to support Member country actions to maintain well-functioning institutions and systems for promoting ethics;

- provide support to Member countries to improve conduct in the public service by, *inter alia*, facilitating the process of information-sharing and disseminating promising practices in Member countries;

- present a report in two years' time analysing the experiences, actions and practices in the Member countries that have proved effective in a particular national context.

Principles for Managing Ethics in the Public Service

Foreword

1.   High standards of conduct in the public service have become a critical issue for governments in OECD Member countries. Public management reforms involving greater devolution of responsibility and discretion for public servants, budgetary pressures and new forms of delivery of public services have challenged traditional values in the public service. Globalisation and the further development of international economic relations, including trade and investment, demand high recognisable standards of conduct in the public service. Preventing misconduct is as complex as the phenomenon of misconduct itself, and a range of integrated mechanisms are needed for success, including sound ethics management systems. Increased concern about decline of confidence in government and corruption has prompted governments to review their approaches to ethical conduct.

2.   In response to the above-mentioned challenges, the attached principles have been developed by the Member countries. The twelve principles are designed to help countries review the institutions, systems and mechanisms they have for promoting public service ethics. They identify the functions of guidance, management or control against which public ethics management systems may be checked. These principles distil the experience of OECD countries, and reflect shared views of sound ethics management. Member countries will find their own ways of balancing the various aspirational and compliance elements to arrive at an effective framework to suit their own circumstances.

3.   The principles may be used by management across national and sub-national levels of government. Political leaders may use them to review ethics management regimes and evaluate the extent to which ethics is operationalised throughout government. The principles are intended to be an instrument for countries to adapt to national conditions. They are not sufficient in themselves – they should be seen as a way of integrating ethics management with the broader public management environment.

Principles for Managing Ethics in the Public Service

1.   Ethical standards for public service should be clear.

Public servants need to know the basic principles and standards they are expected to apply to their work and where the boundaries of acceptable behaviour lie. A concise, well-publicised statement of core ethical standards and principles that guide public service, for example in the form of a code of conduct, can accomplish this by creating a shared understanding across government and within the broader community.

2.   Ethical standards should be reflected in the legal framework.

The legal framework is the basis for communicating the minimum obligatory standards and principles of behaviour for every public servant. Laws and regulations could state the fundamental values of public service and should provide the framework for guidance, investigation, disciplinary action and prosecution.

© OECD 2000

3. Ethical guidance should be available to public servants.

Professional socialisation should contribute to the development of the necessary judgement and skills enabling public servants to apply ethical principles in concrete circumstances. Training facilitates ethics awareness and can develop essential skills for ethical analysis and moral reasoning. Impartial advice can help create an environment in which public servants are more willing to confront and resolve ethical tensions and problems. Guidance and internal consultation mechanisms should be made available to help public servants apply basic ethical standards in the workplace.

4. Public servants should know their rights and obligations when exposing wrongdoing.

Public servants need to know what their rights and obligations are in terms of exposing actual or suspected wrongdoing within the public service. These should include clear rules and procedures for officials to follow, and a formal chain of responsibility. Public servants also need to know what protection will be available to them in cases of exposing wrongdoing.

5. Political commitment to ethics should reinforce the ethical conduct of public servants.

Political leaders are responsible for maintaining a high standard of propriety in the discharge of their official duties. Their commitment is demonstrated by example and by taking action that is only available at the political level, for instance by creating legislative and institutional arrangements that reinforce ethical behaviour and create sanctions against wrongdoing, by providing adequate support and resources for ethics-related activities throughout government and by avoiding the exploitation of ethics rules and laws for political purposes.

6. The decision-making process should be transparent and open to scrutiny.

The public has a right to know how public institutions apply the power and resources entrusted to them. Public scrutiny should be facilitated by transparent and democratic processes, oversight by the legislature and access to public information. Transparency should be further enhanced by measures such as disclosure systems and recognition of the role of an active and independent media.

7. There should be clear guidelines for interaction between the public and private sectors.

Clear rules defining ethical standards should guide the behaviour of public servants in dealing with the private sector, for example regarding public procurement, outsourcing or public employment conditions. Increasing interaction between the public and private sectors demands that more attention should be placed on public service values and requiring external partners to respect those same values.

8. Managers should demonstrate and promote ethical conduct.

An organisational environment where high standards of conduct are encouraged by providing appropriate incentives for ethical behaviour, such as adequate working conditions and effective performance assessment, has a direct impact on the daily practice of public service values and ethical standards. Managers have an important role in this regard by providing consistent leadership and serving as role models in terms of ethics and conduct in their professional relationship with political leaders, other public servants and citizens.

9. Management policies, procedures and practices should promote ethical conduct.

Management policies and practices should demonstrate an organisation's commitment to ethical standards. It is not sufficient for governments to have only rule-based or compliance-based structures. Compliance systems alone can inadvertently encourage some public servants simply to function on the edge of misconduct, arguing that if they are not violating the law they are acting ethically. Government policy should not only delineate the minimal standards below which a government official's actions will not be tolerated, but also clearly articulate a set of public service values that employees should aspire to.

10. Public service conditions and management of human resources should promote ethical conduct.

Public service employment conditions, such as career prospects, personal development, adequate remuneration and human resource management policies should create an environment conducive to ethical behaviour. Using basic principles, such as merit, consistently in the daily process of recruitment and promotion helps operationalise integrity in the public service.

11. Adequate accountability mechanisms should be in place within the public service.

Public servants should be accountable for their actions to their superiors and, more broadly, to the public. Accountability should focus both on compliance with rules and ethical principles and on achievement of results. Accountability mechanisms can be internal to an agency as well as government-wide, or can be provided by civil society. Mechanisms promoting accountability can be designed to provide adequate controls while allowing for appropriately flexible management.

12. Appropriate procedures and sanctions should exist to deal with misconduct.

Mechanisms for the detection and independent investigation of wrongdoing such as corruption are a necessary part of an ethics infrastructure. It is necessary to have reliable procedures and resources for monitoring, reporting and investigating breaches of public service rules, as well as commensurate administrative or disciplinary sanctions to discourage misconduct. Managers should exercise appropriate judgement in using these mechanisms when actions need to be taken.

Annex

Background Note

The need to improve ethical conduct in the public service

1.   OECD Member countries have introduced significant management reforms which have changed the way the public sector operates. However, it is important to ensure that the gains in efficiency and effectiveness are not achieved to the detriment of ethical conduct. New ways of carrying out the business of government are creating situations in which public servants need to be highly attuned to ethical issues, and where there may be few guidelines as to how they should act. Reforms involving decentralisation of power to organisations at sub-national level, devolution of responsibility and greater managerial discretion, increased commercialisation of the public sector and a changing public/private sector interface place public servants more frequently in situations involving conflicts of interest or objectives. At the same time, many countries are finding that the systems that have traditionally governed and guided the behaviour of public servants are insufficient for the new managerial roles public servants are expected to play, and are indeed often in conflict with the demands being made on managers and staff in the new public sector environment. These new situations create dilemmas that need to be resolved, and that require ethical analysis and moral reasoning.

2.   Of further concern is the apparent decline in confidence in government and public institutions in many countries, and the implications this has for the legitimacy of government and public institutions. Weakening confidence is associated, at least in part, with revelations of inappropriate actions - and in some cases outright corruption - on the part of public officials. It is unclear whether standards of conduct are actually falling, or whether mistakes and misdemeanours are simply more visible in these days of open government, an enquiring media and a more sophisticated public. What is clear is that ethics and standards in public life have become more of a public and political issue in some countries demanding effective action by the governments concerned.

3.   Some remedial measures, broadly speaking, have the potential both to promote ethical behaviour and to prevent misconduct. Traditionally, increased regulation and stricter law enforcement have been the first responses to misconduct in the public sector. International initiatives have been concentrated on the development of concrete elements in the ethics infrastructure, mainly to prevent or criminalise certain forms of wrongdoing, such as corruption.

4.   OECD Member countries have taken collective actions to criminalise bribery of foreign public officials They adopted the Convention on Combating Bribery of Foreign Public Officials in International Business Transactions on 21 November 1997. The United Nations passed the Resolution on Action Against Corruption, including the International Code of Conduct for Public Officials, on 12 December 1996. The Organization of American States adopted the Inter-American Convention Against Corruption in March 1996. The European Council adopted an Action Plan to Combat Organized Crime on 28 April 1997 and the Convention on the Fight against Corruption involving Officials of the European Communities or Officials of Member States of the European Union on 26 May 1997. The Council of Europe approved the Programme of Action Against Corruption in November 1996, including the preparation of a model European Code of Conduct for Public Officials, and which underpins the co-operation of 40 countries in fighting corruption, money laundering, computer crimes and organised crimes.

5.   Underlying PUMA's contribution in this area is the conviction that preventing misconduct is as complex as the phenomenon of misconduct itself, and that a combination of interrelated

mechanisms, including a robust ethics infrastructure, sound ethics management systems, specific prevention techniques and effective law enforcement are needed for success.

An ethics infrastructure to promote ethics and prevent misconduct

6.   Significantly, OECD Member countries are increasingly exploring the application of administrative and preventative action. As countries implement more managerial approaches in the public sector, they are finding that a centralised, compliance-based approach to ethics management is incompatible with a devolved, results-based public management system. There is a trend towards a greater reliance on mechanisms that define and promote aspirational values for the public sector and encourage good behaviour.

7.   In 1996 and 1997 PUMA conducted two surveys on the management of ethics and conduct in the public sector involving twenty-three Member countries. The first report, "Ethics in the Public Service: Current Issues and Practice", was based on studies of nine countries,[*] and identified the factors that affect standards of ethics and conduct in the public service, and the initiatives being

---

The Ethics Infrastructure

A well-functioning Ethics Infrastructure supports a public sector environment which encourages high standards of behaviour. Each function and element is a separate, important building block, but the individual elements should be complementary and mutually reinforcing. The elements need to interact to achieve the necessary synergy to become a coherent and integrated infrastructure. The elements of infrastructure can be categorised according to the main functions they serve – guidance, management and control – noting that different elements may serve more than one function.

Guidance is provided by strong commitment from political leadership; statements of values such as codes of conduct; and professional socialisation activities such as education and training.

Management can be realised through co-ordination by a special body or an existing central management agency, and through public service conditions, management policies and practices.

Control is assured primarily through a legal framework enabling independent investigation and prosecution; effective accountability and control mechanisms; transparency, public involvement and scrutiny. The ideal mix and degree of these functions will depend on the cultural and political-administrative milieu of each country.

---

*   Australia, Finland, Mexico, Netherlands, New Zealand, Norway, Portugal, the United Kingdom and the United States. The individual country reports are available on the OECD Home Page on the Internet at *http://www.oecd.org/puma/.*

taken by governments to strengthen ethics management frameworks. The report identified a set of instruments necessary to governments for promoting integrity and preventing corruption, which was termed an "ethics infrastructure".

8.   The key issue addressed in the report is how public servants can be supported in observing the highest standards of integrity and ethics in a rapidly changing public sector environment, without undermining the main thrust of public management reforms, which aim to enhance efficiency and effectiveness. All of the countries included in the study employ a range of tools and processes to regulate against undesirable behaviour and to provide incentives to good conduct.

9.   A second report, based on studies of an additional fourteen countries,* provides further information on the formulation of the principles as an operational document for Member countries in reviewing the national ethics framework, the functions and elements of an ethics infrastructure. New ethics initiatives by governments of Member countries, particularly over the last five years, signal some common directions, as well as an increased concern by governments to examine the effectiveness of their ethics management regimes in relation to wider public management reforms.

10.   The rapidly changing environment requires regular review of policies, practices and procedures affecting public sector ethical conduct. The principles for managing ethics in the public service, set out in this document, are designed to be a reference for carrying out such reviews and to check the validity of existing functions and elements of the ethics infrastructure.

---

*   The participating countries for the survey were Belgium, the Czech Republic, France, Germany, Greece, Hungary, Ireland, Italy, Japan, Korea, Mexico, Poland, Spain, Sweden and Switzerland. The draft report was provided as a background paper for the OECD Symposium on Ethics in the Public Sector: Challenges and Opportunities for OECD Countries in November 1997.

OECD PUBLICATIONS, 2, rue André-Pascal, 75775 PARIS CEDEX 16
PRINTED IN FRANCE
(21 2000 19 1 P) ISBN 92-64-18530-5 – No. 51481 2000